THE VIRGIN BIRTH

The
VIRGIN BIRTH

by THOMAS BOSLOOPER

THE WESTMINSTER PRESS
PHILADELPHIA

LIBRARY OF CONGRESS CATALOG CARD NO. 62–7941

PRINTED IN THE UNITED STATES OF AMERICA

To
Peter, my father
and
Peter, my son

Now the birth of Jesus Christ took place in this way. When his mother Mary had been betrothed to Joseph, before they came together she was found to be with child of the Holy Spirit; and her husband, Joseph, being a just man and unwilling to put her to shame, resolved to divorce her quietly. But as he considered this, behold, an angel of the Lord appeared to him in a dream, saying, "Joseph, son of David, do not fear to take Mary your wife, for that which is conceived in her is of the Holy Spirit; she will bear a son, and you shall call his name Jesus, for he will save his people from their sins." All this took place to fulfill what the Lord had spoken by the prophet:

> "Behold, a virgin shall conceive and bear a son,
>   and his name shall be called Emmanuel"

(which means, God with us). When Joseph woke from sleep, he did as the angel of the Lord commanded him; he took his wife, but knew her not until she had borne a son; and he called his name Jesus.

— Matthew 1:18-25, RSV

And in the sixth month the angel Gabriel was sent from God to a city of Galilee named Nazareth, to a virgin betrothed to a man whose name was Joseph, of the house of David; and the virgin's name was Mary. And he came to her and said, "Hail, O favored one, the Lord is with you!" But she was greatly troubled at the saying, and considered in her mind what sort of greeting this might be. And the angel said to her, "Do not be afraid, Mary, for you have

*found favor with God. And behold, you will conceive in
your womb and bear a son, and you shall call his name Jesus.*

> *He will be great, and will be called the Son of the Most
>   High;*
> *and the Lord God will give to him the throne of his
>   Father David,*
> *and he will reign over the house of Jacob forever;*
> *and of his kingdom there will be no end."*

*And Mary said to the angel, " How can this be, since I have
no husband? " And the angel said to her,*

> *" The Holy Spirit will come upon you, and the power
>   of the Most High will overshadow you;*
> *therefore the child to be born will be called holy,*
> *the Son of God.*

*And behold, your kinswoman Elizabeth in her old age has
also conceived a son; and this is the sixth month with her
who was called barren. For with God nothing will be impossible." And Mary said, " Behold I am the handmaid of
the Lord; let it be to me according to your word! "
And the angel departed from her.*

— Luke 1:26-38, RSV

CONTENTS

PREFACE

SEVERAL CONVICTIONS comprise the foundation for this book. Theology must be the outgrowth of Biblical historical criticism. Criticism has a positive contribution to make to Christian faith. True understanding of the Christian faith both throughout the churches and between the churches and the world can come about only through the highest regard for Christ, Scripture, the church, and the historical-critical method for interpreting them.

The substance of this volume is an answer to the question, What happens when a Biblical and theological doctrine such as the virgin birth is put to the most strenuous tests of historical investigation? The virgin birth is a good subject for this question, since its interpretation is controversial, and its integral connection with Christology, evangelism, ecumenism, and morality makes its importance crucial.

This history of interpretation and historical-critical analysis of the virgin birth cannot possibly be completely objective, since the span of history is long, the complexity of historical, theological, and literary problems is great, and the areas covered are extensive. Serious historians and theologians who specialize in a number of the areas in which this study is involved are therefore welcome to criticize my judgments, correct my errors, and come up with a theology of the virgin birth that will glorify Christ, enrich the church, and strengthen the brethren.

I am indebted to studies such as Albert Schweitzer's *Von Reimarus zu Wrede* (1906), Heinrich Weinel's *Jesus im neunzehnten Jahrhundert* (1907), Chester McCown's *The Search for the Real Jesus* (1940), and Jean Hoffman's *Les Vies de Jésus et le Jésus de l'histoire* (1947). Their sketches of the history of " Lives of Jesus " have been invaluable to me. They have provided the skeletal outline for my history of interpretation of the virgin birth of Jesus.

11

I am grateful to the librarians at the Union Theological Seminary in New York City for making more than one thousand books and articles easily accessible to me; to John Knox and Frederick C. Grant, of Union Seminary, for supplying me with insight, inspiration, and guidance during the early stages of research; and to Norman Pittenger, of General Theological Seminary, for recognizing the potential value of my ideas and encouraging me to write the book.

Grateful acknowledgment is here given to publishers who have given permission to quote extensively from their volumes. Their courtesy has made possible for the reader ready access to numerous important primary sources.

Longmans, Green & Co., Ltd., of London, for *The Homeric Hymns,* by Andrew Lang; J. M. Dent & Sons, Ltd., of London, for *Greek Religious Thought,* by F. M. Cornford, published by E. P. Dutton & Co., Inc., of New York City; Princeton University Press, of Princeton, New Jersey, for *Ancient Near Eastern Texts,* by James B. Pritchard; The Open Court Publishing Company, of LaSalle, Illinois, for *Virgil's Prophecy on the Saviour's Birth,* by Paul Carus, and *The Mysteries of Mithra,* by Franz Cumont, tr. by T. J. McCormack; Random House, Inc., of New York City, for *The Complete Greek Drama,* Vols. 1 and 2, by Whitney J. Oates and Eugene O'Neill, Jr., on Aeschylus' *The Eumenides,* Euripides' *Ion,* and Sophocles' *Oedipus;* G. Bell & Sons, Ltd., of London, for E. P. Coleridge's translations of Euripides' *Helen* and *The Phoenissae* in Vol. 2 of Random House's *The Complete Greek Drama;* A. & C. Black, Ltd., of London, for R. H. Charles's *The Ascension of Isaiah;* T. & T. Clark, of Edinburgh, for Alexander Walker's translation of *Apocryphal Gospels, Acts, and Revelations* and for William Fletcher's translation of *Lactantius;* Houghton Mifflin Company, of Boston, Massachusetts, for T. W. Rhys Davids' translation of *Buddhist Birth Stories or Jātaka Tales,* Vol. I; Luzac & Company, Ltd., of London, for E. A. Wallis Budge's *The History of the Blessed Virgin Mary;* Cambridge University Press, American Branch, New York City, for Montague Rhodes James' *Latin Infancy Gospels;* Clarendon Press, of Oxford, England, for Montague Rhodes James' *The Apocryphal New Testament* and E. A. Wallis Budge's *Legends of Our Lady Mary the Perpetual Virgin;* Methuen & Co., Ltd., of London, for E. A. Wallis Budge's *The Gods of the Egyptians,* Vols. 1 and 2; Wm. B. Eerdmans Publishing Company of Grand Rapids, Michigan, for material on

Saint Augustine from Vol. III of Nicene and Post-Nicene Fathers; the Pali Text Society, of London, for J. J. Jones's *The Mahāvastu,* Vols. 1 and 2, *Sacred Books of the Buddhists;* George Allen & Unwin, Ltd., London, England, for Gilbert Murray's translation of Euripides' *The Bacchae* in Vol. 2 of Random House's *The Complete Greek Drama.*

THOMAS BOSLOOPER

Schenectady, New York

ABBREVIATIONS

ANCL   *The Ante-Nicene Christian Library*
ANET   *Ancient Near Eastern Texts,* ed. James B. Pritchard
ANF   *The Ante-Nicene Fathers*
ANT   *The Apocryphal New Testament,* ed. M. R. James
CGD   *The Complete Greek Drama,* ed. Whitney J. Oates and Eugene O'Neill, Jr.
ET   English translation
HH   *The Homeric Hymns,* ed. Andrew Lang
ICC   *The International Critical Commentary*
JBL   *Journal of Biblical Literature*
LCC   *The Library of Christian Classics*
MS   Manuscript
NPNF   *Nicene and Post-Nicene Fathers*
RSV   *Revised Standard Version of the Bible*
SBE   *Sacred Books of the East,* ed. F. Max Müller

O ne thing may be definitely said, that every time people want to fly from this miracle, a theology is at work, which has ceased to understand and honour the mystery as well, and has rather essayed to conjure away the mystery of the unity of God and man in Jesus Christ, the mystery of God's free grace. And on the other hand, where this mystery has been understood and men have avoided any attempt at natural theology, because they had no need of it, the miracle came to be thankfully and joyously recognized.

— Karl Barth, *Dogmatics in Outline*

INTRODUCTION

THE STORY of Jesus' birth from Mary stands in pristine simplicity in the midst of a constellation of narratives that preface Matthew and Luke. Ancient, medieval, and modern Christian communities, however, have taken complex and widely divergent views of the nature and value of the stories of the origin of our Lord. The history of interpretation of the virgin birth is a history of various uses and multiferous interpretations.

From Ignatius through Origen, the virgin birth was at the crux of the church's controversy with the non-Christian world. With the Jews, the Christians struggled over the relationship of the virgin birth to the Old Testament. With the Gentiles, the Christians carried on a discussion of the relationship of the virgin birth to apparent parallels in other religious traditions. From Lactantius through Aquinas, the virgin birth served as the first step in the ladder that carried the church to heights of speculative Marian theology. A theology of Mary and a body of extracanonical literature to support it developed simultaneously.

Within Protestant Christianity the virgin birth became one of the principal wedges that held supernaturalists and naturalists apart. For the former, the virgin birth was historical and indispensable to the whole structure of Christianity. For the latter, the virgin birth was unhistorical and therefore unimportant.

Modern historians and contemporary theologians tend to perpetuate the naturalistic spirit by attaching the virgin birth to a single historical or theological idea and thereby relegate the story and doctrine to virtual obscurity.

Many scholars have been preoccupied with the attempt to account for the virgin birth as an interpolation, either of the narratives of Matt., chs. 1 and 2, and Luke, chs. 1 and 2, as a whole into their respective Gospels or of the pericope of the virgin birth into each infancy narrative. Harnack suggested that the virgin birth ought to be understood as the outgrowth of a mistranslation of Isa. 7:14. Lobstein propounded the view that the virgin birth is a myth that was created by popular devotion to explain the divine Sonship of Christ. For Percy Gardner, the narratives of the virgin birth are two separate attempts to give a date for the divine origin of Jesus. Soltau made out of the story of Jesus' miraculous conception two separate attempts to reconcile the belief toward the end of the first century that Jesus was born in Bethlehem with the earlier tradition of his origin in Nazareth. Conybeare understood it as a legend that the Catholic Church adopted to effect a reconciliation between opposing Ebionite and Docetic parties. Charles Guignebert saw in the stories of the miraculous birth a solution to a Christological problem that had arisen in the primitive community out of the conflict between the terms " Messiah " and " Son of God."

The contemporary theologians Emil Brunner, Nels Ferré, and Paul Tillich oversimplify the problem of the interpretation and underestimate the significance of the virgin birth by linking it to the early Christian doctrine of the sinlessness of Jesus. They are agreed that by its attachment to the doctrine of the sinlessness of Jesus the virgin birth stands in the way of the true understanding of the incarnation. For Brunner and Ferré, the virgin birth obscures and obstructs the fact of Jesus' true humanity. For Tillich, the virgin birth represents one of the New Testament's rationalizations into a negative form of a positive religious concept.[1]

The history of the interpretation of the virgin birth has had its negative and its positive aspects. Negatively, the history of interpretation has been a history of error. The Old Roman Catholic Church maligned the Biblical narratives by transferring the chief emphasis from Jesus to Mary and from marriage to virginity. Following the Protestant Reformation, the rationalistic naturalists underestimated the importance of the narrative through their a priori judgments against miracle, and the theological supernaturalists by attaching the virgin birth to the deity of Christ and by insisting on the " literal historicity " of the story removed Jesus' origin from the context of history. Historical critics, by being obsessed with the compulsion to demonstrate what was the source

---

[1] Nels F. S. Ferré, *The Sun and the Umbrella* (1953) , pp. 28–29; Emil Brunner, *The Mediator* (1947) , pp. 322 ff.; Paul Tillich, *Systematic Theology*, Vol. 2 (1957) , pp. 126–127, 149.

from which the Biblical narrative was " derived," tended to deprive the church of the significance of the content of the story of Jesus' virgin birth.

Positively, the history of interpretation of the virgin birth is a history of insight and real contributions to our understanding of the Biblical narratives. The Roman Catholic Church has preserved the relevance of the virgin birth to personal morality. The naturalists have helped the church to recognize the true moral character of the narratives and have helped to curb the abuses that had sprung up through apocryphal tradition. The supernaturalists correctly have insisted on the importance of the story of Jesus' origin and have demanded that the church take the doctrine seriously. Historical criticism gave to the virgin birth its proper literary classification, eventually came to the point of recognizing its true role in the world, and provided the basis for an understanding of the true content of its message.

The crux of the problem of interpretation of the virgin birth may be seen in the similarity and extreme diversity between the traditionally Roman Catholic and Protestant positions. Both have taken the virgin birth in the Gospels as literal history, and in so doing have weakened the trust of its morally redemptive message. The former from it produced a Docetic theology of Mary, questioned the sanctity of sex, and idealized virginity. The latter used the virgin birth to prove the deity of Christ and to set forth a moral idealism attached solely to the person of Jesus. As a result the original message that moral order is to be established within the marriage bond has been lost.

Both Roman Catholics and Protestants have been wrong in insisting on the literal historicity of the narratives. The virgin birth is " myth," in the highest and best sense of the word. Both Roman Catholics and Protestants have been correct in insisting on the importance of the virgin birth. The story of Jesus' origin proclaims a vital and provocative universal message. The Roman Catholic tradition of making a plea for individual personal purity on the basis of the Biblical narrative is more nearly correct than the Protestant position which has attached the moral thrust of the narrative exclusively to the person of Jesus. The Protestant tradition of associating the virgin birth with Jesus is more nearly correct than the Roman Catholic position of associating the virgin birth with Mary and with virginity. The truth is to be found between the two. The virgin birth in the New Testament attests the humanity

of Jesus and makes a strong plea for the sanctity of sex and marriage.

The difficulty that the church has had in understanding and interpreting the virgin birth reflects the failure of Biblical scholarship to present the kind of analysis of the story of Jesus' birth
from Mary upon which a satisfactory interpretation can be based.
Recently Oscar Cullmann expressed disappointment over not being able to find a single book on the virgin birth that presents a
historical approach to the subject.[2]

This volume seeks to fill this serious lacuna in Biblical critical
scholarship by presenting a study of the virgin birth that surveys
the history of its interpretation, sets forth in detail relevant literature from extracanonical and non-Christian birth traditions and
compares them with the Biblical writings and with each other, and
analyzes several major historical and theological disciplines that
have been exercised upon the narratives of Jesus' birth.

The hope is here expressed that in viewing and analyzing the
history of interpretation of the virgin birth aids for arriving at a
meaningful interpretation of the story of the origin of our Lord
for our time will emerge.

Because of the tremendous scope of the areas covered in each
chapter and the enormous complexity of the technical problems
that are involved, each presentation and analysis must be considered to be representative and selective rather than exhaustive.
Every attempt has been made, however, to be both extensive and
accurate in the coverage of the material. The relevant literature
in every item in the bibliography has been given thorough and
serious consideration even though references to all of them do not
appear in the content of the individual chapters. Because of the
importance of the problem of the virgin birth, and because of the
complexity and diversity of interpretations of the virgin birth
throughout the history of the church, the approach of necessity has
had to be critical. However, by no means is the intention to be
censorious.

This study is advanced also with the firm conviction in the
utmost importance of the virgin birth. The modern world must be
confronted by a bold church that declares the universality of the
gospel of Jesus Christ, the incarnate Son of God, and stands firm
on its conviction of the sanctity of sex, fidelity in marriage, and the
imperative of the moral life.

2 *The Christology of the New Testament* (1959), p. 295.

If the church continues to deny, neglect, or misinterpret the virgin birth, it will continue to fail to employ one of its chief tools for building a well-ordered and moral society. A truly catholic and ecumenical understanding of the virgin birth of Jesus is demanded by the religious issues and moral climate of the twentieth century. Such an approach to an important Biblical narrative may also help to produce a truly catholic and ecumenical church.

May the Word of God which is Scripture and who is Christ appear powerful and relevant to the modern world!

For in His first nativity, which was spiritual, He was " motherless," because He was begotten by God the Father alone, without the office of a mother. But in His second, which was in the flesh, He was born of a virgin's womb without the office of a father, that, bearing a middle substance between God and man, He might be able, as it were, to take by the hand this frail and weak nature of ours, and raise it to immortality. He became both the Son of God through the Spirit, and the Son of man through the flesh — that is, both God and man.

— Lactantius, *Divine Institutes*, IV. xiii

CHAPTER

1

PATRISTIC TRADITION

F OR THE fifteen hundred years from the times of the apostolic
fathers until the Protestant Reformation the virgin birth was
one of the accepted facts of the Christian faith. Jerome's words
echoed the sentiments of the whole church: " We believe that God
was born of a virgin because we read it " (*Perpetual Virginity of
Blessed Mary* 21, NPNF, VI, p. 344) . Gregory of Nyssa's statement
in *The Great Catechism* 13 placed the doctrine on what appeared
to be an unshakable foundation:

Well, he who has recorded that He was born *has* related also that He
was born of a Virgin. If, therefore, on the evidence stated, the fact of
His being born is established, as a matter of faith, it is altogether incredible, on the same evidence, that He was not born in the manner
stated. (NPNF, V, p. 487.)

The history of this millennium and a half is also significant for
how the story of the origin of our Lord was used. The literature
that has been preserved for us from the ante-Nicene, Nicene, and
post-Nicene fathers shows that the church fathers from Ignatius
through Thomas Aquinas treated the theme of the virgin birth as
a gem which was placed in many different settings: the explanation
of the origin of the redeemer, the answer to the question of how
the Logos entered the world, an aid in describing the relationship
between the two natures of Christ, and the basis for Marianism.
The church fathers, in using the virgin birth, went from a description of Christ in his redemption and incarnation to a portrayal of
Mary in her origin and redemptive office.

A. IGNATIUS OF ANTIOCH, ARISTIDES, JUSTIN MARTYR, MELITO OF SARDIS

Ignatius of Antioch in Syria was the first of the fathers to refer in his writings to the birth of Jesus. In the seven letters that are ascribed to Ignatius, references to Jesus' birth appear in *To the Ephesians* vii, xviii, and xix; in *To the Smyrnaeans* i and ii; in *To the Magnesians* xi; and in *To the Trallians* vi and ix. One of the principal passages is in *To the Ephesians*.

For our God, Jesus the Christ, was conceived by Mary, in God's plan being sprung both from the seed of David and from the Holy Spirit. He was born and baptized that by his Passion he might hallow water. Now Mary's virginity and her giving birth escaped from the prince of this world, as did the Lord's death — those three secrets crying to be told, but wrought in God's silence. How, then, were they revealed to the ages? A star shone in heaven brighter than all the stars. Its light was indescribable and its novelty caused amazement. The rest of the stars, along with the sun and the moon, formed a ring around it; yet it outshone them all. (xviii. 2 to xix. 2, LCC, I, p. 92.)

Although at the turn of the first century the virgin birth was un-doubtedly one of the rudiments of the faith of early believers, and although it is indisputable that the virgin birth has a firm place in the writings and thought of Ignatius, perplexing problems stand out. The setting for the birth narrative is apparently not canoni-cal. A careful reading of Ignatius' letters reveals that there is abso-lutely no allusion to the Lukan birth narrative. It may also come as a surprise that allusion to the Matthaean is highly improbable, and his references betray, as in the quotation above, knowledge of an " apocryphal " tradition. The most that can be said of Ignatius' relation to the canonical narratives of Jesus' birth is that he was acquainted with a Matthaean-type of tradition. The tradition from which he drew was similar to that upon which Matthew's was based.

Careful reading reveals that in *To the Magnesians* xi; *To the Ephesians* vii. 2, xx; *To the Trallians* ix. 1-2; *To the Philadel-phians* viii. 2, b, ix. 2; and in *To the Smyrnaeans* i, " virgin " is mentioned in connection with the Passion and resurrection of Jesus. In Ignatius the birth of Jesus was associated with the close of our Lord's life rather than with his origin.

Two important contextual points, therefore, appear in the writ-ings of Ignatius: the disassociation of the birth of Jesus from the record in the First and Third Gospels and the context for the virgin birth being atonement rather than incarnation.

Aristides, a philosopher in the first half of the second century, presented an *Apology for the Christians to the Roman Emperor.* As there was no clear association in the writings of Ignatius with the canonical Gospels so is there no evidence of such an association in Aristides' *Apology.* Aristides' work reveals that he associated the concept of Jesus as the Son of God with his origin in Mary and that this tradition had come as part of the spoken gospel. This, however, is all that the reference in Aristides reveals.

The Christians then trace the beginning of their religion from Jesus the Messiah, and He is named the Son of God Most High, and it is said that God came down from heaven, and from a Hebrew *virgin* assumed and clothed Himself with flesh, and the Son of God lived in a daughter of man. This is taught in the Gospel, as it is called, which a short while ago was preached among them. (Greek text, XV. 1, ET from Syriac II, ANF, IX, p. 265.)

At the middle of the second century Justin Martyr in his prolific writings made numerous references to the birth of Jesus. They may be found in his *Apology* I. 21–23, 33, 36, 63; *Dialogue with Trypho* 23, 43, 48, 50, 54, 63, 66–68, 70, 78, 84, 100, 105, 113, 127; and in *On the Resurrection* (which may, however, be a spurious work) 3. Justin discussed the virgin birth principally in connection with Isa. 7:14 and the so-called analogies in Greek mythology.

Dialogue with Trypho 43 clearly shows that in Justin's time the interpretation of " virgin " as " young woman " was current, and the judgment of Jewish interpreters was that the prophecy applied only to the immediate situation described by the prophet. Justin argued that it was the modern scribe who had perverted the old and accepted interpretation and had introduced a new one because he did not want to admit that the prophecy was fulfilled in Jesus.

Justin deliberated a great deal on the association of passages in the Old Testament with the advent of Jesus. In addition to his discussion on Isa. 7:14 he interpreted several other passages with relation to the birth of our Lord. This is characteristic of his *Dialogue with Trypho,* where he used Isa., ch. 11 (86; 87) ; Isa., ch. 53 (76); Dan. 2:34 and 7:13 (76) ; and passages in The Psalms (34; 76; 83; 88).

The famous second-century apologist was also vitally concerned with the analogy between Jesus' birth and stories in pagan mythology (*Dialogue with Trypho* 67, 70; *Apology* I. 21–22, 33, 54) . One of his major contentions against the Greeks was that they devised fables to take the place of prophetic truth. It was also incredible to him that the Greeks, who were steeped in traditions of the birth of pagan deities, would hesitate to accept the virgin birth of Jesus. He argued, however, that they were analogous only in a very general way, the stories of Jesus being completely free from the gross sensuality that characterized heathen stories.

In saying that the Word, who is the first offspring of God, was born for us without sexual union, as Jesus Christ our Teacher, and that he was crucified and died and after rising again ascended into heaven we introduce nothing new beyond [what you say of] those whom you call sons of Zeus. (*Apology* I. 21, LCC, I, p. 255.)

When we say, as before, that he was begotten by God as the Word of God in a unique manner beyond ordinary birth, this should be no strange thing for you who speak of Hermes as the announcing word from God. (*Apology* I. 22, LCC, I, p. 256.)

Lest some, not understanding the prophecy which has been referred to, should bring against us the reproach that we bring against the poets who say that Zeus came upon women for the sake of sexual pleasure, we will try to explain these words clearly. For " Behold, the Virgin shall conceive " means that the Virgin would conceive without intercourse. For if she had had intercourse with anyone, she would not have been a virgin; but God's power, coming upon the Virgin, overshadowed her, and caused her to conceive while still remaining a virgin. The angel of God who was sent to this Virgin at the time brought her this good news, saying, " Behold, you shall conceive in the womb by the Holy Spirit and will bear a son, and he will be called Son of the Highest and you shall call his name Jesus, for he will save his people from their sins," as those who recorded everything about our Saviour Jesus Christ have taught us. (*Apology* I. 33, LCC, I, p. 263.)

Besides, in Greek mythology there is a story of how Perseus was born of Danae, while she was a virgin, when the one whom they call Zeus descended upon her in the form of a golden shower. You Christians should be ashamed of yourselves, therefore, to repeat the same kind of stories as these men, and you should, on the contrary, acknowledge this Jesus to be a man of mere human origin. (The Fathers of the Church, ed. by Ludwig Schopp, *Writings of Saint Justin Martyr,* p. 254.)

This last quotation from Justin's *Dialogue with Trypho* 67 is a remonstrance from Trypho. Justin countered that the Greek myths had been invented by Satan to counterfeit the subsequent and true miraculous birth of Jesus. He argued in similar fashion in *Dia-*

logue with Trypho 70:1, where he charged the devotees to Mithraism with having imitated the dictum of Dan. 2:34 by the story of
Mithra's being born from a rock and having the place where his
believers are initiated being called a cave.

Justin was concerned with the mission of Jesus as the Son of
God. For him that mission had as its ultimate basis a birth that
was unique in character and that was foreshadowed in prophecy.
Jesus' birth according to Justin was brought about by God through
the instrumentality of a virgin in a miraculous and superhuman
manner. Justin made a didactic connection between his doctrine
of the incarnation and his doctrine of redemption. The virgin
birth helped to explain how Jesus was able to redeem mankind
from sin, that is, how Jesus was able to save, transform, purify, and
restore the human race.

It is possible to make a clear delineation of Justin's doctrine of
the virgin birth. The relationship, however, of the virgin birth in
Justin's writings to his sources is puzzling. Bruno Bauer was probably right when he proposed that Matthew and Luke were unknown to Justin.[1] Justin himself referred to his sources as " Memoirs " (*Dialogue with Trypho* 105:1c, 106; *Apology* I. 33:5) . It is
not clear from the context of any of his references to the virgin
birth that these " Memoirs " were the Gospels as we now have
them or the canonical birth narratives themselves.

A few examples should suffice to illustrate the problem. His
references to the census under Cyrenius, recorded in Luke (*Apology* I. 46:1 and *Dialogue with Trypho* 78:4) , are given in the context solely of Matthaean incidents. The matter is further compli-
cated by his use of the Matthaean incidents themselves, since he
uses them out of the context in which they appear in the First Gospel. In Justin's narrative, the Herod incident and the Magi come
before Joseph's vision in which he was commanded not to " put
her [Mary] away."

In *Dialogue with Trypho* 100:5, he clearly seems to be quoting
from the Lukan Annunciation, but in the First *Apology* 33 he has:

And the angel of God who was sent to the same virgin at that time
brought her good news, saying, " Behold, thou shalt conceive of the
Holy Ghost, and shalt bear a Son, and He shall be called the Son of
the Highest, and thou shalt call His name Jesus; for He shall save His
people from their sins." (ANF, I, p. 174.)

---

[1] *Kritik der Evangelien* (1850) , p. 306.

Here is a combination of ideas from the Annunciation to Mary
as recorded in the Third Gospel and the Annunciation to Joseph
as we find it in the First Gospel. Justin presented these two separate ideas as a single quotation. Two alternatives are possible.
Either he had two sources which he combined to appear as one
quotation, or he had a source which already had this material combined into one continuous narration. The second alternative is
possible, since such a source did exist which combined the two
ideas into a single quotation.

The *Book of James* XI. ii has:

For a power of the Lord shall overshadow thee: wherefore also that
holy thing which shall be born of thee shall be called the Son of the
Highest. And thou shalt call his name Jesus: for he shall save his
people from their sins. (ANT, p. 43.)

The similarity between Justin's reference and the quotation
from the apocryphal writing does not mean that Justin knew the
Book of James. It may mean that Justin used a source that was
common to both, a source in which these two ideas were combined.

Justin makes matters even harder for us by his reference in the
First *Apology* 33:8, where he quoted: " Wherefore, too, the angel
said to the virgin, ' Thou shalt call His name Jesus, for He shall
save His people from their sins ' " (ANF, I, p. 174). This pro-
nouncement of the angel to Mary, of course, exists nowhere in the
canonical narratives. This may be looked at as Justin's mistaking
Mary for Joseph as the proper point of reference for this part of
the Annunciation.

It is puzzling, too, when in discussing John the Baptist as forerunner of Christ, he alluded only to " Elisabeth who bore John the
Baptist " (*Dialogue with Trypho* 84:4, ANF, I, p. 241). In 49-51,
84, and 88 details of John's birth and infancy are conspicuous by
their absence.

Justin Martyr is guilty either of extreme carelessness and exces-
sive freedom with regard to his use of the text, leaving him easily
open to the criticism of his opponents, or else he is relying upon a
tradition that was as yet not at all established and was itself am-
biguous. In this case his source hardly appears to have been canonical Matt., chs. 1 and 2, and Luke, chs. 1 and 2.

Evidence for the belief in the virgin birth in the writings of
Tatian may be derived from his *Diatessaron* (ANF, IX, pp. 43 ff.) .

From this and from his *Address to the Greeks* (ANF, II) it may be seen that Tatian stressed that Jesus' conception in Mary came about through a divine and not a human agency, the prenatal existence of Jesus as Logos of the Father, and his position as the " Son of the Father " came by virtue of his divine paternity. According to Theodoret, Tatian cut out of the Gospels all the passages which show that Jesus was born of the seed of David according to the flesh; thus, he omitted the genealogies, following the Encratite views which he adopted in later life. It is possible that in his later adaptation of his thinking to Valentinian Gnosticism he lost sight of a real birth, but at least his earlier writings reveal the evidence of the existence of definite views concerning Jesus' virginal origin.

References to the virgin birth in Melito of Sardis are clear in the *Discourse on the Soul and Body,* in a fragment entitled *From Melito the Bishop, On Faith,* and in the *Discourse on the Cross* (66, 70, 104) .[2] In the last two references, 70 and 104, Jesus' birth from a virgin is distinctly referred to. In 66, Jesus' pre-existence and unusual conception are implied, but the virgin birth is not stated directly.

Although both the authorship and authenticity of these writings have been questioned, they may be assumed to represent the probable location and period of Melito of Sardis' activity. These fragments teach that the mother of Jesus was a virgin at his birth, and that the birth was an incarnation of a divine person.

B. IRENAEUS, CLEMENT OF ALEXANDRIA, HIPPOLYTUS, TERTULLIAN, ORIGEN

A distinct development may be seen in the use of the tradition of Jesus' birth made by Irenaeus, Clement of Alexandria, Hippolytus, Tertullian, and Origen.

References become more numerous, they are obviously derived from canonical materials, and they demonstrate a shift in theological emphasis. The most notable change is in the shift of orientation of the virgin birth from the motif of atonement to the motif of incarnation.

Irenaeus' numerous references to Jesus' origin in his *Against Heresies* (ANF, I, pp. 315 ff.) must be understood in the light of his polemic against those who held extreme views. His polemic was

---

[2] *Studies and Documents* XII, " The Homily on the Passion," Kirsopp and Silva Lake (London, Christophers, 1940) .

addressed against Gnostics of two general types: those who accepted the view that Jesus was a *Man* in whom dwelt an Aeon from
the Pleroma of Deity, and those who believed that although he was
a manifestation of the Supreme Being, yet, as regarded his body,
he was a mere Phantasmal Appearance. Some Gnostics, like the
Sethians and Ophites, accepted the doctrine of Jesus' birth from a
virgin through the procreative energy of God, but held that he was
only constituted the Christ by the subsequent descent into him of
the Christ-Aeon united to Sophia.

Irenaeus discussed these views in the context of their being contrary to the teaching of John, ch. 1, and Matt., ch. 1 (III. xvi. 1-2)
and as contrary to the meaning of the virgin birth (V. 1. 1-3). He
also discussed the virgin birth in terms of Isa. 7:14, insisting
that the word be " virgin " (*parthenos*) and not young woman
(*neānis*).

Irenaeus is the first of the church fathers of whom it can be con-
fidently said that he had as a source for his ideas on the birth of
Jesus the narratives as we know them in Matt., chs. 1 and 2, and in
Luke, chs. 1 and 2. His references to the infancy narratives of the
First and Third Gospels may be tabled:

Matthew 1:20; 2:15; 1:23; 2:2	III. ix. 2
Luke 1:6; 1:8; 1:15	III. x. 1
Luke 1:26; 1:32; 1:46; 1:78	III. x. 2
Luke 2:11	III. x. 4
Luke 2:22, 29, 38	III. x. 5
Enumeration of Lukan incidents	III. xi. 8
Luke 2:29	III. xvi. 4
Matthew 1:20 ff.	IV. xxiii. 1

As well as being the first of the fathers to demonstrate a knowledge of the canonical infancy narratives, Irenaeus was also the first
to appeal to the authority of the New Testament on a level of authority similar to that of the Old Testament, the first to appeal to
apostolic tradition and to the church as responsible for and the re-
pository of true tradition, and the first to shift definitely from
apologetics to polemics.

Throughout Clement of Alexandria's *The Instructor* and *Miscellanies* there are numerous references to the virgin birth and the
incidents of Matt., chs. 1 and 2, and Luke, chs. 1 and 2. In *The Instructor* (ANF, II, pp. 209 ff.), the Instructor is the Word (I. i. ii)
who became flesh by way of birth by a virgin mother (I. vi. 41:2b,

42) . The Lord Christ was " The Fruit of the Virgin " (I. vi) . The description of the Logos who was born as a child is to be found in Isa. 9:6. As a child, the characteristics of the redeemer's manner are insured and typified in his gentle and tender qualities (I. v. 1:1, 19:3) . His work as redeemer is central (reference to Isa. 53:6; I. viii. 67:3 ff.) . Clement integrally related the redemption theme to the Logos born as a child [3] (I. v. 23:1 ff.) . This idea is fully expressed in Clement's " Hymn to Christ the Saviour."

O King of saints, all subduing word of the most high Father, Ruler of wisdom. . . . Babes nourished with tender mouths, filled with the dewey spirit of the rational pap, let us sing together simple praises, true hymns to Christ [our] King . . . let us sing in simplicity the powerful Child. O choir of peace, the Christ-begotten, O chaste people, let us sing together the God of peace. (*The Instructor,* III. xii. 101:3b.)

Clement's references to the infancy tradition in *Miscellanies* are puzzling, however. He mentioned John, Anna and Simeon, and Zacharias (I. xxi. 136:2) . He seemed to have known the Matthaean genealogy (I. xxi. 147:5-6) and the story of the visit of the Magi (II. viii. 63:4) . By the former references he seemed to know Luke, chs. 1 and 2. Yet in trying to establish the date of Jesus' birth he referred back no farther than Luke 3:1 (I. xxi. 145:1-2) :

And our Lord was born in the twenty-eighth year, when first the census was ordered to be taken in the reign of Augustus. And to prove that this is true, it is written in the Gospel by Luke as follows: " And in the fifteenth year, in the reign of Tiberius Caesar, the word of the Lord came to John, the son of Zacharias." And again in the same book: " And Jesus was coming to His baptism, being about thirty years old." (ANF, II, p. 333.)

Hippolytus carried on the battle with the Valentinians and Gnostics which Irenaeus had started. His *Refutation of All Heresies* (ANF, V, pp. 9 ff.) carries a criticism of essentially the same Christological " heresies " as those attacked by Irenaeus — Naasseni, Peratae, Sethians, Valentinians, Marcus, Basilides, Saturnilus, Marcion, Carpocrates, Cerinthus, Theodotus, Apelles, Hermogenes, Justinus, Elchasai, Melchisedecians, Docetists.

According to Marcus' typically Gnostic theory, the power that

---

[3] The " child " motif appears throughout the writings of the early fathers: Clement of Rome, " To the Corinthians," LIX.2.b, LIX.4; " The Didache," IX. ii, iii, X. ii, iii; " The Martyrdom of Polycarp," XIV.3, XX.2.a; " The Epistle to Diognetus," VIII–X. In the apostolic fathers the child motif seems to be associated closely with redemption and the servant motif. In Clement of Alexandria it is more closely associated with Logos.

emanated from the second tetrad fashioned Jesus. Jesus was born through Mary, but completely in Gnostic conceptions; substituting Greek concepts for the figures in the narrative: Gabriel was the Logos, the Holy Spirit was Zoe, the Power of the Highest was Anthropos, and the Virgin was Ecclesia (VI. 1:1, xlvi, li:1).

Against this array of ideas which ranged from the rejection of Jesus' generation (Marcion) and the assertion that Jesus was never a man (Theodotus) to the insistence that Jesus was the son of Joseph and Mary (Cerinthus) and the denial of the virgin birth (Apelles), Hippolytus stated his doctrine of the truth, which he began by stating the relationship between the Father and the Logos. The first and only God, both Creator and Lord of all, had nothing coeval with himself, but was One, alone in himself (X. 32:1). This solitary and supreme Deity by an exercise of reflection brought forth the Logos (X. 33:1) who was the first-begotten child of the Father (X. 33:11). He received his body from a virgin (X. 33:14), and in order that he might not seem different from man he even underwent toil, hungered and thirsted, slept, did not protest against his Passion, died, resurrected — all in order that man when he is in tribulation might not be disquieted (X. 33:14-17).

In Hippolytus' system the virgin birth is significant in its association with the Logos as the means by which the latter becomes incarnate. Hippolytus used it as well in an anti-Docetic setting as a means of stressing Jesus' humanity.

In his exegetical and homiletical writings the same point of view is amplified. The Logos came down from heaven and was incarnate in Mary (*Treatise on Christ and Anti-Christ* I), Jesus is described as born of the Holy Spirit and the Virgin (*On Proverbs* XXIV), and neither in mere appearance nor by conversion but " in truth " he became man (Fragment VIII, *Against Beron and Helix*). Christ was of heavenly nature by virtue of his being the Word and was of earthly nature by virtue of his flesh received from the Virgin.

Let us believe then, dear brethren, according to the tradition of the apostles, that God the Word came down from heaven, [and entered] into the holy Virgin Mary, in order that, taking the flesh from her, and assuming also a human, by which I mean a rational soul, and becoming thus all that man is with the exception of sin, He might save fallen man, and confer immortality on men who believe His name. (*Against the Heresy of One Noetus* XVII, ANF, V, p. 230.)

Contemporaneous with the activity of Irenaeus and Hippolytus at Rome and with Clement at Alexandria, Tertullian was busy at Carthage with the great Christological controversy. His writings were conditioned by a strong polemical attitude, which he directed primarily against Marcion. He was acquainted with the birth narratives. *On the Flesh of Christ* II to IV contain all the Matthaean and Lukan incidents. For Tertullian, like Clement and Hippolytus, the virgin birth was the means by which the Logos became incarnate. The Logos was " brought down by the Spirit and Power of the Father into the Virgin Mary, was made flesh in her womb, and, being born of her, went forth as Jesus Christ" (*The Prescription Against Heretics* XIII, ANF, III, p. 249). For Tertullian the virgin birth was a confirmation of the belief in the Lord's nativity (XXVI).

Against Praxeas, Tertullian tried to give a description of Jesus' birth that would do justice to the narratives in Matthew and in Luke. Praxeas maintained that the Father, himself, came down into the Virgin's womb, was himself born of her, himself suffered, and was himself Jesus Christ (XXI). Praxeas is described as having substituted " Father " for " Power of the Highest " in Luke 1:35 (XXVII).

Tertullian's chief interest in this work was to maintain a doctrine of Christ that would bring out the proper relationship between the Father and the Son. He took issue with those who denied the Father by saying that he was the Son and with those who denied the Son by supposing him to be the same as the Father. *Against Praxeas* is really a discussion in which Tertullian maintained that the Father and the Son are distinct persons. References to Jesus' birth were used to illustrate this position.

Tertullian contended hard with Marcion, who apparently in contradiction to Luke, chs. 1 and 2, had stated that Jesus Christ had come down from heaven in the fifteenth year of Tiberius Caesar (*Against Marcion* I. xix).[4] Jesus suddenly appeared and was suddenly Christ (*Against Marcion* III. ii).

[4] In *Against Marcion* IV. i and in *The Prescription Against Heretics* XXXVIII, he tried to establish the view that Marcion sought to destroy the character of those Gospels which were published as genuine and under the names of the apostles, in order to secure for his own Gospel the credit that he took away from the others. His theory was that Marcion cut out what was not suitable to him (whereas Valentinus perverted the true Scriptures by rearranging the record). Being late in coming to Christianity, Tertullian accepted uncritically the views about Scripture which the churches at Rome and Alexandria had just established. He adapted these views and elaborated upon them. Since the heretics did not possess the Scriptures just as

At all events, he who represented the flesh of Christ to be imaginary
was equally able to pass off His nativity as a phantom; so that the
virgin's conception, and pregnancy, and child-bearing, and the whole
course of her infant too, would have to be regarded as putative. [These
facts pertaining to the nativity of Christ] would escape the notice of
the same eyes and the same senses as failed to grasp the full idea of
His flesh. (*On the Flesh of Christ* I, ANF, III, p. 520.)

In struggling in *Against Marcion* to articulate the significance
of Jesus' nature, Tertullian brought out that Christ is the Son of
God, the Creator of the world (III), the incarnation was real
(III. viii), the manner of Jesus' birth is in fulfillment of the prophecy in Isa. 7:14, his humility is described in Isa., ch. 53, and in
Isa. 11:1-2 (III. xii, xiii, xvii; also in *An Answer to the Jews* IX,
XIV), and his Davidic descent can be traced through Mary (III.
xx). The crux of the interpretation came at the point of explaining the relationship between Jesus as the Son of Man and Jesus as
the Son of God. Christ was constituted Son of Man by virtue of
his birth from a virgin mother. He was Son of God, not having had
a human father (*Against Marcion* IV. x, ANF, III, p. 358).

Tertullian waged a similar controversy with Apelles, who advocated that Christ was of solid flesh without having been born. Tertullian was very careful to distinguish whether or not Christ had
been born *through* or *of* a virgin, *in* or *of* a womb, *in* her or *of* her.
Gnostics such as Valentinus had taught that the divine Christ
" passed through Mary as water through a tube." Tertullian maintained the reality of Christ's human birth (*On the Flesh of Christ*
XX, ANF, III, pp. 538, 539).

Set in full creedal context, the virgin birth is presented in chapter I of *On the Veiling of Virgins*.

The rule of faith, indeed, is altogether one, alone immovable and ir-
reformable; the rule, to wit, of believing in one only God omnipotent,
the Creator of the universe, and His Son Jesus Christ, born of the
Virgin Mary, crucified under Pontius Pilate, raised again the third day
from the dead, received in the heavens, sitting now at the right [hand]

---

he possessed them, his only conclusion was that the heretics must have cut or rearranged these Scriptures. It did not occur to him that the heretics may not have
possessed these Scriptures. Because his own immediate orthodox predecessors had
them, he assumed everyone contemporaneous with them and preceding them must
have had them because of the recently formed (unknown to him) doctrine of
apostolic succession and authorship of the Gospels. A reading of the fathers up to
Irenaeus reveals no such concept of Scripture as that which Tertullian was inclined
to think the fathers possessed.

of the Father, destined to come to judge the quick and dead through the resurrection of the flesh as well [as of the spirit]. (ANF, IV, p. 27.)

In chapter VI of this same writing, Mary was mentioned as a virgin and as a woman, and Tertullian then proceeded to interpret Paul's reference to " born of a woman " in Gal. 4:4 as virgin birth.

From statements made by Origen to Celsus it is apparent that the virgin birth of Jesus was well known in the first half of the third Christian century. Not only was it well known, it was a topic for increasing discussion. In his writing in refutation of the ideas of Celsus, the Jew, Origen proudly exclaimed that the virgin birth was a doctrine with which almost the entire world was acquainted because it was an integral part of that which Christians preached. " For who is ignorant of the statement that Jesus was born of a Virgin, and that he was crucified, and that His resurrection is an article of faith among many? " (*Against Celsus* I. vii, ANF, IV, p. 399.) However, along with its popularity the virgin birth acquired notoriety. Celsus insisted that Jesus was really illegitimate and that the Christians had " invented his birth from a virgin."

This is what may be called the Pandera tradition. It probably arose somewhere in the second century and flourished among the opponents of Christianity for several more.[5] The tradition appeared in the Babylonian Talmud in the fifth or sixth century A.D. and is also to be found in the *Toledoth Jeshua,* which dates from about the fourth century and may have had its origins in the second. The Huldreich (1708) Vindobona MS. reads:

During the second Temple in the days of the Emperor Tiberius and of Herod II, King of Israel . . . there was a man of the descendants of the House of David, who was called Joseph Pandera. He had a wife named Maria; the same man feared God and was a disciple of the Rabbi Shimeon ben Shetach. The neighbor of this Joseph was a rascal named Jochanan, the wicked, an evil doer and an adulterer. Maria was a beautiful woman on whom the wicked Jochanan had cast his eyes desiring to possess her. So he used to place himself behind the modest woman and she perceived it not. What follows occurred in the month Nisan at the end of the Feast of the Passover at midnight. Joseph had departed at this early hour to his school. What did that miscreant do? He arose betimes and when Joseph had departed, the rascal entered the house and found Maria lying apart from her husband since it was the time of her period.

---

5 Origen in *Against Celsus* I, 26, 28–29, 33–34–35, 37–38; II. 7. See also Tertullian's *De Spectaculis* 30: " *Hic est ille fabri aut quaestuariae filius."*

Then follows the description of how Mary thought the intruder was Joseph and how she scolded him for defiling her, how Joseph soon became aware of what had really happened and how he deserted his family for Babylon after the illegitimate son was born, and how Mary was always of the opinion that Joseph was the father of Jesus.

In the Talmud, and according to Celsus, Pandera is the seducer. In the *Toledoth Jeshua,* Pandera is the father of Joseph and Jochanan is the seducer. Another variation is in the Strassburg MS. and the Adler of Jemen MS. of the *Toledoth Jeshua* where the husband of Mary is Jochanan, and the seducer is Joseph, the son of Pandera.[6]

The strangest conclusion that has ever been drawn from this scurrilous tradition was made by Alfred Resch in his *Das Kindheitsevangelium nach Lucas und Matthäus* (1897). He said that the source for the infancy narratives in Matthew and Luke was an " original " *Toledoth Jeshua.* Resch reconstructed the original out of extracanonical traditions and insisted that this " original " document underlies not only Matthew and Luke but also the Fourth Gospel, the Pauline Epistles, the Apocalypse, and the writings of Ignatius, Aristides, and Justin Martyr. Resch's " original document " begins with the birth of John and concludes with the Lukan genealogy which has been remodeled along the lines of the Matthaean.

In opposition to Celsus' views, Origen argued that it could be expected that those who would not believe the miraculous birth of Jesus would invent some falsehood (I. 32) and that the rationale of his day was that a man's origin must be in keeping with his life. Since Jesus' life and ministry demonstrated great character, so must his birth be within the context of purity. Therefore, Celsus must be completely mistaken (I. 33).

In chapters 34 and 37 of Book I, Origen developed the defense for the virgin birth. He based this doctrine on accepted and popular tradition, the relation of the birth narrative in the Gospels to the prophecy in Isa. 7:14, and on the fact that in his time there was known to be a female animal species that gave birth as the result of a parthenogenetic process. He added that spermatic elements exist within the earth.

His doctrine of incarnation was summarized in the process of

---

6 Elwood Worcester, *Studies in the Birth of the Lord* (1932), pp. 231–249, gives a detailed account of these stories.

his contentions with Celsus: " Jesus, on entering into the world, assumed, as one born of a woman, a human body, and one which was capable of suffering a natural death. For which reason, in addition to others, we say that He was also a great wrestler; having, on account of His human body, been tempted in all respects like other men, but no longer as men, with sin as a consequence, but being altogether without sin " (I. 69; ANF, IV, p. 428).

The relationship of the canonical form of Matt., chs. 1 and 2, and Luke, chs. 1 and 2, to the writings of the early church fathers is one of the most perplexing problems in historical research. Although it is certain that the idea of the virgin birth was prominent in the Christian community in the first century, and this fact is attested in the writings of the early church fathers, no clear reference to the Matthaean stories appears until after the first part of the second century, and Lukan references begin to appear in the writings of the fathers only as late as the end of the second century. A most baffling question is, Why did no Lukan birth or infancy incidents appear prior to the writings of Irenaeus? Does this mean that they just did not know Luke, chs. 1 and 2, or does this mean that Luke, chs. 1 and 2, in its present form was not composed and did not become part of the canonical record until after the middle of the second century?

C. LACTANTIUS, JEROME, ATHANASIUS, AUGUSTINE, THE " SEVEN ECUMENICAL COUNCILS," THOMAS AQUINAS

By A.D. 300 the virgin birth came to be associated with the Logos as the means by which the former explained the method by which the latter entered the world. Lactantius in his *Divine Institutes* related the Son of God to the Greek Logos and discussed the concept in terms of " Word " or " Speech."

With good reason, therefore, is He called the Speech and the Word of God, because God, by a certain incomprehensible energy and power of His majesty, enclosed the vocal spirit proceeding from His mouth, which He had not conceived in the womb, but in His mind, within a form which has life through its own perception and wisdom, and He also fashioned other spirits of His into angels. (IV. viii, ANCL, XXI, *The Works of Lactantius* I, p. 225.)

Lactantius also related the birth of the Lord to the activity of the Holy Spirit.

Therefore the Holy Spirit of God, descending from heaven, chose the holy Virgin, that he might enter into her womb. But she, being filled by the possession of the Divine Spirit conceived; and without any intercourse with a man, her virgin womb was suddenly impregnated. But if it is known to all that animals are accustomed to conceive by the wind and the breeze, why should any think it wonderful when we say that a virgin was impregnated by the Spirit of God, to whom whatever He may wish is easy? (IV. xii, ANCL, XXI, *The Works of Lactantius* I, p. 233.)

The author of *Divine Institutes* in this discussion referred to Virgil's *Georgic* iii. 274 and to Isa. 7:14 and 9:6. Lactantius' discourse on the incarnation of the Word is noteworthy for its use of the vivid terminology, the " first nativity " and " second." This is a classic statement of the orthodox theory of the two origins of Christ which corresponded to his two natures.

For in His first nativity, which was spiritual, He was motherless, because He was begotten by God the Father alone, without the office of a mother. But in His second, which was in the flesh, He was born of a virgin's womb without the office of a father, that, bearing a middle substance between God and man, He might be able, as it were, to take by the hand this frail and weak nature of ours, and raise it to immortality. He became both the Son of God through the Spirit, and the Son of man through the flesh — that is, both God and man. (IV. xiii, ANCL, XXI, *The Works of Lactantius* I, p. 237.)

The same idea of a twofold nativity is also to be found in Lactantius' *Epitome of the Divine Institutes* (XLIII and XLIV, ANCL, XXI, *The Works of Lactantius* II, p. 126) , where he specifies that the purpose of the incarnation is to send to the world a teacher of righteousness who will establish true worship.

At the beginning of the fourth century A.D. emphasis was transferred from the virgin birth of Jesus to the virginity of Mary. In his " Oration in Praise of Constantine," Eusebius posed the question which for centuries remained in the forefront of the church's mind: " And why is it impossible that she who was with child of the Holy Spirit should be, and ever continue to be, a virgin? " (XIX, NPNF, I, p. 576.) Jerome's discourse on " Perpetual Virginity of Blessed Mary," written at about A.D. 383 against Helvidius, who held the contrary view, was a subject picked up by Augustine and continued to be developed through the centuries until it reached its culmination in the writings of Thomas Aquinas.

I must call upon the Holy Spirit to express His meaning by my mouth and defend the virginity of the Blessed Mary. I must call upon the Lord Jesus to guard the sacred lodging of the womb in which He abode for ten months from all suspicion of sexual intercourse. And I must entreat God the Father to show that the mother of His Son, who was a mother before she was a bride, continued a Virgin after her son was born. (*Perpetual Virginity* 2, NPNF, VI, p. 334.)

You say that Mary did not continue a virgin: I claim still more, that Joseph himself on account of Mary was a virgin, so that from a virgin wedlock a virgin son was born. For if a holy man he does not come under imputation of fornication, and it is nowhere written that he had another wife, but was the guardian of Mary whom he was supposed to have to wife rather than her husband, the conclusion is that he who was thought worthy to be called father of the Lord, remained a virgin. (*Perpetual Virginity* 21, NPNF, VI, p. 344.)

Athanasius argued with those who said that the Word was co-essential with the body of our Lord. In his *Letter to Epictetus* he wrote: Scriptures " say that God came in a human body. But the fathers who also assembled at Nicaea say that, not the body, but the Son himself is coessential with the Father, and while He is of the Essence of the Father, the body, as they admitted according to the Scriptures, is of Mary " (NPNF, IV, p. 571). Athanasius had also insisted that Jesus' birth from Mary was to reveal that he was really a human being. Augustine maintained the same view — Jesus was both God and man, and his birth illustrated this.

By Augustine's time, however, the discussion centered upon the means by which the miraculous action of God had taken place within Mary. Augustine's basis for belief in the virgin birth, like that of his predecessors, was the acceptance of the fact that the narrative in the New Testament was the fulfillment of the prophecy in Isa. 7:14, and his basic formula for the Christian doctrine was: " Jesus Christ who is the only-begotten, that is, the only Son of God, our Lord, was born of the Holy Ghost and of the Virgin Mary " (*Enchiridion* 37, NPNF, III, p. 250).

At this point, however, Augustine was forced to deal with a question that arose in the minds of some and that continued for years to be a debatable issue: " Nevertheless, are we on this account to say that the Holy Ghost is the father of the man Christ, and that as God the Father begat the Word, so God the Holy Spirit begat the man, and that these two natures constitute the one Christ; and that as the Word He is the Son of God the Father, and as man the Son of God the Holy Spirit, because the Holy Spirit as His father begat Him in the Virgin Mary? " (*Enchiridion* 38, NPNF, III, p. 250). Augustine pleaded that in no sense is Jesus the son of the Holy Ghost. To the question, his answer was a resounding " No! "

Whether or not the Holy Spirit was the " father of Jesus " was a serious point of contention for several centuries beginning in Augustine's time. Later in the church's history this became one of the points of Christian doctrine at which followers of Muhammed became most provoked. Many of them interpreted this to mean that " God married a woman from whom He begot a Son." [7]

Augustine, like many who followed him, discussed the sinlessness of Jesus in terms of the absence in his conception of " carnal lust."

Begotten and conceived, then, without any indulgence of carnal lust, and therefore bringing with Him no original sin, and by the grace of God joined and united in a wonderful and unspeakable way in one person with the Word, the Only-begotten of the Father, a son by nature, not by grace, and therefore having no sin of His own; nevertheless, on account of the likeness of sinful flesh in which He came, He was called sin, that He might be sacrificed to wash away sin. (*Enchiridion* 41, NPNF, III, p. 251.)

Similar theologically speculative elements may be observed in his treatise *On the Holy Trinity*, where, in Book XIII, ch. 18, he tried to explain why the Son of God took upon himself flesh from the race of Adam and from a virgin. " But God judged it better both to take upon Him man through whom to conquer the enemy of the human race, from the race itself that had been conquered; and yet to do this of a virgin, whose conception, not flesh but spirit, not lust but faith, preceded." (NPNF, III, p. 180.) He insisted that it was necessary that carnal concupiscence should be entirely absent, when the offspring of the Virgin was conceived.

Gregory of Nyssa had also insisted that the feeling of sensual pleasure precedes human birth, " and as to the impulse of vice in all living men, this is a disease of our nature " (*The Great Catechism* 16, NPNF, V, p. 488). Gregory had summarized the matter in this way: in his birth he had no connection with sensual pleasure, and in his life he had no connection with vice.

The tendency within the church to give centrality to the nature

[7] See J. Windrow Sweetman's *Islam and Christian Theology*, Vol. I (1945), pp. 72–73.

of the mother of Jesus may be seen clearly within the results of the
" Seven Ecumenical Councils." This period of church history is
characterized by a highly developed monastic life and the parallel
of virginity being extolled as the highest of Christian virtues. The
early writings of this period such as *The Epistle of Cyril to Nes-
torius* (ca. 431) show that the interest began with the attempt to
relate the two natures of Christ.

The Word having personally united to himself flesh animated by a
rational soul, did in an ineffable and inconceivable manner become
man, and was called the Son of Man, not merely as willing or being
pleased to be so called, neither on account of taking to himself a person, but because the two natures being brought together in a true
union, there is of both one Christ and one Son; for the difference of
the natures is not taken away by the union, but rather the divinity and
the humanity make perfect for us the one Lord Jesus Christ by their
ineffable and inexpressible union. (NPNF, XIV, p. 198.)

In the same writing may be observed an increasing interest concerning the nature of the woman who bore God's Son:

This the declaration of the correct faith proclaims everywhere. This
was the sentiment of the holy Fathers; therefore, they ventured to call
the holy Virgin, the Mother of God, not as if the nature of the Word
or His divinity had its beginning from the holy Virgin, but because of
her was born that holy body with a rational soul, to which the Word
being personally united is said to be born according to the flesh.
(NPNF, XIV, p. 198.)

Mary had been called " Mother of God " by Origen, Alexander
of Alexandria, Athanasius, Eusebius, and Cyril of Jerusalem.
" Mother of God," however, soon became more than an appellation. It had become part of the confession of the church.

We confess therefore, our Lord Jesus Christ, the Only Begotten Son
of God, perfect God, and perfect Man of a reasonable soul and flesh
consisting, and the last days, for us and for our salvation, of Mary the
Virgin according to his humanity, of the same substance with his
Father according to his Divinity, and of the same substance with us
according to his humanity; for there became a union of two natures.
We therefore confess one Christ, one Son, one Lord. . . . According
to this understanding of this unmixed union, we confess the holy Virgin to be the Mother of God; because God the Word was incarnate
and became Man, and from this conception he united the temple taken
from her with himself. (*Letter of Cyril to John of Antioch,* NPNF,
XIV, p. 251.)

The next step in logic was to demand of the Mother of God that she be " ever Virgin." The concern for her perpetual virginity was evidenced in the writings of the church fathers after the third century and had a place in the Council of Constantinople II (A.D. 553). One of the " Sentences of the Synod " was directed against those who deny that " God the Word was incarnate of the holy Mother of God, and ever Virgin Mary." The same council defined the incarnation in terms of Lactantius' " Double Nativity " but added perpetual virginity and made of the whole a confessional statement: " If anyone shall not confess that the Word of God has two nativities, the one from all eternity of the Father, without time and without body; the other in these last days, coming down from heaven and being made flesh of the holy and glorious Mary, Mother of God and always a virgin, and born of her: let him be anathema " (NPNF, XIV, p. 312).

At Constantinople III (A.D. 680, 681) the confession took on an additional flourish.

Moreover we confess that one of the same holy consubstantial Trinity, God the Word, who was begotten of the Father before the worlds, in the last days of the world for us and for our salvation came down from heaven, and was incarnate of the Holy Ghost, and of our Lady, the holy, immaculate, ever-virgin and glorious Mary, truly and properly the Mother of God, that is to say according to the flesh which was born of her; and was truly made man, the same being very God and very man. (In the *Letter of Agatho and of the Roman Synod of 125 Bishops Which Was to Serve as an Instruction to the Legates Sent to Attend the Sixth Synod,* NPNF, XIV, p. 340.)

At the Council in Trullo (A.D. 692) the concept became fixed. " As the Catholic Church has always taught the Virgin-birth as well as the Virgin-conception of our Blessed Lord, and has affirmed that Mary was ever-virgin, even after she had brought forth the incarnate Son, so it follows necessarily that there could be no child bed nor puerperal flux." (Canon LXXIX, NPNF, XIV, p. 400.)

In the next century those who did not confess the perpetual virginity of Mary were anathematized, and the image of Mary came to be venerated along with the image of the crucifixion. At the Iconoclastic Conciliabulum held at Constantinople in A.D. 754 the following appeared as number fifteen in a list of nineteen anathemas: anathema to anyone who does " not confess the holy ever-virgin Mary, truly and properly the Mother of God, to be higher than every creature whether visible or invisible, and does not with sincere faith seek her intercessions as of one having confidence in her access to our God " (NPNF, XIV, p. 546). Later in A.D. 787 at Nice II it was stated: " Likewise we venerate the image of the Virgin Mary, we lift up our mind to her the most holy Mother of God, bowing both head and knees before her; calling her blessed above all men and women, with the Archangel Gabriel " (NPNF, XIV, p. 554). At the same council reference was made to Mary as " our spotless Lady, the holy Mother of God " (NPNF, XIV, p. 533).

By the thirteenth century these ideas had reached their culmination in the writings of Thomas Aquinas and were a part of the unchallenged traditions of the church. They were a part of the piety as well as the rationale of the Christian faith. " And we give Thee thanks because, as by Thy Son Thou didst create us, so by thy true and holy love with which Thou hast loved us, Thou didst cause Him, true God and true Man, to be born of the glorious and ever-Virgin, most Blessed holy Mary and didst will that He should redeem us captives by His Cross and Blood and Death." (Francis of Assisi, *Rules of the Friars Minor* 23.) [8]

Anselm, in the eleventh century, represented one exception to this development in which the purity of Mary was being made to account for the sinlessness of Jesus. He made claims for the Virgin's perfect and unrivaled purity which classed him with those to whom the doctrine of the immaculate conception was the true formula for the explanation of Mary's purity. However, in his *Cur Deus Homo?* he expressed the view that Mary's purity was derived " from Him." " But that Virgin from whom the Man we are speaking of was taken, was one of those who, before His birth, had been purified by Him from sins. And it was in her state of purity He was taken from her." (II. xvi, tr. Edward S. Prout, p. 151.)

The *Summa Theologica* of Thomas Aquinas crystallized the traditions of preceding centuries. Part III of the *Summa* is a treatise on the incarnation and on Christology. A number of chapters are devoted to the nature of Christ's birth and the nature of Mary. What had happened in the history of the church with regard to balance between the two doctrines is apparent just from his listing of the chapters. One chapter, 35, is devoted to Christ's nativity. The preceding eight chapters are devoted to the nature of Mary, her virginity, and our Lord's conception. In the first of these chapters appears a classic illustration of the kind of theological reason-

[8] Father Paschal Robinson, *The Writings of Saint Francis of Assisi* (1906), p. 60.

ing that led to the appearance of such ideas in the life of the church.

The Church celebrates the feast of Our Lady's Nativity. Now the Church does not celebrate feasts except of those who are holy. Therefore even in her birth the Blessed Virgin was holy. Therefore she was sanctified in her womb.

Nothing is handed down in the canonical Scriptures concerning the sanctification of the Blessed Mary as to her being sanctified in the womb; indeed, they do not even mention her birth. Just as Augustine, in his tractate on the Assumption of the Virgin, argues with reason, since her body was assumed into heaven, and yet Scripture does not relate this; so it may be reasonably argued that she was sanctified in the womb. For it is reasonable to believe that she, who brought forth the Only Begotten of the Father full of grace and truth, received greater privileges of grace than all others. (*Summa Theologica* Part III, Vol. 16, p. 3.)

Aquinas was also convinced that the Christian confession must contain the belief that the Blessed Virgin committed no actual sin, neither mortal nor venial (Q. 27, Art. 4), and that she was a virgin even in giving birth to Jesus (Q. 28, Art. 2). He argued that it was fitting that Christ should be born of a virgin for four reasons: (1) in order to maintain the dignity of the Father who sent him, (2) this was fitting to a property of the Son himself, who is sent, (3) this was befitting the dignity of Christ's humanity in which there could be no sin, (4) on account of the very end of the incarnation of Christ, which was that men might be born again as sons of God (Q. 28, Art. 1).

The great Aristotelian Christian got around the problem of how the body of Jesus was formed from the body of the Virgin and remained free of sin by having taken his form not from actual flesh, but from blood, which he termed that which is " potentially flesh."

Since the Blessed Virgin was of the same nature as other women, it follows that she had flesh and bones of the same nature as theirs. Now, flesh and bones in other women are actual parts of the body, the integrity of which results therefrom: and consequently they cannot be taken from the body without its being corrupted or diminished. But as Christ came to heal what was corrupt, it was not fitting that He should bring corruption or diminution to the integrity of His mother. Therefore it was becoming that Christ's body should be formed not from the flesh or bones of the Virgin, but from her blood, which as yet is not actually a part, but is potentially the whole. (Q. 31, Art. 5, Vol. 16, p. 67.)

Aquinas took up the problem of the role of the Holy Spirit in the conception of Jesus where Augustine had left off. According to Aquinas the conception of Christ's body was effected by the whole Trinity, but should be attributed to the Holy Ghost (Q. 32, Art. 1). However, Christ is not called the Son of the Holy Ghost, even though the third person of the Trinity was active in his conception, because he was not in the likeness of the same species (Q. 32, Art. 3).

Other questions were posed by Aquinas and answered by him: whether the Blessed Virgin co-operated actively in the conception of Christ's body, whether Christ was sanctified in the first instant of his conception, whether Christ as man had the use of free will in the first instant of his conception, whether Christ could merit in the first instant of his conception, whether nativity regards the nature rather than the person, whether a temporal nativity should be attributed to Christ, and whether the Blessed Virgin should be called the Mother of God. Aquinas, in addition to answering these questions, dealt with another that had for a number of years been raised in Christian circles. Was Christ born without his mother suffering? He stated in logical and doctrinal form what pseudepigraphal stories had been telling and what had been posed since Augustine: "Because she conceived Christ without the defilement of sin, and without the stain of sexual mingling, therefore did she bring Him forth without pain, without violation of her virginal integrity, without detriment to the purity of her maidenhood" (Q. 35, Art. 6, Vol. 16, p. 118).

Thus, Thomas Aquinas represented the culmination of a long history of interpretation and reinterpretation of the virgin birth of Jesus. The history of early Christianity shows that the primary significance of the birth of Jesus was not the virginity of the mother but the fact that the Savior came into the world as a child. In the days of the apostolic fathers and the early apologists the virgin birth was inseparably connected with the redemption motif. The redeemer first appeared as a child. He was the Holy Child. The crucified and resurrected one, whose life was so surrounded by an aura of the divine, entered human society normally, in human form, as a child. He was God's wonderful *pais:* servant-child.

In Ignatius and other early writers, the virgin birth and the child motif are associated with the redemption motif and Passion of Christ in relationship to Isa., ch. 53. What was important was the incarnation of the redeemer. In the apologists, redemption remains important, but the incarnation is more fully described as the incarnation of the Son of God. From Tatian through Tertullian, the central context of the incarnation is the Logos becoming man, and the virgin birth is used to explain how the Logos became incarnate. Late in the second century, when the discussion centered around a Christological controversy with the Gnostics and Docetists, the virgin birth was used to describe and account for the true humanity of Jesus. The Biblical description of birth by the Holy Spirit and the Virgin Mary maintained the dualism of spirit and flesh. From the writings of the ante-Nicene fathers it can be seen that from the middle of the second century on, Logos and virgin birth were united. By means of virgin birth the Logos was made flesh. Later the concern for the virgin birth of Jesus, the Logos, was supplanted by interest in the virginity of Mary, the Lady.

After the second century the story of the virgin birth of Jesus gradually became separated from Christology and became attached to Mariology. This development came about in conjunction with monasticism and probably was also closely associated with the reaction of the church against attacks made on the legitimacy of Jesus. The content of Jerome's " The Virgin's Profession " [9] must also be considered. This essay glorifies virginity in order to offset immoralities among the populace of that time. All of this formed the background for the development in theology that culminated in Marianism. Eventually the church made a total substitution for the truth that the Biblical narratives conveyed.[10] The church substituted a moral idealism based on virginity for a moral idealism

[9] F. A. Wright, *Fathers of the Church* (1929), pp. 225–267.

[10] One of the oddities in the history of Christianity is the little attention given by Luther and Calvin to the virgin birth especially in view of the predominance of this highly developed theme in Roman Catholicism and the excesses that had sprung up around it. The two Reformers stood in agreement with Roman Christianity on several basic issues. Luther agreed with Roman Catholic dogma on the virgin birth at two points: that " virgin birth " meant that Christ's birth was without co-operation of a man and that Mary remained a virgin. (Luther's Works, Vol. 22, *Sermons on The Gospel of St. John Chs. 1 to 4,* ed. by Jaroslav Pelikan [1957], p. 23.) Calvin showed accord with Roman tradition by his observation that " the secret and heavenly manner of generation has separated him from the ordinary rank of men." (*Commentary on a Harmony of the Evangelists Matthew, Mark, and Luke,* Vol. I, The Calvin Translation Society, Edinburgh, 1845, p. 43.) Luther and Calvin left to the rationalistic philosophers who followed them the task of evaluating and criticizing the vast complex of Marian tradition and Mariology.

based on marriage, and the erroneous concept of the inherent evil of sexuality was substituted for the primitive Christian ideal of the sanctity of sex. The Roman Catholic Church is to be commended for its deep concern for personal purity. It is unfortunate, however, that the church developed and used the Biblical narratives in a way opposite from what they were originally intended.

*A*nd God looked at her, and descended into the womb of the holy woman, and all the saints rejoiced over her, the deliverer of the world, and when they saw her they prostrated themselves before her, and said, " O Mother of God, our Lady and redeemer, pray for us! Thou hast become the habitation of glory. He shall be conceived, and formed, and brought forth from thy womb, and shall put on thy flesh. O Mother of God, thou shalt carry [Him] in thy belly, and thou shalt become the habitation of the Godhead."

— *The Annunciation of Gabriel to Mary,* Ethiopic

CHAPTER

2

PSEUDEPIGRAPHAL AND APOCRYPHAL TRADITION

As THE CHRISTIAN FAITH spread after the first century, popular traditions that reflected the thinking of the growing Christian community flourished. A literature circulated that not only represented the thinking of the eras in which they arose but also provided source material and reference for many of the ideas expressed in the theological writings of the church fathers. Although the extant texts of this literature are of late date, the development of the traditions themselves goes back to very early Christian times. By means of these extracanonical writings Christian authors attempted to increase the range of application of the gospel message. Christian ideas were rewritten over against the background of pagan thought. These traditions grew and became fixed in the millennium preceding the Protestant Reformation. The infancy of Jesus was one of the major themes of this literature, and alongside it there developed a literature associated with Mary. After the second century, Mary replaced Jesus as the center of interest in the infancy traditions.

The fathers of the church reveal in their writings the knowledge of and use of noncanonical traditions. The extant pseudepigraphal literature contains some materials relevant to the birth and infancy of Jesus. Apocryphal literature contains much that is pertinent.

A. PSEUDEPIGRAPHAL WRITINGS

The extant Greek books of the *Sibylline Oracles* (ET, Milton S. Terry; Hunt & Eaton, New York, 1890) are not identical with those of antiquity to which reference is made by old classic authors.

Those which are known at the present time belong to the large body of pseudepigraphal literature that flourished in Christian circles beginning in the second century and continued to be of considerable importance for several centuries. The present twelve Sibylline books include literary activity that extended from the second century B.C. through the sixth century of the Christian era.

A passage in the *Oracles,* Book III, displays probable pre-Christian expectations of the Alexandrian Jewish mind.

> And then will he a kingdom for all time
> Raise up for all men, and a holy law
> Give to the pious to whom he has pledged
> To open up the land, and the wide world,
> And portals of the blessed, and all joys,
> And mind immortal, and eternal bliss.
> And out of every land unto the house
> Of the great God will they bring frankin-
> cense,
> And gifts, and there shall be no other house
> To be inquired of by men yet to be;
> But whom God gave to honor faithful men,
> Him mortals shall call Son of the great God.
> And all paths of the field and the rough
> hills,
> And lofty mountains, and the sea's wild
> waves,
> Shall in those days be easy to pass over,
> For all peace of the good shall come on
> earth.
> And the sword shall God's prophets take
> away,
> For they shall be the judges of mankind,
> And righteous kings; for of the mighty God
> This is the judgment and the sovereignty.
>   (912–931, pp. 107–108.)

The text continues with ideas strikingly reminiscent of passages in Isaiah introduced with the thought of a wonder that shall befall a maiden (*kore*).[1]

> Be of good cheer, O maiden, and exult;
> For the Eternal, who made heaven and
> earth

---

[1] This word is usually used of a maiden, girl, or damsel. Sometimes it refers to a newly married woman or young wife.

> Has given thee joy, and he will dwell in
>   thee,
> And for thee shall be an immortal light.
> And wolves and lambs promiscuously shall
>   eat
> Grass in the mountains, and among the
>   kids
> Shall leopards graze, and wandering bears
>   shall lodge
> Among the calves, and the carnivorous lion
> Shall eat straw in the manger like the ox,
> And little children lead them with a band.
> For tame will be on earth the beasts he
>   made,
> And with young babes will dragons fall
>   asleep,
> And no harm, for God's hand will be on
>   them.
>
> (932–944, p. 108.)

Where direct reference is made in the *Oracles* to Christ's birth, the idea of pre-existence is combined with incarnation in the Virgin. Judging from references in the church fathers, this material ought then to be dated from the close of the second or at the beginning of the third century A.D.

The present Book VI is brief and consists in its entirety of allusions to Christ.

> The Immortal's mighty Son, renowned in
>   song,
> Proclaim I from the heart, to whom a
>   throne
> The most high Father gave for a possession
> Ere he was born; and then he was raised up,
> In flesh given him, and washed in Jordan's
>   stream,
> Which bears with gleaming foot the waves
>   away.
> He having fled from fire first shall behold
> The blessed Spirit of God descending down
> With white wings of a dove. And he shall
>   bloom
> A blossom pure, and all things shall burst
>   forth.
>
> (1–10, p. 159.)

The lines that follow speak of his " boasting a descent from a celestial Father " and combine elements of both Jewish and Gentile traditions.

> And from one root shall come
> Enough bread for men, when David's house
> A scion shall bring forth, and in his hands
> Shall be the whole world — land and heaven
>   and sea.
> He will flash lightning on the earth, as once
> The two born from each other's sides be-
>   held
> The light appear. And this shall come to
>   pass
> When earth rejoices in hope of a son [*pais*].
>   (18–25, pp. 159–160.)

The outstanding feature of these references is the concept of the " child " who will usher in the new age.[2] This idea has its parallel in Virgil's " Fourth Eclogue " and in the writings of the early fathers of the church (cf. Clement of Alexandria). The same idea precedes the most elaborate reference to Christian birth traditions in Book VIII of the *Oracles*. It is with the advent of the holy child (*pais*) that a new reign shall come upon men.

> Let me not live when the gay one shall reign,
> But then, when heavenly grace shall rule
>   within,
> And when a holy child the murderous guile
> Of all shall utterly destroy with chains.
>   (241–244, p. 183.)

The language of the following description is typical of the combination in the fathers of the late second and early third Christian century of the idea of incarnation of the Logos and virgin birth.

> Thus spakest thou to the Word, and by thy
>   mind
> All things occurred, and all the elements
> At once obeyed thy order, and a creature
> Eternal was in mortal image formed;
> Heaven also, air, fire, earth, and the sea's
>   wave.
>   (561–565, p. 196.)

[2] In the apocryphal *Acts of Paul*, ca. A.D. 160, the same motif appears. " Wherefore God hath sent his own Child, whom I preach and teach that men should have hope in him who alone hath had compassion upon the world that was in error."

In several lines following, other aspects of the created world are enumerated. Then comes a remarkable passage on the birth of Jesus.

> But in the latest times
> The earth has changed itself, and there has
> come
> A humble one, from the Virgin Mary's
> womb;
> A new light rose, and coming from the
> heavens
> He entered mortal form.[3] And therefore
> first
> Did Gabriel show his strong and holy frame.
> And second to the virgin he by voice
> Spoke, being himself a messenger and said:
> " Virgin, receive God in thy holy breast."
> So speaking God breathed grace. But as for
> her,
> Always a virgin, terror and surprise
> Seized her at once as she heard, and she
> stood
> In trembling, and her mind was filled with
> fear,
> Her heart leaped at the messages unknown.
> But she again was gladdened, and her heart
> Was by the voice cheered, and the maiden
> laughed,
> And her young cheek blushed, merry with
> the joy;
> And she was spell-bound in her heart by awe.
> But confidence came to her, and the Word
> Flew in her womb,[4] and became flesh in
> time,

[3] Cf. Tertullian (Apol. 21). When Gabriel visited Mary and announced to her that she should bring forth the Messiah, " a divine ray of light glided down into her, and descending, was made concrete as flesh in her womb." Herodotus told how a ray of light fell from heaven upon the sacred cow which afterward gave birth to Apis. Plutarch in Isis and Osiris says the same about the moonlight (Conybeare, Myth, Magic, and Morals, p. 230).

[4] Ephrem, the fourth-century Syrian Father, Rufinus of Aquileja, and others describe how the Word of God entered, as divine seed, through the ears of Mary. This is reminiscent of the Egyptian tradition of which Plutarch speaks in Isis and Osiris that the cat conceives through its ears and brings forth its young through the mouth. This for Plutarch symbolized the mystery of the generation of the Logos, which is also conceived through the ears and expressed through the mouth (Conybeare, op. cit., pp. 230–231).

Was gendered and was made a human form,
And came to be a youth, of virgin born,
This was a mighty wonder to mankind,
But it was nothing greatly wonderful
To God the Father, and to God the Son.
  And the glad earth received the new-
    born babe,
The heavenly throne laughed, and the
  world exulted.
The new appearing and prophetic star
Was honored by the wise men, and the babe
In the manger and wrapped in his swad-
  dling-clothes
Was shown to those obedient unto God.
And of the Word was Bethlehem fatherland
Called by the keepers of herds, goats and
  sheep.

                    (573–605, pp. 196–197.) [5]

The *Sibylline Oracles* convey two principal motifs, that of the " child " and that of the Logos being virgin born. The first motif is important for demonstrating the kind of background which syncretistic thought presented in early Christian times. The second is significant for showing how the virgin birth tradition was developed and used at the beginning of the Old Catholic era.

Another composite work that is of great interest for the development of Christian thought is *The Ascension of Isaiah,* which is accessible in R. H. Charles's book of the same title. This composite work consists of three basic parts, all of which may have circulated separately in the first Christian century. The three are: the *Martyrdom of Isaiah,* the *Vision of Isaiah,* and the *Testament of Hezekiah.* The only one of these which contains a section on the virgin birth is the second, the *Vision of Isaiah.*

And I indeed saw a woman of the family of David the prophet, named Mary, a Virgin, and she was espoused to a man named Joseph, a carpenter, and he also was of the seed and family of the righteous David of Bethlehem Judah. And he came into his lot. And when she was espoused, she was found with child, and Joseph the carpenter was desirous to put her away. But the angel of the Spirit appeared in this

---

[5] See Book I, ET, lines 381–420, where it is mentioned that " the Child of the great God to men shall become incarnate, being fashioned like to mortals of the earth."

world, and after that Joseph did not put her away, but kept Mary and did not reveal this matter to any one. And he did not approach Mary, but kept her as a holy virgin, though with child. And he did not live with her for two months. And after two months of days while Joseph was in his house, and Mary his wife, but both alone, it came to pass that when they were alone, that Mary straightway looked with her eyes and saw a small babe, and she was astonied. And after she had been astonied, her womb was found as formerly before she had conceived. And when her husband Joseph said unto her: " What has astonied thee? " his eyes were opened and he saw the infant and praised God because into his portion God had come. And a voice came to them: " Tell this vision to no one." And the story regarding the infant was noised abroad in Bethlehem. Some said: " The Virgin Mary hath borne a child, before she was married two months." And many said: " She has not borne a child, nor has a midwife gone up [to her], nor have we heard the cries of [labour] pains." And they were all blinded respecting Him and they all knew regarding Him, though they knew not whence He was. And they took Him, and went to Nazareth in Galilee. And I saw, O Hezekiah and Josab my son, and I declare to the other prophets also who are standing by, that [this] hath escaped all the heavens and all the princes and all the gods of this world. And I saw: in Nazareth He sucked the breast as a babe and as is customary in order that He might not be recognized. And when he had grown up He worked great signs and wonders in the land of Israel and of Jerusalem. And after this the adversary envied Him and roused the children of Israel against Him. (xi. 2–19, *The Ascension of Isaiah,* R. H. Charles [Adam and Charles Black, 1900], pp. 74 ff.)

Charles believed that this passage dated from the close of the first or beginning of the second Christian century. In view of this early date, he concluded that it provides the source or background for certain ideas in Ignatius and in the *Book of James.* The injunction to " tell this vision to no one " is paralleled in *James* xx. 4: " Tell none of the marvels which thou hast seen, until the child enter into Jerusalem." That which " hath escaped all the heavens," etc., is thought by Charles to be the source for Ignatius' *To the Ephesians* xix and the whole passage x. 8 to xi. 19, in which the concealment of the real nature of Christ is the entire theme and in which the concealment of Mary's virginity is a subordinate theme.

The Odes of Solomon, forty-two in number, were first translated and published in 1909 by J. Rendel Harris from the Syriac version. Throughout the *Odes,* Christ is regarded as a pre-existent being and as the Divine Logos. Ode 19, which may come from another hand and postdate the others in the collection, elaborates a noncanonical birth tradition.

A cup of milk was offered to me: and I drank it in the sweetness of the delight of the Lord. The Son is the cup, and He who was milked is the Father: and the Holy Spirit milked Him: because His breasts were full, and it was necessary for Him that His milk should be sufficiently released; and the Holy Spirit opened His bosom and mingled the milk from the two breasts of the Father; and gave the mixture to the world without their knowing: and they who receive in its fulness are the ones on the right hand. [The Spirit] opened the womb of the Virgin and she became a Mother with many mercies; and she travailed and brought forth a Son, without incurring pain; and because she was not sufficiently prepared, and she had not sought a midwife [for He brought her to bear], she brought forth, as if she were a man, of her own will; and she brought Him forth openly, and acquired Him with great dignity, and loved Him in His swaddling clothes, and guarded Him kindly, and showed Him in majesty. Hallelujah. (J. Rendel Harris, *The Odes and Psalms of Solomon* [Cambridge University Press, 1909], p. 114.)

Ode 19 is attested by Lactantius. His *Divine Institutes* has a quotation from the Ode with regard to the painless delivery of the Virgin and even gives the number of the Ode as 19 or 20.[6]

The pseudepigraphal writings reveal a complex pattern of traditions that are comprised of Christian, Jewish, and Gentile elements. The child motif appears to have been the principal one, and this motif in turn seems to have been closely associated with the struggle of the times to achieve a concept of sexual purity.

B. APOCRYPHAL WRITINGS

What is most significant in the apocryphal writings is the departure of this tradition from the canonical and the affinity that the legends within them increasingly bear to pagan stories. They form a depository of popular ecclesiastical traditions that repre-

---

[6] Harris, p. 8. As a parallel to this, Harris quoted from the Chinese Classics the *Shi-King* III. ii. 1, where the delivery of the mother of Hou-tsi, the founder of the dynasty of Tchū, is described.

> "Lo! when her carrying time was done,
> Came like a lamb her first-born son,
> No pains of labour suffered she —
> No hurt, no pain, no injury."

In Ephrem's commentary on the Gospel there is a statement that "it was indecent that she who had been a habitation of the Spirit should bring forth with pains and curses."

sent the beliefs of the church from the second Christian century on through the Middle Ages and witness to the historical process in which the child motif, which developed early in the Christian era, became subordinate to the Lady motif.

The *Acts of Paul*, the *Acts of Peter,* and the *Epistle of the Apostles* date from the close of the second century and thus represent relatively early apocryphal traditions that include references to Jesus' origin.

In the *Acts of Paul*, we read these words:

For I delivered unto you in the beginning the things which I received of the HOLY apostles which were before me, who were at all times with Jesus Christ: namely, that our Lord Jesus Christ was born of Mary WHICH IS of the seed of David ACCORDING TO THE FLESH, the Holy Ghost being sent forth from heaven from the Father unto her BY THE ANGEL GABRIEL, that he [JESUS] might come down into this world and redeem all flesh by his flesh, and raise us up from the dead in the flesh, like as he hath shown to us in *himself* for an ensample. (III. 4 ff., ANT, pp. 289–290.)

The passage in the *Acts of Peter* that refers to Jesus' origin is significant for the attempt made in it to combine several apocryphal traditions. Peter is contending with the Romans and with Simon.

In the last times shall a child be born of the Holy Ghost: his mother knoweth not a man, neither doth any man say that he is his father. And again he saith: *She* hath brought forth and not brought forth. And again: Is it a small thing for you to weary men . . . ? Behold, a virgin shall conceive in the womb. And another prophet saith, honouring the Father: Neither did we hear her voice, neither did a midwife come in.[7] Another prophet saith: Born not of the womb of woman, but from a heavenly place came he down. (XXIV. ANT, pp. 324–325.)

In the *Epistle of the Apostles,* the apostles confess their faith:

In God the Lord, the Son of God, we do believe, that he is the word become flesh: that of Mary the holy virgin he took a body, begotten of the Holy Ghost, not of the will [lust] of the flesh, but by the will of God: that he was wrapped in swaddling clothes in Bethlehem and made manifest, and grew up and came to ripe age, when *also* we beheld it. (ANT, p. 485.)

The *Book of James* is typical of the apocryphal Gospels and served as the principal source for most subsequent similar tradi-

7 Cf. *The Ascension of Isaiah* xi. 14.

tions. Its present form was reached after the time of Origen and before the middle of the fourth century. Parts that refer to the birth of Jesus perhaps originated in the second century. The " History of the Childhood of Mary " may come from shortly before the time of Origen.[8]

The infancy narrative in *James* commences with a description of the miraculous manner in which the parents of Mary, Ioacim and Anna, were assured of offspring. Beneath a laurel tree Anna prayed that God would hearken unto her as he had unto Sarah and bless her with a child. An angel and then two messengers appeared to Anna and an angel to Ioacim assuring them of the answer to the prayer and giving proper ceremonial directions. In nine months she brought forth a daughter, who at six months was strong enough to walk seven steps. From three years of age, she was brought up in the Temple " as a dove that is nurtured: and she received food from the hand of an angel " (viii. 1, ANT, p. 42).

When she was twelve, the high priest summoned all available widowers, and the one to whom the Lord revealed a sign would be her husband. The lot fell on Joseph when a dove came forth from his rod and flew upon his head. At first Joseph refused because he was old, had several sons, and did not want to be the laughingstock to the Children of Israel. When the priest threatened, Joseph feared and finally consented to take her home with him. While she was under the protection of his house, this Annunciation was related to her by an angel as she went forth to fill a pitcher with water.

Fear not, Mary, for thou hast found grace before the Lord of all things, and thou shalt conceive of his word. And she, when she heard it, questioned in herself, saying: Shall I *verily* conceive of the living God, and bring forth after the manner of all women? And the angel of the Lord said: Not so, Mary, for a power of the Lord shall overshadow thee: wherefore also that holy thing which shall be born of thee shall be called the Son of the Highest. And thou shalt call his name Jesus: for he shall save his people from their sins. And Mary said: Behold the

---

[8] Harnack, *Gesch. Altchrist. Litt.*, p. 725. Ludwig Conrady attempted to prove that the infancy narratives in James had an origin independent of the canonical narratives and actually provided the source for the canonical. He likened the relationship of *James* to its source unto the relation which a butterfly bears to its chrysallis (p. 85, *Die Quelle der kanonischen Kindheitsgeschichte Jesus'* [1900]). This theory has been ably refuted by A. Hoben and James Moffatt. Some scholars have felt that at least the Lukan phrase, " How shall this be, seeing I know not a man? " is derived from other passages in *James,* where the phrase appears in more suitable context. See Conybeare, *op. cit.,* p. 203.

handmaid of the Lord is before him: be it unto me according to thy word. (xi. 2, ANT, p. 43.)

Mary returned to her work of making the purple and scarlet for the veil of the Temple and soon brought her finished product to the priest, who blessed her and reiterated the fact that " thou shalt be blessed among all generations of the earth." Mary thereupon rejoiced and went to visit her relative, Elizabeth, who exclaimed: " Whence is this to me that the mother of my Lord should come unto me? For behold that which is in me leaped and blessed thee " (xii. 2) . At this time Mary was sixteen years old and she stayed with Elizabeth for three months.

When Mary was six months pregnant, Joseph discovered her and chastised himself for having allowed her virginity to be defiled. After denying that she had been defiled by any man, Mary said: " As the Lord my God liveth, I know not whence it is come unto me " (xiii. 3) . Then Joseph found himself in the dilemma of hiding her sin and breaking the law or revealing his discovery and exposing himself to the responsibility for shedding innocent blood, thinking it possible that she was pregnant with the seed of an angel (xiv. 1) . An angel appeared to him that night in a dream, however, and allayed his fears.

Shortly thereafter Annas, the scribe, discovered him with Mary, who was obviously great with child. Annas reported this immediately to the priest, thinking that Joseph had gone unto Mary before he had made public declaration before the Children of Israel of his intentions of marriage. Both Mary and Joseph persisted in their innocence. Both were given the water test, sent away into the hill country, and returned whole. The people marveled.

In response to the decree of Augustus that all who were in Bethlehem should be recorded, Joseph proceeded to Bethlehem with the problem of whether to record Mary as his wife or as his daughter. While on the journey, riding on an ass, Mary became uncomfortable because of her burden and alighted from the animal. Then Joseph left Mary in a cave nearby with his sons while he went to look for a midwife. On his way he had wonderful celestial visions, and when he met a midwife, having answered several of her questions, he said to her in reply to who it was that was bringing forth in the cave: " It is Mary that was nurtured up in the Temple of the Lord: and I received her to wife by lot: and she is not my wife, but she hath conception by the Holy Ghost." Then the midwife went with him to see what was coming to pass.

one in *James*. Whereas in the latter the Matthaean and Lukan formulas were freely combined, in this Gospel they are again separate, the " he will save his people from their sins " again appearing in an annunciation to Joseph.

Pseudo-Matthew's use of the Annunciation tradition is more closely parallel to the canonical accounts than to *James*.

Whereas the " water test " is stated only in *James*, it is explained in *Pseudo-Matthew*. Instead of being sent into the hill country while the effects are expected to take hold, the accused appeared in the Temple and walked around the altar seven times. The narrative explains: " And when any one that had lied drank this water, and walked seven times round the altar, God used to show some sign in his face " (ch. 12) . When Joseph and then Mary had drunk in safety, the people rejoiced and praised Mary.

The incident in *James* of Joseph's seeking a midwife is omitted. Instead, after the birth he suddenly appears with two midwives.

The light from God so shone in the cave, that neither by day nor night was light wanting as long as the blessed Mary was there. And there she brought forth a son, and the angels surrounded Him when He was being born. And as soon as He was born, He stood upon His feet, and the angels adored Him, saying: Glory to God in the highest, and on earth peace to men of good pleasure. (Ch. 13, ANCL, Vol. XVI, pp. 31–32.)

Then Joseph appears with two midwives, Zelomi and Salome, who feared to enter the cave because of the exceeding brightness inside.

And when the blessed Mary heard this, she smiled; and Joseph said to her: Do not smile; but prudently allow them to visit thee, in case thou shouldst require for them thy cure. Then she ordered them to enter. And when Zelomi had come in, Salome having stayed without, Zelomi said to Mary: Allow me to touch thee. And when she had permitted her to make an examination, the midwife cried out with a loud voice and said: Lord, Lord Almighty, mercy on us! It has never been heard or thought of, that any one should have her breasts full of milk, and that the birth of a son should show his mother to be a virgin. But there has been no spilling of blood in his birth, no pain in bringing him forth. A virgin has conceived, a virgin has brought forth, and a virgin she remains. And hearing these words, Salome said: Allow me to handle thee, and prove whether Zelomi have spoken the truth. And the blessed Mary allowed her to handle her. And when she had withdrawn her hand from handling her, it dried up, and through excess of pain she began to weep bitterly, and to be in great distress, crying out and saying: O Lord God, Thou knowest that I have always feared Thee, and that without recompense I have cared for all the poor; I have taken nothing from the widow and the orphan, and the needy have I not sent empty away. And, behold, I am made wretched because of mine unbelief, since without a cause I wished to try Thy virgin.

And while she was thus speaking, there stood by her a young man in shining garments, saying: Go to the child, and adore Him, and touch Him with thy hand, and he will heal thee, because He is the Saviour of the world, and of all that hope in Him. And she went to the child with haste, and adored Him, and touched the fringe of the cloths in which He was wrapped, and instantly her hand was cured. (ANCL, Vol. XVI, pp. 32–33.)

In *Pseudo-Matthew*, subsequent incidents are: the transfer from the cave to the stable, the circumcision of the child, the appearance of the Magi (when the child was two years old), the anger and edict of Herod, and the flight into Egypt which enjoys the greatest embellishment in the tradition. On the journey they are accompanied by three boys and a girl. They encounter dragons and are adored by lions and panthers. When Mary feared because of the animals, the infant Jesus " looked into her face with a joyful countenance, and said: be not afraid, mother, for they come not to do thee harm, but they make haste to serve both thee and me " (ch. 19). Then all the animals — lions, oxen, asses, and sheep — walked side by side along the way.

The *Gospel of the Nativity of Mary* was attributed to Jerome and finds its place among the spurious works that bear his name. Even though it is a poor reproduction of *Pseudo-Matthew* and the canonical Gospels, it is valuable for showing the increasing interest given to Mary in the growing infancy traditions. The most interesting feature of this Gospel is the elaborate Annunciation, which takes up most of chapter 9.

And in those days, that is, at the time of her first coming into Galilee, the angel Gabriel was sent to her by God, to announce to her the conception of the Lord, and to explain to her the manner and order of the conception. Accordingly, going in, he filled the chamber where she was with a great light; and most courteously saluting her, he said: Hail, Mary! O virgin highly favoured by the Lord, virgin full of grace, the Lord is with thee; blessed art thou above all women, blessed above all men that have been hitherto born. And the virgin, who was already well acquainted with angelic faces, and was not unused to the light from heaven, was neither terrified by the vision of the angel, nor astonished at the greatness of the light, but only perplexed by his words; and she began to consider of what nature a salutation so unusual could be, or what it would portend, or what end it could have. And the angel, divinely inspired, taking up this thought, says: Fear not, Mary, as if anything contrary to thy chastity, thou hast found favour with the Lord; and therefore thou, a virgin, shalt conceive without sin, and shalt bring forth a son. He shall be great, because He shall rule from sea to sea, and from the river even to the ends of the earth; and He shall be called the Son of the Most High, because He who is born on earth in humiliation, reigns in heaven in exaltation; and the Lord God will give Him the throne of His father David, and He shall reign in the house of Jacob forever, and of his kingdom there shall be no end, forasmuch as He is King of kings and Lord of lords and His throne is from everlasting to everlasting. The virgin did not doubt these words of the angel; but wishing to know the manner of it, she answered: How can that come to pass? For while, according to my vow, I never know man, how can I bring forth without the addition of man's seed? To this the angel says: Think not, Mary, that thou shalt conceive in the manner of mankind: for without any intercourse with man, thou, a virgin, wilt bring forth; thou, a virgin, wilt nurse: for the Holy Spirit shall come upon thee, and the power of the Most High shall overshadow thee, without any of the heats of lust; and therefore that which shall be born of thee shall alone be holy, because it alone, being conceived and born without sin, shall be called the Son of God. Then Mary stretched forth her hands, and raised her eyes to heaven, and said: Behold the handmaiden of the Lord, for I am not worthy of the name of lady; let it be to me according to thy word. (ANCL, Vol. XVI, pp. 58 ff.)

In 1927, M. R. James published a book by the title *Latin Infancy Gospels,* which consisted of a new form of the apocryphal infancy narratives. Its sources consisted of several previously known, such as *James, Pseudo-Matthew,* and the *Nativity of Mary.* The innovation was a source which presented a Docetic Christ, who was born from a light which gradually took the form of a child, had no weight, needed no cleansing, did not cry, and had intelligence from the moment of birth.

James printed the translation of two separate texts, the " Arundel " (fourteenth century MS.) and the " Hereford " (thirteenth century MS.) side by side. The following quotation is from the " Arundel."

When therefore the hour drew near the power of God came forth openly and the maiden standing looking toward heaven became like a vine. For now was coming forth the end of good things. But when the light had come forth she adored him whom she saw she had brought forth.

Now that child was shining round about like the sun, mightily, pure and most pleasant in aspect, inasmuch as he alone hath appeared wholly peace making peace. Now in that hour wherein he was born there was heard a voice of many invisible ones saying with one voice Amen.

And that light which was born was multiplied and with the brightness of its light it darkened the light of the sun and this cave also was filled with bright light, with a most sweet perfume. Now this light was so born like as dew from heaven descended upon the earth. For the perfume of it is fragrant more than all the scent of ointments.

Now I stood amazed and marveling, and fear laid hold upon me, for I was looking upon so great brightness of the light that was born. But that light by little and little withdrawing into itself, made itself like to an infant, and in a moment it became an infant as infants are wont to be born, and I put on boldness and bowed myself and touched him and lifted him up in my hands with great fear, and I was smitten with fear for there was no weight in him as of a man that is born.

And I looked upon him, and there was not in him any defilement, but he was as it were all shining [or washed] with the dew of the most high God, light in body to bear and bright to look upon. And as I wondered much because he did not cry like as infants newborn are wont to cry and as I held him, looking upon his face, he smiled upon me with a most merry smile, and opening his eyes he looked upon me sharply and suddenly there came forth a great light from his eyes, as a great lightning. (Pp. xx–xxi.)

At the conclusion of his *Latin Infancy Gospels,* James presented a translation of what he called " The Irish Testimony," which was introduced to the world by Father E. Hogan, S. J., in his *Legends and Homilies from the Lebar Brecc* in 1895. This is an Irish version of much of the material of the new Latin text. Every phase of the tradition is rewritten in terms of varying details.

At the time of the birth of the infant, all the elements were silent and motionless, doing homage to their creator. While Joseph stood outside the house with Mary giving birth within, a shining light cloud came down from heaven and hovered over the cave and city, as if the sun were rising over the middle of the city and cave. Simultaneously, a fragrance equal to the smell of precious ointment and wine and tree-perfume from the whole world flooded the surroundings. All the irrational animals recognized their creator and licked and adored the newborn child.

And when the animals had offered their licking and worship, Mary takes her Son in her bosom then, and she was perfectly healthy in body and mind, for she had no pains or birth pangs, and there was not ache or soreness for her in body or in flesh, but as the sun's light would pass through glass, without sigh, without sickness, without harm.

Joseph went afterwards into the cave, and saw Mary, and her Son on her bosom; she giving her breast to Him, for she had indeed paps flowing like the gushing of spring-water. (P. 106.)

The History of Joseph the Carpenter is an Egyptian book which dates after the fourth century and was produced originally from Sahidic and Bohairic into Arabic and then into Latin. The purpose of the narrative was to clarify Joseph's past family relationships. He was described as sprung from a family of Bethlehem, wise, and a priest in the Temple. He was also a skilled carpenter and had a family consisting of a wife (unnamed), four sons: Judas, Justus, James, and Simon; two daughters: Assia and Lydia. All this was related by Jesus, himself, to his disciples. He added: " At length the wife of righteous Joseph, a woman intent on the divine glory in all her works, departed this life. But Joseph, that righteous man, my father after the flesh, and the spouse of my mother Mary, went away with his sons to his trade, practising the art of a carpenter." (Ch. 2, ANCL, Vol. XVI, p. 64.) Jesus then tells that Mary was twelve years old at the time Joseph became a widower: " And I chose her of my own will, with the concurrence of my father, and the counsel of the Holy Spirit. And I was made flesh of her, by a mystery which transcends the grasp of created reason." (Ch. 5, ANCL, Vol. XVI, p. 64.) [9]

Throughout the remaining narrative, Joseph's advanced age is stressed, along with the recognition that he gave to Jesus as the Savior.

In *The Arabic Gospel of the Infancy,* the infant at birth announces to the world who he is: ". . . when He was lying in His cradle said to Mary His mother: I am Jesus, the Son of God, the Logos, whom thou hast brought forth, as the angel Gabriel announced to thee; and my Father has sent me for the salvation of the world." (ANCL, Vol. XVI, p. 100.)

[9] For the " mystery," see the Sahidic *Pistis Sophia* (Gnostic), where Jesus as Gabriel chooses beforehand and assists in the conception of both John and himself. (*Pistis Sophia,* ed. George Horner [1924], pp. 6–7.)

In this narrative several incidents in the birth scene vary from earlier tradition. Here the midwife is simply an " old woman " and it is she herself who is cured of palsy, with which she has been afflicted for some years, by touching the child.

Wherefore, after sunset, the old woman, and Joseph with her, came to the cave, and they both went in. And, behold, it was filled with lights more beautiful than the gleaming of lamps and candles, and more splendid than the light of the sun. The child, enwrapped in swaddling-clothes, was sucking the breast of the Lady Mary His mother, being placed in a stall. And when both were wondering at this light, the old woman asks the Lady Mary: Art thou the mother of this child? And when the Lady Mary gave her assent, she says: Thou art not at all like the daughters of Eve. The Lady Mary said: As my son has no equal among children, so his mother has no equal among women. The old woman replied: My mistress, I came to get payment; I have been for a long time affected with palsy. Our mistress the Lady Mary said to her: Place thy hands upon the child. And the old woman did so, and was immediately cured. Then she went forth, saying: Henceforth I will be the attendant and servant of this child and all the days of my life. (Ch. 3, ANCL, Vol. XVI, p. 101.)

This narrative is filled with magic. One of the most interesting bits of magic involves the swaddling cloth. Mary gave the Wise Men one of the bands of swaddling cloth in exchange for their gifts. Later they threw the cloth into a fire, but the cloth was un-affected by the flames. (Chs. 7 and 8.)

The History of the Blessed Virgin Mary consists of a fairly full summary of apocryphal books among which are included the *Book of James,* the *Gospel of Pseudo-Matthew,* the *Gospel of Thomas,* the *Gospel of the Infancy,* the *Gospel of the Nativity of Mary,* and the *Assumption of Mary.*[10] Some of these traditions about the Virgin and the Child were current in Syria and Palestine as early as the end of the fourth century of our era. Some were incorporated into the whole at a later date. Although this Syrian version seems to be a compilation of the aforementioned writings, incidents and details are noted in this one which differ from those which have already been described.

In *James,* Mary's early ability to walk was emphasized. In this narrative the emphasis is not on her ability to walk but upon care

[10] E. A. Wallis Budge, *The History of the Blessed Virgin Mary* (Syriac text in *Luzac's Semitic Text and Translation Series,* Vol. IV [1899]) , ET, Vol. V (1899) .

which is taken to assure that as a child she will not have contact with the earth.

Hannâ ordered her husband, Yônâkhîr, to build a chamber for Mary in which she would be carried to Jerusalem. " So Yônâkhîr her father built for his daughter a beautiful chamber wherein was a shrine; and they strewed the ground with costly stuffs, saying, ' She shall not walk upon the earth until she hath gone up to the temple of the Lord.' " (P. 15.)

When Mary was three years old, her father made a great feast in her honor to which priests and Levites and many people, in addition to many virgins, were invited. The priests blessed her, and the people shouted, " Amen."

When Mary was ten years old, her mother had a second daughter, Parôghîthâ. Since Mary belonged to the Lord, the second offspring was to be Yônâkhîr's and Hannâ's personal delight.

At the age of twelve, Mary went up to Jerusalem to the Temple, accompanied by seven virgins each with lamps in their hands. The following narrative records a drawing of lots that precedes the familiar one in which Mary became the property of Joseph. In this scene at the Temple, Mary first came under the care of the priest, Zadok, who was elderly and whose wife was about to die. The priests cast lots for Mary, and she became Zadok's charge.

At the beginning of Mary's thirteenth year, both her parents died, and when she was fourteen, Sham'î the wife of Zadok died also. When Zadok made known that the time for the question of Mary's marriage had come, an assembly was called to which Joseph appeared and eventually became Mary's guardian as the result of being the recipient of a favorable omen.

The narrative continues in a manner similar to other traditions, but at the point of the Annunciation of the angel to Mary an interesting detail may be noted. Here Gabriel is fashioned as aged. " Gabriel, the angel of the Lord, appeared unto her in the form of a venerable old man, so that she might not flee from him." (P. 22.)

In the growing infancy legends Joseph and Gabriel were depicted as aged so as to contradict the stories of opponents that either Joseph or Gabriel could have been the father of Jesus.

The Annunciation follows generally the usual lines, but toward the end there is a marked variance from other tradition when the angel introduces new material, all of which is in accord with the early tradition in the church fathers of explaining the incarnation in terms of a mystery.

The prophets prophesied concerning thee in the spirit, and concerning thy bringing forth did they speak in their revelations. Moses, the first of the prophets, depicted the type of thee by means of the rock from which he made water to flow down, and Aaron the priest by means of the rod which he made to blossom; and Jeremiah called thee the woman-earth; and Gideon surnamed thee the fleece which received the dew from on high; and Daniel taught the mystery of thee by means of the rock which he saw and which had been hewn from the mountain without hands; and Isaiah spake openly of thee, saying, "Behold, a virgin shall conceive, and shall bear a son, and his name shall be called Immanuel." Moreover, this shall be a sign unto thee in thy days: thy kinswoman Elizabeth, even she, shall conceive a son, and she shall give birth unto him in her old age; and behold she is now in her sixth month. And from thee the True Light willeth to rise upon the world. And Mary answered and said unto Gabriel, "Behold, I am the hand-maiden of the Lord; let it be to me according to thy word." (Pp. 23–24.)

The ensuing description is also interesting. The angelic host directs itself to Mary:

Then straightway great joy dwelt in Mary, and all her body was glori-fied and became like light. And at that moment Mary saw the angelic hosts glorifying God, and ascribing praise unto herself, and proclaim-ing hope for mortals. And their hosts came round about Mary like the troops and horsemen of a king when he cometh and taketh up his abode in his palace; and, having followed in his train to the palace, then returned from the door thereof with joy and gladness. (P. 24.)

Later in the story the old woman midwife appears, but the nar-rative leaves out the incident of the difficulty with her hand. In the story of the visiting Wise Men, it is stated specifically that they presented three pounds of myrrh, three pounds of gold, and three pounds of frankincense. The narrative is elaborated with details of their angelic guidance, swiftness of the journey, and at their arrival at the cave the star changed itself into a pillar of light. The incident of the magic swaddling band was also further embellished. Not only was it untouched by the fire, it was better than before.

And when the fire had been put out, they brought out the swaddling-band, which was like the snow and was firmer than it was before. Then they took it and kissed it, and laid it upon their eyes, and said, "In truth, and beyond all doubt, this is a garment of the God of gods; for the fire of our gods was unable to consume it." And they received it in faith and with great honour. (P. 39.)

In his volume entitled *Legends of Our Lady Mary the Perpetual Virgin and Her Mother Hannâ,* E. A. Wallis Budge has collected and translated a number of texts that show how the infancy legends were developed in Abyssinia. The traditions which this volume contains reflect the thought of that Christian community into the fifteenth century. *The Conception and Birth of Our Lady Mary, the Bearer of God* (pp. 122–142) is principally the same legend as those contained in *James* and *Pseudo-Matthew,* with interesting variations.

Joseph's vision as he looks for a midwife [11] is picturesquely outlined:

And as he was going along the road, behold, he saw the earth trembling. And again, he saw oxen feeding, and they lifted up their eyes to heaven. And again, he saw a great river [or valley] wherein were many sheep, and they wished to drink, but only lifted up their eyes to heaven. And then JOSEPH [lifted up] his eyes toward the mountains of BETHLEHEM, and he saw a woman coming, and he came to her and saluted her. (Pp. 135–136.)

When Joseph and the midwife arrived at the cave, " they saw a cloud of light which crowned MARY, and also there went forth from the inside of the cave a great light, and it shone in all lands; and they saw a child lying in a manger." After the midwife expresses her joy, she goes outside the cave where she meets Salome, who had been sent by God unto Mary. Salome's unbelief at the probability of virgin birth is stressed. When she stretched out her hands to examine Mary, " fire went forth from the body of our Lady MARY, and consumed the two hands of SALOME." Heeding an injunction of an angel, Salome showed her hands to the child and was healed.

The most amazing Ethiopic text is *The Annunciation of Gabriel to Mary* (pp. 102–121). Here a substantial part of the whole infancy tradition is presented in the form of the Annunciation of the angel to Mary. The narrative reflects a time in the history of the church when Mary was thought of as the Mother of God. In it, too, is the concept that the Word became flesh by being virgin born, and the virgin is addressed as a " White Dove." There is also

[11] The role of the midwife which is emphasized in the apocryphal narratives may have its roots in the kind of tradition which is reflected among Islamic peoples that the birth of a child must be authenticated by the presence at the birth of either of one of two persons, the father of the child or a midwife. Since Joseph presumably was not the father of Jesus, a midwife had to be present in order to validate his birth.

mixed therein the idea that it was God, himself, who was incarnate.

And God looked at her, and descended into the womb of the holy woman, and all the saints rejoiced over her, the deliverer of the world, and when they saw her they prostrated themselves before her, and said, " O Mother of God, our Lady and redeemer, pray for us! Thou hast become the habitation of glory. He shall be conceived, and formed, and brought forth from thy womb, and shall put on thy flesh. O Mother of God, thou shalt carry [Him] in thy belly, and thou shalt become the habitation of the Godhead." (P. 105.)

Several other ideas are prominent. They include: that the Son will come to be born in Mary out of choice, that during her pregnancy Mary will be unaware of any occurrence within her, and the activity within her is as a burning fire. The " burning fire " is reminiscent of the teaching of the monophysite churches of Armenia and Syria in the fifth century that Christ's body was made of ethereal fire.

In *The Narrative of the Virgin Mary as Told by Herself to Timothy, Patriarch of Alexandria*, the child to be born appears as a gem within the expectant mother. Mary is speaking:

And from that time my heart became strong. And I reckoned nine months His time, like all women. And when I returned from her I did not know the appearance of His coming until my pearl shone brightly by His good pleasure, and became lighted up throughout, and I saw the splendor of His light and heard His voice. (P. 82.)

Conybeare tells how the " pearl " idea is related to the idea by which Christ is conceived by a ray of light. It is probably, he thought, Syrian in origin. " Pearls were supposed to be generated by rays of sunlight striking down through the sea, on the floor of which they coagulated and took a material consistency in the oyster shell. They are thus a precipitate of sunlight. Jesus, engendered by rays of divine light or fire striking down through the Virgin's ears and consolidated within her, was by analogy and metaphor termed the Pearl." [12]

In the same narrative Mary went on to say, " And I knew nothing about the way wherein I brought Him forth, nor the mystery of my conception, and I was ignorant about the one matter and the other."

Just preceding this in the same narrative, Mary calls attention to the lack of disturbance created within her by her pregnancy.

[12] *Myth, Magic, and Morals*, p. 232.

And I knew nothing about the operations that were effected in women nor about their desires when they were with child. And I saw no sign in my breasts that I had conceived, and my belly did not grow large, and I did not remove from my body my habitual apparel. And He came to me and I knew not how He came, and He dwelt in my belly, and I did not hear any voice [speaking] to Him, and I did not see that He had any chariot, and I saw nothing of His throne. And I did not know whether He dwelt in my belly or not, until my kinswoman ELISABETH informed me concerning Him.

What is most significant in all this literature is the increasing emphasis on Mary and the condition of her body. Another Ethiopic writing gives forty-two " salutations " in praise of Mary. Most of them bring out the excellence of some part of her body. Salutations are made to her name, the hairs of her head, her face (the splendor of which is greater than the splendor of the sun and moon), her eyelashes (which were set to guard her eyes), her eyes (which are like two lamps that have been suspended by a cunning workman in the exalted palace of her body), her ears (whereinto were poured the glad tidings by the mouth of the Creator, thy Son, that thy Pearl should be preserved), her cheeks (which are like roses and pomegranates), her nostrils (the double opening of life), her lips, her mouth, her teeth (which are like unto a flock of sheep that have been shorn, and have gone forth from the bath brilliantly white), her tongue, her voice, her breathings (which bring health and heal the souls of sinners), her throat (sweet and beautiful), her neck (the appearance of which is as the tower of David), her noble shoulders (which have received a blessing and not a curse), her back (which is the resting place of God), her breast and bosom and twin nipples, her arms and forearms, arms and wrists and hands, her palms of her hands, her fingers and white nails and two breasts (which are the doors of the milk that is to be desired), her heart, her navel (which is like unto a round goblet), her virginity (wherein are included the five senses of the body), and two thighs (which are the pillars of the roof of the sanctuary), her knees, the soles of her feet and insteps, the toes on her two feet and the nails which belong to each of them. (*Salutations to the Members of the Body of the Blessed Mary,* pp. 236–244.)

Budge's volume opens with *The History of Hannâ, the Mother of the Blessed Virgin Mary.* In this narrative many of the virtues that earlier tradition had confined to Mary were added to Hanna.

Before notice is made of how this tradition took form, it is well to observe how the narrative of Mary was elaborated in it.

When the VIRGIN MARY, the daughter of JOACHIM and HANNA, gave birth unto CHRIST the King, the mountains became the bread of life, and the hills produced grapes of blessing, and the waters of the sea became milk and honey. In this house there are none of the many spirits of sickness that have been smitten with the sharp arrows of sin. (P. 3.)

Within this context also the White Pearl theme is developed. The narrative speaks of God's creation of the world, which included the heavens, the earth, the Garden of Life, the sun, the moon, and stars, the seas, marine life, and man.

And when He had made an end of creating His creation, He created our father ADAM in His own form and likeness, and He breathed upon him the spirit of life. At that time MARY, the daughter of JOACHIM, existed in the belly of ADAM in the form of a White Pearl, which shone in his right side, and was a perfect likeness [of her]; and the similitude of her flew up into the heights of heaven. (P. 4.)

Apparently the apocryphal stories were dealing with a theme in a legendary fashion which the theologians dealt with doctrinally. In Augustine and in Thomas Aquinas there is considerable discussion of " original sin " and the relation of Christ and Mary to Adam and Abraham.

The matter of Christ's body was not the flesh and bones of the Blessed Virgin, nor anything that was actually a part of her body, but her blood which was her flesh potentially. Now, whatever was in the Blessed Virgin, as received from her parents, was actually a part of her body. Consequently that which the Blessed Virgin received from her parents was not the matter of Christ's body. Therefore we must say that Christ's body was not in Adam and the other patriarchs according to something signate, in the sense that some part of Adam's or of anyone else's body could be singled out and designated as the very matter from which Christ's body was to be formed: but it was there according to origin, just as was the flesh of other men. For Christ's body is related to Adam and the other patriarchs through the medium of His mother's body. Consequently Christ's body was in the patriarchs, in no other way than was His mother's body, which was not in the patriarchs according to signate matter: as neither were the bodies of other men. (*Summa Theologica*, Q. 31, Art. 6, Part III, Vol. 16, pp. 69–70.)

Besides the transfer of the Pearl idea — Jesus within Mary to Mary within Adam — the opening of the *History of Hannâ* is conspicuous for another incident; namely, the miraculous cure that the unborn Mary was able to effect. Six months after Hanna had conceived, a woman who was blind in one eye touched the belly of Hanna, saying: " Is it true, what I have heard? My sister, how canst thou conceive, being an old woman? " Immediately she received her sight. And many sick folk came and touched Hanna, as the woman had done, and they were healed of their sicknesses (Budge, *op. cit.*, p. 7).

Following this is a series of " salutations " similar to those quoted above with reference to Mary. Here members of Hanna's body are saluted. Toward the close of the salutations, the traditional figures of speech are rearranged so as to apply to Hanna, and the affinities of Christian thought to pagan are very close.

SALUTATION to thee, O HANNA, thou who art the morning, and to thee, O MARY, who art the heaven that gave birth unto Christ, the Sun, Who burneth up the thorns of error.

SALUTATION to thee, O thou stone of chalcedony, HANNA, thou brilliant pearl, wherefrom went forth MARY the Virgin, who gave birth to the Flame. (Budge, p. 10.)

Later in the narrative, the " pearl theme " is highly developed. Mary is the pearl of great renown, who was in the belly of Adam. She was passed on from Adam down through the genealogical tree. At the appointed season " and after long delay," the White Pearl entered into the womb of Hanna. At the appropriate hour, when God had seen Hanna's sorrow at not having a child,

He appeared unto her that day in a vision of the night, in the form of a White Bird which came down from heaven. Now this Bird had its being [i.e., existed] in the days of old, for it overshadowed the Cherubim of glory; and there was the hand of a man beneath the wing thereof, and held in it the cord of life. Now this was the Spirit of Life, in the form of a White Bird, and it took up its abode in the person of HANNA, and became incarnate in her womb, at the time when the Pearl went forth from the loins of JOACHIM, and when, according to the ordinance of carnal union HANNA received the Pearl, which was the Body [*or*, Flesh] of our Lady MARY. Now the White Pearl is mentioned because of its purity, and the White Bird because her soul [existed] aforetime [with] the Ancient of Days, and it was with Him on the right hand of His Father; thus the White Bird and the White Pearl are alike and equal. And when it [i.e., the Pearl] took up its abode in the womb of HANNA, her womb was moved even like the water of the sea, for it was unaccustomed to this thing. (Budge, p. 19.)

Mary is unique in her heavenly virginity. No one is pure in body and in mind like the Lady Mary. Hanna shares with Mary the spotlight among women. Only Mary is superior to Hanna. Hanna is even described in language that in other tradition was ascribed to Mary. " She is more beautiful than the Sun, and the Moon, and all created beings and things that are in the heavens and on the earth. No woman can be compared with her for beauty, and grace, and majesty, and honour, although she was inferior to our Lady MARY." (Budge, p. 24.) Her odour was more fragrant than any flower. Her whole pleasure was her blessed child Mary.

The record is clear that throughout the Middle Ages a view of the virgin birth was maintained which had substituted interest in the virginity of Mary for concern for the humanity of Jesus. This phenomenon arose out of the necessity that the church felt for Christianizing the " Lady " and " Queen " and " Mother " ideas which for centuries had been current in pagan religions. Out of the competition between the cult of Mary with the cult of Isis and other non-Christian cults [13] the growing legend of Mary's virginity evolved into a Marian theology which centered on her Docetic and superhuman qualities. She was at first remarkable mainly because of her virginity, but as the tradition grew, everything about her became of special quality. She was exquisite. She was the ideal woman.

The interest in the virginity of Mary developed in Christian circles at the time when orthodox Christianity was combating a Docetic theology of Christ and trying to establish and account for the humanity of Jesus. It is ironic that from the point in history at which the churchmen sought to establish the non-Docetic character of Jesus there developed the tradition that was to culminate in the establishment of a Docetic theology of Mary. This was also a turning point in the history of the church when it began to lose its real moral impact on society. The glorification of the virginity of Mary and the idealization of personal virginity subverted the original impact of the Biblical narrative that was to show that the Savior was human and that a moral ordering of society was to come about through marriage. For centuries Christians struggled to maintain moral purity by means of an idealism that was the opposite of the Christian ethic.

[13] See Budge, *Legends of Our Lady Mary*, Introduction, pp. 1 ff., for his discussion of " Cults of Isis and Mary Compared."

The historian who approaches his subject imbued with the faith of the Church finds himself confronted at the very outset with the most stupendous of miracles, the fact which lies at the root of Christianity being in his eyes that the only-begotten Son of God descended from the eternal throne of the God-head to the earth, and became man in the womb of the Virgin. He who regards this simply as a miracle, steps at once outside of all historical connection.

— Ferdinand Christian Baur, in *The Church History of the First Three Centuries*

3

NATURALISTIC PHILOSOPHICAL INTERPRETATION

B EGINNING with the Protestant Reformation the story of Jesus'
origin was interpreted along rigid and contrasting philosophical and theological lines. The naturalistic philosophers and the
supernaturalistic theologians are important for having provided
two completely diverse interpretations: the rejection of the virgin
birth as unhistorical and the acceptance of the virgin birth as historical. The whole question was whether the story in Matt. chs.
1 and 2, and Luke, chs. 1 and 2, took place literally as described.
On the basis of certain theological presuppositions, supernaturalists insisted that it did. Using their own presuppositions the
naturalists insisted that it did not, and then proceeded to explain
what really happened or upon what basis the narrative ought to be
understood.

The central figure in the whole history of interpretation of the
virgin birth from the Protestant Reformation to the present was
David Strauss. Strauss's mythical interpretation of the virgin birth
was directed primarily against the "rationalistic" interpretation
which preceded. Strauss's criticism in turn gave rise to the whole
school of supernaturalistic interpretation that developed from
Olshausen through Machen and has been the fortress for conservative theologians in modern times. All important interpretation of
the virgin birth from the theologically conservative point of view
is directed against Strauss and his successors. In order to gain a
perspective of the context of supernaturalistic theological interpretation of the virgin birth it is necessary to have insight into its
naturalistic philosophical antecedents.

Rationalistic or naturalistic philosophical interpretation of the
virgin birth served the dual function of preparing the way for
purging the interpretation of the virgin birth of its old Roman

Catholic excesses and of providing the impetus for the development of the traditionally conservative Protestant interpretation of the birth of Jesus.

A. FROM THE REFORMATION TO STRAUSS

Rationalistic interpretation of the virgin birth before Strauss falls under two main categories: that which was motivated by the naturalistic philosophy, which developed in the Renaissance and the Enlightenment, and that which was determined by the idealistic philosophy, which was the immediate outgrowth of the Enlightenment. The principal interpreter of the first group was Paulus, and the primary representative of the second was Schleiermacher. What is characteristic of each is his rejection of the virgin birth as historical on philosophical grounds. What distinguishes them is their particular type of rationalism and the different consequence to which their methodologies led them.

1. THE TRANSFER OF AUTHORITY FROM SCRIPTURE TO REASON

The first premise upon which the philosophical negation of the virgin birth is based is the rejection of authority and the insistence upon rational freedom. This revolt had its roots in the Protestant thinkers of the Reformation. Although Luther and Calvin transferred the central point of authority from the ecclesiastical hierarchy to the Sacred Writings, others during the Reformation completed the revolt against the existing authority by challenging the authority of the Bible itself. Sebastian Franck (1499–1542), for example, in his *Das mit sieben Siegeln verbütschierte Buch* (1539) attempted to show that the Bible is full of discrepancies and contradictions when interpreted literally.

Early in the seventeenth century, the " Natural Science Period of the Renaissance," Francis Bacon's *Advancement of Learning* (1605) and *Novum Organum* (1620) ; René Descartes's *Discourse on the Method of Rightly Conducting the Reason and Seeking the Truth in the Sciences* (1637) ; and Thomas Hobbes's *Leviathan* (1651) in new methods of approach to the problems of the universe, God, and man, decisively, although unintentionally, deepened the roots of resistance to Biblical authority. The methods were intended to be applied only to philosophy, but the successors

to Bacon, Descartes, and Hobbes applied their scientific methodology to all religious questions.

Bacon was able to accept the views of the orthodox Anglican
Church and maintain at the same time his scientific methodology,
since he held the realm of revelation on which faith was based to
be outside the concern of philosophy. Descartes's revolt against
tradition was in philosophy. His principle, " Cogito ergo sum,"
the consequence of which was the establishment of reason as the
focal point of authority, was intended by him to be applied chiefly
to matters pertaining to philosophical inquiry.

Thomas Hobbes's Leviathan (subtitled " The Matter, Forme
and Power of a Commonwealth, Ecclesiastical and Civill ") showed
that for him, as well as for Descartes, religion was outside the realm
of philosophy and to be understood on the basis of theology and
accepted on the authority of the state.

Hobbes accepted miracles as a form of God's direct revelation.
He made an important distinction, however. The private man is
always at liberty to believe or not to believe those acts which are
described as miracles; nevertheless " when it comes to confession
of that faith, the Private Reason must submit to the Publique."
Hobbes included the virgin birth among those miracles which
attest to the belief that " Jesus is the Christ " and which ought to
be a part of the public confession.

The great English philosopher was " Protestant " in accepting
the virgin birth while rejecting the use of the image of " the Virgin Mary and of her Sonne our Saviour " which he interpreted as
a mark of idolatry in the church and a carry-over from paganism
of the image of Venus and Cupid. He was severely critical of " all
the Legend of fictitious Miracles, in the lives of the Saints; and all
the Histories of apparitions, and Ghosts, alleged by the Doctors
of the Romane Church, to make good their Doctrines of Hell, and
Purgatory, the power of Exorcisme, and other doctrines which
have no warrant, neither in Reason, nor Scripture."

In this period of the development of philosophy in which natural science was the preoccupation, the application of the rationalistic method was made primarily to philosophy itself and secondarily to some of the dogmas of the church. These were chiefly the
most offensive Roman Catholic dogmas. Incidentally, but effec-
tively, however, the concept of reason was introduced into matters
of faith and authority of the Scripture. Bacon's scientific attitude

and Descartes's and Hobbes's rationalism would soon be no longer limited by the boundary of faith.

The philosophers of the Enlightenment inherited the task of carrying the principle of reason to its logical conclusions.[1] Whereas Bacon, Descartes, and Hobbes placed revelation and miracle in a special precinct to which the principles of their philosophy were not directly applicable, David Hume (1711–1776), and others such as John Toland, Thomas Chubb, and Voltaire, turned the full force of naturalistic philosophy upon religion. Instead of conceiving philosophy and religion to exist in separate spheres, according to Hume's notion, religion as such and not just the abuses of religion must be subject to the scrutiny of reason.

Hume set the world of nature over against the world of religion. A miracle had come for him to be " a transgression of a law of nature by a particular volition of the Deity, or by the interposition of some invisible agent." [2] Philosophically, he could not deny that no event could take place in violation of these laws, but he was convinced that experience demonstrates that man can depend much more upon the uniformity of natural events than upon the accuracy of human testimony. His theory on the nature of the universe and its relation to God excludes the concept of a particular providence and its counterpart miracles. In Hume, philosophy gained an esteem which it was never to relinquish. No longer were philosophy and religion supreme in separate spheres. Now religion was to be held accountable to philosophy.[3]

The most influential mark in the criticism of the Biblical record was made in this period by Herman Samuel Reimarus (1694–1768) and Gotthold Ephraim Lessing (1729–1781). Since Lessing was responsible for the publication of Reimarus' works, the two are inseparably connected in the history of philosophy. Lessing was the philosopher who brought before the world the philosophical criticism of Scripture of Reimarus, whose life work was at Hamburg as a Professor of Oriental Languages. Lessing met Rei-

---

[1] John Locke, 1632–1704, is an exception. His views on the relation of philosophy to religion and on revelation and reason were almost identical to those of Descartes and Hobbes (Essay on Human Understanding, Book IV, chs. XVI and XIX). Locke is reported to have said of the Scriptures: " Therein are contained the words of eternal life. It has God for its author, salvation for its end, and truth without any mixture of error for its matter." (A Commonplace-Book to the Holy Bible, p. 16.)

[2] " Enquiry Concerning Human Understanding " (1748), Section X, n. 1, p. 115.

[3] Hume's position was the result of the influence of the monistic philosophy of Spinoza (1632–1677) and Leibniz (1646–1716) as well as the logical consequence of what followed from Descartes and Hobbes.

marus in 1768, the last year of Reimarus' life, and began publishing Reimarus' *Fragments* in 1774.

Reimarus is of primary importance for his views on miracles. Miracles belong to the unessential elements of faith. He added that the miracles of the New Testament are not as outrageous or disgusting as those of the Old. As far as he was concerned, it is always a sign that a doctrine or history possesses no depth of authenticity when one is obliged to resort to miracles in order to prove its truth. For him, miraculous meant nonhistorical, and nonhistorical meant lack of reliability for a reasonable faith. Reimarus entertained no conception of myth or legend by which the meaning of the miraculous character of a narrative might be explained and some reliable truth indicated (*Fragments*, Sections XLVI to XLIX).

For all the philosophers of the Enlightenment the problem of the virgin birth was simple. It was a miracle. Miracle must be rejected on rationalistic and naturalistic grounds. Therefore, the miracle of the virgin birth of Jesus must be rejected. Not much more need to be said.

The first attempts to apply the rationalistic principle to the miracle stories of the Gospels were made by Karl Friedrich Bahrdt (1741–1792), Karl Heinrick Venturini (1768–1849), and Heinrich Eberhard Gottlob Paulus (1761–1851). When they did this, the problem of the virgin birth became the question of what actually happened. It was no longer satisfactory simply to reject the miracle on naturalistic grounds. These men felt that they had to explain the miracle on naturalistic grounds. The virgin birth interpretations of Bahrdt, Venturini, and Paulus were the inevitable consequence of the doctrine of miracle, which was formulated in the Enlightenment by Hume, Reimarus, and Lessing.

According to Bahrdt, the miracle of the birth of Jesus is one of several " illusions " produced by the Essenes, which depict the life of Jesus only as seen by the populace from the outside and must be understood as an " illusion," which conceals the natural fact of Mary's delusion and probable seduction (*Ausführung des Plans und Zwecks Jesu*, Vol. 2).

Venturini agreed that the birth of Jesus has a naturalistic explanation. After the death of her parents, Mary went to live in the house of Elizabeth, where she had intercourse with the priest, Zacharias, and entertained the enthusiastic wish of becoming the mother of the Messiah. She was betrothed on the Day of Pentecost to the aging Joseph, whom she had known since her youth as a friend of her family, he, like herself, having been descended from the house of David. She spent the day before her wedding in the house of Clopas in Nazara. A storm came up; she dreamed; the door opened; and a shining form entered. The Annunciation inspires her to desire that God do unto her according to his will. Joseph was beside her when she awoke from her ecstasy. She was ashamed to meet his eye. Only later is her secret revealed. In Venturini's scheme, the "angel" turns out to be Joseph of Arimathea, a rabbi, member of the high council, an Essene, and known in Jerusalem as an eccentric character who is anxious for Israel's future (*Natürliche Geschichte des grossen Propheten von Nazareth*, Vol. 4, 1802, pp. 112 ff., 165 ff., 247 ff., 352).

Paulus is the most famous representative of the rationalistic interpretation of the Gospel narratives. In his *Life of Jesus* he started from the principle that interpretation of the Gospels should deal strictly with the determination of what are actual facts.

The commentator, according to him, must view the stories of the Evangelists as simple events with natural causes. He began his criticism of the virgin birth with carefully guarded language, but soon he showed that he had simply taken over Bahrdt's theory of seduction and Venturini's illicit theory and reworked them into his own theory of imposture. The virgin birth could be looked at, he claimed, in terms of viewing the conception as an act of self-consciousness of Mary in which, through holy inspiration, she received the power of conceiving her son. The "holy spirit" is not an objective or external influence operating upon Mary. It is her own imagination. Paulus then suggested that some unknown man as a fanatic impostor assumed the role of Gabriel, and by him Mary conceived Jesus. This resulted from a ruse of the ambitious "*Priesterfrau*" Elizabeth. It was she who was supposed to have sent an unknown man to play the part of the angel Gabriel and deceive the simple Mary (*Das Leben Jesu*, 1828).

Venturini's and Paulus' theories are reminiscent of the early Pandera tradition and demonstrate how crude and banal rationalistic criticism could become.

2. THE TRANSFER OF THE VALUE OF THE BIBLICAL RECORD FROM HISTORICITY TO MEANING

The primacy of reason was permanently established by Immanuel Kant (1724–1804) and George Wilhelm Friedrich Hegel

(1770–1831). They focused attention on the meaning of the narratives in the Biblical record and refused to judge a Biblical idea solely on the basis of its credibility. For them the crux of interpretation of a Biblical passage became the moral significance and religious meaning of the narrative, rather than the determination of its historical or scientific value. Kant and Hegel provided the immediate philosophical background for Schleiermacher and established the groundwork for Strauss's whole system.

Kant, by locating the seat of religion in the moral consciousness, and Hegel, by emphasizing the " double meaning " of the Biblical narratives, rescued Biblical interpretation from the abuses it was suffering at the hands of naturalists and established the principal points with which all succeeding criticism has had to deal.

Even though Kant rejected the virgin birth on various moral, doctrinal, and physiological grounds and disliked the story of Jesus' origin since he felt that emphasis on the miraculous origin or nature of the Son of God might tend to diminish the force of his example,[4] he did make an advance over the older rationalism. The basis upon which the miracle was to be judged was a more realistic one. Johann Gottfried Herder (1744–1803) [5] and Johann Jacob Hess (1741–1828),[6] who had become apprehensive over the Kantian critique of the virgin birth, applied Kant's own principle more sympathetically to the infancy narratives. They encouraged readers to pay little attention to the outward details of the stories and seek instead the truth of their " inner realities." The meaning of the miracle should be sought in its ethical teaching.

In Kant's *Critique of Pure Reason* the rationalistic principle, the spontaneity and autonomy of the human mind, was brought into great prominence. In it the Ego was established as *the* principle of the entire phenomenal world. Then Fichte (1762–1814) and Schelling (1775–1854) developed the logical conclusion that the phenomenal world is derived from the Ego. The ultimate consequence of this was to be the philosophical unity of mind with nature.

This movement reached its high point in Hegel. His *Lectures on the Philosophy of Religion,* published in German in 1832, show how he developed the Kantian tradition. He accomplished the

---

4 *Die Religion Innerhalb der Grenzen der Blossen Vernunft,* first published in 1794; in Kant's *Sämmtliche Werke* (1838), pp. 71 ff., footnote, p. 94.

5 *Vom Erlöser der Menschen* (1796).

6 Hess explained many miracles on the basis of " natural causes." He, however, did not do so to the birth narratives. *Lebensgeschichte Jesu* (1822), pp. 1–120.

reuniting of philosophy and religion and ascribed value to miracle by his definition of the relationship between philosophy and religion and by his theory of the "double meaning" and moral value of the Biblical narratives.

According to Hegel, every narrative contains not only an external series of occurrences and actions, but it has also " the Divine for its content, divine action, divine timeless events, a mode of working that is absolutely divine." He added that this is the true, inward, and substantial element of history, and " it is just this that is the object of reason " (p. 146). This is true of every type of narrative including myth. Hegel distinguished Biblical myths from Homeric by establishing the principle that the latter are not to be taken seriously but figuratively even though stated in historical fashion; whereas the former are to be regarded in the strict sense as history. Also, myths of Plato usually contain an allegory.

The concept of the double meaning in every Biblical narrative originated in Hegel's general philosophical analysis of the religious attitude and in his distinction between what he called an idea (*Vorstellung*) and a picture (*Bild*).

A picture derives its content from the sphere of sense, and presents it in the immediate mode of its existence in its singularity, and in the arbitrariness of its sensuous manifestation. But since the infinite number of individual things, as they are present in immediate definite existence, cannot, even by means of the most detailed or ample representation be rendered as a whole, the picture is necessarily always something limited; and in religious perception, which is able only to present its content as a picture, the Idea splits up into a multitude of forms, in which it limits itself and renders itself finite. The universal Idea [*Idee*], which appears in the circle of these finite forms, and only in these, and which is merely their basis, must, as such, remain concealed. General idea or ordinary thought [*Vorstellung*], on the other hand, is the picture lifted up into the form of Universality, of thought, so that the one fundamental characteristic, which constitutes the essence of the object, is held fast, and is present before the mind which thus forms the idea. (P. 142.)

It is this analysis which led him inevitably to his concept of the double element in the Biblical narrative. For Hegel the substantial part of any history is the moral that it contains. The moral forces recognizable even in the detached and isolated character of the narrative are identified with the universal laws. This is the genuine spiritual content with which he felt philosophy and religion are essentially concerned (p. 147).

According to Hegelian reasoning, on the following basis the proper relationship between faith and miracle can also be understood: negatively, faith that begins in the external manner of attaching itself to the miracle is yet formal and not essential. True faith has no accidental content, so faith that attaches itself to content that is finite and contingent is not true faith. Faith that has miracle as its object is nonspiritual from its very nature. Miracles can produce verification of truth only for the man who is guided by his sense, but this is only the beginning of verification, an unspiritual kind of verification by which what is spiritual cannot really be verified. Miracles are changes connected with the world of sense and should, therefore, be distinguished from the realm in which reason operates. Positively, faith that attaches itself to the meaning of miracle is true faith.[7]

True to the Kantian-Hegelian tradition, Friedrich Ernst Daniel Schleiermacher (1768–1834) had a strong distaste for both the naturalistic rationalism and the supernaturalism of his day. The error of both parties with which he was so dissatisfied was their common notion that Christian faith consists of a number of doctrines that stand in contradiction to rational thought and in need of defense by orthodox theologians. The Christian faith, he claimed, does not consist primarily in any number of doctrinal propositions that can be made either by philosophers or theologians, but in a condition of devout feelings, in a fact of inward experience based on personal self-consciousness.

In his *Life of Jesus*,[8] the extent to which his historical criticism of the story of Jesus' birth went was the scope of his own philosophical and theological perception. Throughout this work he exposited the life of Jesus in terms of a dialectic that sought to avoid the extremes of both an Ebionism that would diminish the divine in Jesus and a Docetism that does away with his humanity. He rejected the probability of the miraculous element in the stories of Jesus' birth and childhood and made the question of miracle secondary by emphasizing that the phenomena in the birth narratives are to be accounted for out of the author's poetic imagination. The narrative is important only for its doctrinal viewpoint of the relationship of the Messianic nature of Jesus to his human nature,

---

[7] *Lectures on the Philosophy of Religion*, Vol. 1, p. 219; Vol. 2, p. 338.

[8] 1864. This work is based on notes taken by a student from class lectures which terminated in 1832.

which, for Schleiermacher, does not need to be maintained on the foundation of a superior or perfect origin based on an historically questionable narrative, but on his nature and superior self-consciousness of God.

The same idea may be found in Ritschl's *The Christian Doctrine of Justification and Reconciliation* (1st German ed., 1870–1874). A singular observation in ch. VI on "The Doctrine of Christ's Person and Life-Work" shows his kinship to Schleiermacher: the essential nature of Christ is not to be found in his physical origin, which can never be, and never has been, reconciled with his historical appearance; it is, rather, to be located in "His world-conquering will, which marks Him as the God-man." "If Christ is to be judged by categories that are applied to no other object than Himself, then He is rendered unintelligible." Ritschl found in the New Testament no consistent doctrine of the nature of Christ. He observed a dialectical tension between two basically distinct views, one exalting Jesus to the equivalent of God, and the other stressing how God, in Jesus, became a human person. Ritschl not only denied the virgin birth as history, but he lifted the whole concept of the person of Jesus out of historical connection. The main question in the life of Jesus for him was not historical reliability but moral superiority.[9]

Before Strauss, the problem of the virgin birth was the question of whether the story of Jesus' origin was historically acceptable. The period of the Renaissance provided the philosophical machinery for the rejection of the virgin birth. Once authority had been established in the reason, the primacy of reason and the dominance of natural science combined to deny the virgin birth because the idea was thought to be contrary to reason and to natural law. Certain rationalists deemed it necessary, however, to go a step farther and explain the narrative on purely naturalistic grounds, and so Bahrdt's and Paulus' theories of seduction and imposture were forthcoming.

Realizing the inadequacies of naturalistic rationalism, the post-Enlightenment and idealistic philosophers shifted the crux of the problem from the question of the historicity or credibility of the miracle to the meaning or the moral and religious value of the story of the miraculous conception. While they denied the historical value of the virgin birth, Kant and Schleiermacher attested its doctrinal and religious value.

9 ET, 2d ed. (1902), pp. 400–404, 467–468.

In the earlier period, the virgin birth was worthless. In the latter, it was of secondary or minor importance. The chief questions concerning the virgin birth which various rationalists raised were: how ought miracle to be interpreted, has a miracle story any value, and if so, in what does the value consist? On these questions rationalists reached greatly divergent points of view. All were unanimous, however, in wresting from the story of the virgin birth all historical value.

The problem of the virgin birth was not given serious consideration by any of the rationalists, since it was either secondary to the question of miracle, or subsidiary to the question of Jesus' moral character. As miraculous conception, the solution to the problem was a foregone conclusion based on the rationalistic estimate of miracle. As a story of Jesus' origin, the problem was obscured by the much greater importance of his life and ministry.

Kant, Hegel, and Schleiermacher prepared the way for Strauss by providing him with the philosophical setting in which to work. Kant and Schleiermacher showed that the solution of the naturalistic rationalists to the problem of the virgin birth was far too simple and naïve. Hegel provided him with the dialectic into which he forced his entire system. Strauss intended to supercede rationalistic philosophy (as well as supernaturalism) by providing a new methodology by which to interpret the life of Jesus. However, by placing all his historical material into a single cast which was constructed on the basis of a philosophical dialectic, Strauss himself never got beyond the bounds of rationalism.

B. STRAUSS'S MYTHICAL INTERPRETATION

The rational method of interpretation of the life of Jesus reached its climax in David Friedrich Strauss's (1808–1874) *Das Leben Jesu* (1835),[10] which was written while he held the position of "Repetent" (assistant lecturer) on the philosophical faculty at Tübingen. Strauss's chief contribution to Biblical learning lies in his effort to prove that the concept of myth is to be applied to the New Testament. His criticism of the infancy narratives is the most brilliant and comprehensive in all the literature on the subject.

[10] According to Hase, Strauss began his studies for the "Life of Jesus" by writing a detailed critical review of his (Hase's) first Life of Jesus (1829) for the *Jahrbücher für wissenschaftliche Kritik* in Berlin. The review was turned down. Hase, *Das Leben Jesu* (1876), p. 124.

1. APPLICATION OF HEGELIAN DIALECTIC TO THE GOSPEL HISTORY

In his analysis of the different modes that had been employed by scholars before him to explain sacred histories, he discovered two chief methods: supernaturalistic allegorism and rationalistic euhemerism. Being convinced of the numerous difficulties and inconsistencies that either method presented, he turned to another method, one that heretofore had been applied only to the Old Testament.[11] Logic had forced Eichhorn to regard much of the material in the Old Testament as mythic in nature. George Lorenz Bauer (1755–1806), in *Hebräische Mythologie*, 1 Thl., Einleitung 5 (1802), asserted that " eine total mythische Geschichte " is not to be sought in the New Testament, although single myths could be discovered. These he believed could be found in the narrative of Jesus' birth. Bauer was convinced that after the death of a celebrated personage it was natural for his life to be embellished with wondrous (legendary) elements. Strauss accepted this point of view and expressed keen disappointment with most of the theologians of his day who felt that the narratives of Jesus' birth required a mythical interpretation but declined to apply the mythical theory to the remainder of the Gospel. Strauss was convinced that the interpretation of the New Testament demanded application of the mythical principle throughout. The application of this principle he thought would provide the synthesis for the thesis and antithesis created by supernaturalistic allegorism and rationalistic euhemerism.

2. THE DEFINITION OF " MYTHUS "

In the introduction to the third edition of Strauss's *Life of Jesus* (1838) his own theory of myth and how it should be applied to the life of Jesus is clearly stated: myth, when it is applied to the Gospel narratives, is " evangelical mythus," a narrative that relates directly or indirectly to Jesus. An " evangelical mythus " is not to be considered as the expression of a fact, but as the product of an idea of Jesus' earliest followers. The " evangelical mythus " was classified into two main categories: what Strauss called " pure mythus," which constitutes the substance of the narrative, and

---

[11] Johann Gottfried Eichhorn (1752–1827), *Urgeschichte* (1790–1793); *Einleitung in das A.T.* (1823–1824).

" historical mythus," which is an accidental adjunct to the actual history. The former has two different sources out of which the mythus arises: one, the Messianic ideas and expectation that existed in several forms in the Jewish mind before the time of Jesus and independently of him; two, in the particular impression that was left by Jesus' character, action, and fate, as it served to modify the Messianic idea in the minds of Jesus' contemporaries (pp. 113 ff.).

The " historical mythus " is the outgrowth of a single fact that has been grasped by religious enthusiasm and embellished with mythical conceptions taken from the idea of Christ or from certain natural occurrences in his life.

Strauss used the word " legendary " to describe those parts of the evangelical history which are characterized by indefiniteness, lack of connection, misconstruction, strange combinations, and confusion, which for him were the natural results of the long course of oral transmission, and by highly colored and pictorial representations.

The three categories designated for Strauss the boundaries of the unhistorical element in the Gospels. He insisted, however, that these classifications do not involve the renunciation of the " historical " which these narratives themselves may contain (p. 115).

3. The Distinction Between Myth and History

In establishing criteria by which to distinguish the unhistorical element in the Gospel narrative, Strauss pointed out first of all, negatively, that mythus is not history. This can be determined when aspects of the narrative are irreconcilable with the known and universal laws that govern the course of events and when an account reveals inconsistencies within itself and points of contradiction with other parallel accounts.

In the second place, positively, the myth is fiction. Sometimes the fictitious aspect is to be recognized in the form, i.e., when the actors converse in hymns, and sometimes in the substance of the narrative, i.e., when the ideas seem to be the products of preconceived opinions rather than of practical experience such as narratives of origin. When details of the life of Jesus are found to be evidently sketched according to the pattern of prophecies and prototypes, they are to be taken as mythical rather than as historical (pp. 115–124).

Strauss conceded that the most difficult question in historical criticism is the determination of the boundary line between the historical and the unhistorical when two accounts of the same event contradict, and he believed that the boundary line between the historical and the unhistorical in such accounts will forever be unsusceptible to accurate delineation (p. 124).

4. MIRACLE

In the 1864 edition of his *Life of Jesus,* Strauss prefaced his section on the definition of mythus with several paragraphs on the idea of miracle.[12] From the standpoint of critical philosophy Strauss considered Hume's *Essay on Miracles* as having definitely settled the question, yet Strauss did not feel that the criticism did complete justice to the proper evaluation of the Biblical event (p. 148). For Strauss, the solution to the problem which the miraculous incident presents is not to be found solely in the determination of whether the incident is contrary to natural law or whether the author was deliberately attempting to deceive his audience.

5. THE MYTHICAL INTERPRETATION OF THE NARRATIVES OF JESUS' BIRTH

Part I of *Das Leben Jesu* (1835) is " Geschichte der Geburt und Kindheit Jesu." In this section Strauss noted the striking gradation in the different representations of the conception and birth of Jesus described in the canonical and in the apocryphal gospels, and he felt that the fathers of the church held a superiority over most of the theologians of his own time in that they interpreted both the canonical and the apocryphal accounts by the same method, treating both as miraculous or both as natural. They did not take the former as history and the latter as fiction. Strauss believed that neither the canonical nor the apocryphal accounts should be understood as history.

Generation of the human species without the concurrence of the two sexes, said Strauss, is sufficient cause to question the narratives. Theology supplied the sufficient cause for suspension by God of a natural law in the redemption of mankind which required the impeccability of the redeemer. The canonical narrative of Jesus' conception implies that the exclusion of participation of a sinful

---

[12] *Das Leben Jesu,* " Für das deutsche Volk bearbeitet," pp. 146–150.

father renders Jesus exempt from sin. Strauss agreed with Schleiermacher and others that the exclusion of paternal participation is insufficient to render the child exempt from sin, but since the Gospel narratives represent an actual paternal participation, a divine intervention that would sanctify the participation of the sinful human mother in the conception of Jesus must be supposed in order to maintain his assumed necessary impeccability.

According to Strauss, the most conclusive exegetical basis for a negative decision regarding the supernatural conception of Jesus is to be found in the two genealogies. The express purpose of these tables is to prove that Jesus through Joseph is of the lineage of David. He did not think that the genealogy and the history of the birth of Jesus in Matthew could come from the same author. He who had regarded Joseph as nothing more than the adopted father of Jesus probably would not have troubled himself to trace the Davidic descent of Joseph. It is indisputable that these genealogies were composed in belief that Jesus was the actual son of Joseph and Mary. The author who received them altered them to conform to his belief in the divine origin of Jesus: Matthew changing an original " Joseph begat Jesus of Mary " and Luke inserting at the beginning of his genealogy " Jesus as was supposed " in place of " Jesus the son of Joseph." The genealogies are to be regarded as memories of a time in the primitive church when Jesus was regarded as a naturally begotten man.

Strauss discovered that Origen indirectly suggested the correct interpretation of this narrative when he placed the miraculous conception of Jesus alongside the story of Plato's conception by Apollo (*Against Celsus* vi. 8), and when he stated that the story concerning Plato belongs to those myths by which the distinguished wisdom and power of great men was exhibited. Origen pointed out the similarity of the two narratives and interpreted the Platonic as mythical in character. The conclusion that this should also apply to the Biblical narrative did not occur to Origen, but Strauss thought that it should occur to modern interpreters of the Gospel narrative.

Strauss was convinced that the mythical explanation of the story of Jesus' conception avoids the difficulties that are inherent in both the supernatural and the natural explanations of Jesus' birth. Historically Jesus was the son of Joseph and Mary. Philosophically (dogmatically) Jesus was born of a virgin by means of divine agency in accord with prevailing belief in the origin of the Mes-

siah on the basis of the interpretation of Isa. 7:14 in the early
Christian church. In addition, Jesus' title as "Son of God" was
understood Messianically in terms of Ps. 2:7 and suggested physical relationship. Very early, "Son of God" and "Son of a virgin"
were complementary ideas which brought about the substitution
of the divine agency for human generation.[13]

The narratives in Matthew and Luke, Strauss judged, are equally
unhistorical. The balance between their similarity and diversity
indicates that they are separate variations of the same theme, composed independently of each other. In different ways, each attempted to reconcile the historical fact that Jesus was universally
reputed to be a Nazarene with the prophetic requisition that the
Messiah should be born at Bethlehem. Matthew effected the reconciliation more favorable to Messianic interpretation by giving great
prominence to Bethlehem as the original home of Jesus' parents
and by representing Nazareth as only a place of refuge; whereas
Luke, more interested in historical detail, attached greater importance to Nazareth, making it the original dwelling place of Jesus'
parents and regarding the visit to Bethlehem as temporary. Each is
contrary to fact.

Without question, Strauss's criticism of the birth narratives was
the best up to his time, and in comprehensiveness it is superior to
all since his era. His fairness in presenting all the positions opposed to his own, his clear insight into the problems involved, and
the value that he ascribed to the narratives according to his mythical interpretation demonstrate his greatness as a historian, philosopher, and theologian. The obvious deficiency of his criticism was
his sole intended purpose of proving that the narratives are mythical in character and the decidedly negative character of his mythical interpretation. However, although Strauss's view on the virgin
birth was predetermined by a philosophical presupposition that
resulted in his denial of the virgin birth, he made a positive contribution to the history of its interpretation. By exposing the
inadequacies of both the old supernaturalistic and the current naturalistic interpretations, he prepared the way for a new supernatu-

[13] Karl August Hase (1800–1890), Professor of Theology in the University of
Jena, adopted the same view: The virgin birth pericopes are legends occasioned by
a first-century interpretation of Isa. 7:14 and Ps. 2:7. The idea itself is a legendary
formulation of the spiritual purity and divinity of Jesus as stated in Rom. 1:3. *Das
Leben Jesu*, 1853 and 1865. An analysis of the virgin birth pericopes was absent
from his first edition of 1829. This shows his obvious dependence upon Strauss,
even though his second and third editions were intended to be critical of Strauss.

ralism, which was to retain for Christianity the importance of the virgin birth, and for the historical-critical study of the birth narratives which would eventually clarify the significance of the story of the origin of our Lord.

C. FROM STRAUSS TO THE TÜBINGEN SCHOOL

1. THE SURVIVAL OF THE "OLDER" RATIONALISM

Strauss's work did not immediately silence the advocates of the older rationalism. Christoph Friedrich von Ammon (1766–1850), in his *Life of Jesus*,[14] showed that he had neither surpassed the philosophical insights of Kant nor the naturalistic method of Paulus in his treatment of the Gospel narrative. Daniel Schenkel (1813–1855), who was Professor of Theology in the University of Heidelberg, seeking to purify and glorify Christianity by removing supernatural elements and pointing out the moral values, betrayed his lack of insight into what Strauss had revealed, namely, the value which even accounts of supernatural events may contain when interpreted mythically. For Schenkel the narrative of Jesus before his public career is scarcely worthy of mention because of its unhistorical character. Because it can give us no accurate picture of the birth and childhood of Jesus, he thought, the stories are not worthy of consideration.[15] Schenkel's view is characteristic of the approach of Kant, Herder, Schleiermacher, and Ritschl. Unfortunately he looked at Strauss's *Life of Jesus* as a destructive effort and perpetuated an approach which previously had been rendered obsolete.[16]

---

[14] *Die Geschichte des Lebens Jesu mit steter Rücksicht auf die vorhanden Quellen* (3 vols., 1842–1847), Vol. 1 (1842), pp. 169 ff.

[15] *Das Charakterbild Jesu nach den biblischen Urkunden wissenschaftlich untersucht und dargestellt,* Vierte vermehrte und völlig umgearbeitete Auflage, Wiesbaden, 1873, pp. 34 ff. (1st ed., 1864).

[16] Even more disappointing was the continuance of the old rational method of the imaginative type reminiscent of Bahrdt and Venturini in the writings of the following:

Charles C. Hennell, *An Inquiry Concerning the Origin of Christianity,* 1838.

August Friedrich Gfrörer (1803–1876), *Kritisch Geschichte des Urchristentums,* Vol. 1, 1831; Vol. 2, 1838.

Friedrich Wilhelm Ghillany (1807–1876), *Theologische Briefe an die Gebildeten der deutschen Nation,* 1863.

Ludwig Noack (1819–1885), *Die Geschichte Jesu auf Grund freier geschichtlicher Untersuchungen über das Evangelium und die Evangelien,* 4 vols., 2d ed., 1876, first published in 1870–1871 under the title *Aus der Jordanwiege nach Golgatha; vier*

Schenkel's *Das Charakterbild Jesu* (1864), although avowedly
in criticism of Strauss, was comparable in significance only to
Strauss's *Das Leben Jesu* of 1864, the popularized version, and
Ernest Renan's *Vie de Jésus* of 1863.[17] Both Schenkel and Renan
attempted in their own way to make Christianity explicable to intelligent laymen. Unlike Schenkel, who endeavored to revitalize
Christology, and Strauss, who desired to establish a new system of
dogma, Renan's purpose was purely historical. In Renan the rational historical method reached a high point of subjectivity. The
chief characteristic was romanticism, but he gained esteem by being the first to make a rational interpretation of Christianity which
appealed to the cultured masses.[18]

Like Schenkel, Renan in opening the discussion of Jesus' childhood brushed aside the beginnings of Matthew and Luke.

Jesus was born at Nazareth, a small town of Galilee, which until his
time had no celebrity. During the whole of his life he was designated
by the name of " the Nazarene," and only by a very confused inference
is it made out in the legend constructed about him that he was born
at Bethlehem.[19]

Bücher über das Evangelium und die Evangelien. Also, *Der Ursprung des Christenthums,* 2 vols., 1857.

For all these men, the birth narratives were fictitious.

[17] The fifteenth edition, thoroughly revised, appeared in 1876 as Vol. 1 in the
series *Histoire des Origines du Christianisme.*

[18] The combined effect of Strauss and Renan precipitated a storm of controversy.
Besides the multitude of criticisms that appeared in book and periodical form to
counter the theory in general, certain major works were produced to offset the " Life
of Jesus " of each. Of these the outstanding are:

Contra Strauss —

Johann Ernst Osiander, Professor at the Evangelical Seminary at Maulbronn,
Apologie des Lebens Jesu, gegen den neuesten Versuch, es in Mythen aufzulösen,
1837.

Friederic Augustus Tholuck (1799–1877), Professor of Theology at the University of Halle, *Die Glaubwürdigkeit der evangelischen Geschichte, zugleich eine
Kritik des Lebens Jesu von Strauss,* 1837.

Rev. J. R. Beard, editor of collected essays in defense of Christianity as the first
reply in the English language with a history of the earliest German replies to
Strauss, *Voices of the Church,* 1845.

Contra Renan —

Edmond D. de Pressensé, *Jésus-Christ, son temps, sa vie, son oeuvre,* 1865.

For an excellent sketch, see " Renan and His Interpreters," by Dora Bierer in
The Journal of Modern History, Vol. XXV, No. 4 (December, 1953), pp. 375–389.

Contra Strauss and Renan —

Philip Schaff, *The Person of Christ,* 1865.

[19] Pp. 11–15, French ed., 1863; p. 89 in ET, 1903.

Unlike Schenkel, however, he did not drop the subject here. Later he discussed the narratives of Matt., chs. 1 and 2, and Luke, chs. 1 and 2, in terms of the assumption by Jesus of a Messianic role.

2. THE OUTCOME OF STRAUSS'S NEGATIVE CRITICISM

a. *Complete skepticism — the Christ-Myth School*

Bruno Bauer (1809–1882) started out to elucidate and refine Strauss's concept of myth. He felt that Strauss's concept of myth was too vague to explain adequately the transformation of the personality of Jesus. The " experience " of the church, he suggested, is the real cause of the portrait in the Gospel history, the starting point of the Gospel narrative is the belief in the sacrificial death and resurrection of Jesus, and the formation of the church and the development of the idea that Jesus is the Messiah are one and the same thing. Bauer pictured Christianity as a new religion, the spirit of which was Roman and the outward frame of which was furnished by Judaism. In his *Christus und die Cäsaren. Der Ursprung des Christentums aus dem römischen Griechentum* (1877) he sketched Christianity as the outgrowth of a spiritual movement inspired by Seneca and Josephus. The role of Josephus he had previously developed in *Philo, Strauss, und das Urchristenthum* (1874).

Since he received severe criticism of his views throughout his professional life, Bauer was driven by an almost insane desire to ruin the theological systems of his adversaries. This motivation behind the rational-mythical method that he employed propelled him to interpret every point in the early Christian tradition with increasing skepticism until he denied the historicity of Jesus and the genuineness of all the Pauline Epistles.

Bauer laid the foundation for his general criticism of the origin of Christianity in his earlier work, *Kritik der Evangelien und Geschichte ihres Ursprungs* (1850–1851) . In his treatment of " Die Geburt und Kindheit Jesu " (pp. 253 ff.) he criticized the idea of Jesus' Davidic descent, the Lukan infancy narrative, Jesus' supernatural conception, and the origin of the Lukan and Matthaean birth stories. The birth narratives in Matthew and in Luke were for him literary inventions that were based on originally separate accounts, and the individual stories were in keeping with a uni-

versal motif that pictured a mother and child. The Jesus they portray never lived. " Seine Natur, seine Geschichte, seine Familie
sind in Himmel." (P. 294.)

Bauer's skepticism influenced Daniel Völter, the Professor of
Theology in Amsterdam, who denied the historicity of Jesus. In
*Die Evangelischen Erzählungen von der Geburt und Kindheit
Jesu, kritisch Untersucht* (1911) he traced the idea of the birth
of the Messiah to a Jewish legend, denied the historicity of the narratives, and accounted for the stories out of the dogmatic reflection
of the church. Völter had the advantage in his criticism of the use
of the Sinaitic Syriac text of Matt. 1:16, which gave an account of
the natural descent of Jesus.

Strauss's mythical theory combined with Bauer's skepticism
heralded an outbreak of radical criticism that commanded the attention of the theological world at the turn of the century. Jesus
himself had become a myth, and numerous real and pseudo scholars tried to reconstruct what for them was the true portrayal of
early Christianity. These taskmasters now carry the appellation
" The Christ-Myth School." The development of this movement is
difficult to trace because of the number of writers, the criticism of
them, the numerous editions with replies, counterreplies, and rebuttals in prefaces and introductions.

The publication in the spring of 1909 of *Die Christus-mythe,*
by Arthur Drews, who was lecturer in the College of Technology
at Karlsruhe, highlighted the development of the Christ-Myth
School, and his preface to the second edition (1911) furnishes an
excellent history of the Christ-Myth theory.

Of those whom Drews considered to have contributed most to
this trend in historical investigation, Kalthoff, Robertson, Mead,
Jensen, and Smith were among the foremost.[20] He felt that each

[20] Albert Kalthoff (1850–1906), *Das Christus-Problem Grundlinien zu einer Sozialtheologie,* Zweite Auflage, 1903; *Die Enstehung des Christenthums* (1904), according to whom Christianity is explained as a social movement combining Roman,
Greek, and Judaistic elements. The birth narratives form the introduction and setting for the Gospel narrative. The virgin mother and the spirit of God as begetter
signifies that the Son of God cannot have been an individual human being (p. 178,
1904 ed.).

John M. Robertson, *Christianity and Mythology,* 2d ed., enlarged, 1910 (1st ed.,
1900). A sociological-anthropological interpretation. Birth narratives, based on ideas
borrowed from non-Christian religions, are an example of the superimposition of a
myth on a cult (p. 124). The cult of Jesus, survival of an ancient solar myth or
another worship of the babe Joshua, son of Miriam (p. 285).

G. R. S. Mead, *Did Jesus Live 100 B.C.?,* 1903, an inquiry into the Talmud, identifies Jesus with Jeschu, who is described as a contemporary of Jannai (pp. 137–138);

had penetrated into different aspects of the total problem. His own work was intended to represent the refinement and crystallization of the process.

Basing his theories on the main lines of the mythological method which sought analogies to all Biblical ideas in non-Christian religions, Drews tried to show that the ideas of a dying Messiah, his rising again, and stories that relate to the miraculous birth of such a figure date back to pre-Christian times: the clue to the origin of the legend of Jesus' birth is to be found in the canonical Rev., ch. 12, which portrays the ancient Babylonian mythical idea of the birth of a divine child whose immediate birth is threatened by the Dragon. This motif was common throughout the ancient world in Greek, Roman, Egyptian, and Assyrian mythologies. The original source of all stories in the ancient world of the birth of Fire-Gods and Sun-Gods is to be traced to the Vedic Agni Cult (Krishna) which lies behind a pre-Christian Buddhist legend. The resemblances between the Christian and Buddhist legends are too close to avoid close comparison. Both Jesus and Buddha are said to be born of a " pure virgin," honored by heavenly spirits, prayed to by kings, and loaded with presents. Every point in the birth legends of Jesus has its parallel in the narratives of Buddha's

---

interprets " Birth " and " little one " in terms of mystic and cryptic expressions in the Talmud (pp. 145–147) ; idea of virgin birth has basis in first-century Hermetic literature.

Peter Jensen (1861–1936), Professor of Semitic Philology at Marburg, *Das Gilgamesh-Epos in der Welt-literatur,* Erster Band, 1906, who found practically all characteristics of the Bible in the Babylonian Gilgamesh Epic, the oldest in the world. In the Gospel narrative, Jesus and John represent Gilgamesh and Eabani. (Also in a short appeal to laymen as *Moses, Jesus, Paulus, Drei Varianten des babylonischen Gottmenschen Gilgamesh,* Zweite, 1909) . Jensen and Adolf Jülicher, Professor of Theology in Marburg, waged a private controversy over this issue. Jülicher's *Hat Jesus gelebt?* (1910), in answer to Jensen, was in turn replied to by Jensen's *Hat der Jesus der Evangelien wirklich gelebt?* (1910) .

William Benjamin Smith (1850–1934), Professor of Mathematics and later of Philosophy at Tulane University in New Orleans, *Ecce Deus,* published first in German at Jena in 1911, expounds the theory he first advocated in 1906 in *Der vorchristliche Jesus.* Disappointed by the shadowy Christ of Harnack, Loisy, Wellhausen, and Burkitt, concluding that nothing remains of Jesus as a historical personality, taking a clue from Origen that the Gospel narratives should be interpreted as symbolical, and combining this with Mead's idea of a pre-Christian Jesus cult, he tried to establish what he called the " Secret of Primitive Christianity," which was essentially a monotheistic as over against a polytheistic view of the gods. The true " germ " of Christianity is the monotheistic impulse, the instinct for unity which lies at the heart of all great philosophy and noble religion. The Gospels represent the success of the Christian community in the second century in combating polytheism. By his theory, he intended as much to counter the views of Kalthoff, Robertson, and Jensen as he did the liberal theologians and historians listed above.

early life. Mary and Joseph, too, are mythological characters whose prototypes may be located in Indian religion. The historical Jesus was from the beginning a dogma, a fiction caused by the religious and practical social needs of the growing and struggling Christian church.

Many able scholars hastened to the defense of the historical Jesus in reply to Drews and his colleagues. The most significant writing was done by Johannes Weiss in *Jesus von Nazareth Mythus oder Geschichte?* (1910); Friedrich Loofs in *What Is the Truth About Jesus Christ?* (1913); Shirley Jackson Case in *The Historicity of Jesus* (1912); Arnold Mayer in *Le Christ Mythique* (1912); Fred C. Conybeare, *The Historical Christ* (1914); Johannes Leipoldt, *Sterbende und auferstehende Götter* (1923); Maurice Goguel, *Jésus de Nazareth — Mythe ou Histoire?* (1925); and by Martin Dibelius in *Gospel Criticism and Christology* (1935).

Replies of able historians could not, however, answer or suppress this left-wing radical movement. Transplanted into the French mentality, it flourished at the hands of several gifted authors. M. Paul-Louis Couchoud, former physician turned littérateur and archaeologist, attempted to refine the Christ-Myth theory by proposing that Jesus was not a myth or a symbol but a spiritual reality,[21] and that the clue to the origin of Christianity is to be found in the canonical Apocalypse which indicates the existence of a cult of Jesus. The portrayal of the earthly Jesus in the Gospels and the harmonious original community in The Acts of the Apostles are two legendary variations of the ancient legend of the birth of a God.[22]

The same theory is exposited by Couchoud along with P. Alfaric and Albert Bayet in *Le Problème de Jésus et les origines du Christianisme* (1932). Their procedure was to discredit the testimony of Josephus and Tacitus, elaborate on the inconsistencies of the Christian testimonies, point out numerous mythological analogies, and to show how the cultic conception of the Apocalypse was applied in various ways by the anonymous author of Hebrews, by Paul, and by the Evangelists (pp. 52–55).

Two applications of the mythological theory that did not deny outright the historicity of Jesus were prevalent in French criti-

21 *Le Mystère de Jésus* (1924), pp. 91, 179.
22 Paul-Louis Couchoud, *The Book of Revelation,* trans. from the French (1932), pp. 78–79.

cisms. One type used the method to destroy the whole theological artifice of the Roman Catholic hierarchy. Specific application of this kind of criticism is exemplified in the writings of Louis Coulange (pseudonym for Joseph Turmel), who felt deceived by the Roman Catholic Church and consequently devoted himself to a study of Christian origins. His *Histoire des Dogmes,* II, consists of three parts: " La Trinité," " L'Incarnation," " La Vierge Marie." The latter, before its enlargement and revision, was published separately in 1925. In it Coulange outlined the historical development of the concept of Mary as Mary Ever-Virgin, the Virgin Mother, the Holy Virgin, and the idea of the Immaculate Conception from the beginning to the proclamation of Pope Pius IX on December 8, 1854. In his analysis of the canonical narratives he concluded that the virgin birth is a part of the apotheosis of Jesus, the doctrine arose after the Christian community had bestowed on Jesus the title Son of God, and the virgin birth idea was associated with Son of God as an adaptation to the pagan world whose religious thought was accustomed to the idea of a God mating with a woman (*Dogmes* II, pp. 254–255). Coulange took the narratives as legendary and inferior. They reflected for him the mentality of primitive Christianity about A.D. 60 and were the first step in a development of Christology of which John's Logos idea was the next.

A second French variation of the mythological theme was the " Psychological Life " of Jesus. It was exemplified by P. de Régla in his *Jésus de Nazareth* (1891); E. Bosc, *La Vie ésotérique de Jésus de Nazareth* (1902); C. Binet-Sanglé, *La Folie de Jésus* I–IV (1908–1915); and by G. Bergeur in his *Quelques traits de la Vie de Jésus au point de vue psychologique et psychanalytique* (1920). This kind of interpretation was popularized elsewhere by G. Lomer, *Jesus Christus* (1905); W. Hirsh, *Conclusions of a Psychiatrist* (1912); and E. Rasmussen, *Jesus* (1905). G. Stanley Hall's *Jesus the Christ* (1917) represented the flowering of this French import on American soil.

In this type of writing the historicity of Jesus is not denied, but the whole portrait of Jesus is considerably altered. The theory received its impetus from Strauss's *Das Leben Jesu* (1835), page 1480, where he hinted in speaking of Jesus' conception of an immediate future kingdom ushered in with a blaze of supernatural glory, that Jesus, from our point of view, must be considered a fanatic. In the method of interpretation that ensues, the imagina-

tion runs wild in its attempt to understand Jesus from the standpoint of psychology and psychoanalysis. That the narratives of
Matt., chs. 1 and 2, and Luke, chs. 1 and 2, all belong to legend,
not to history, became a foregone conclusion. Albert Schweitzer,
in his pamphlet *Die psychiatrische Beurteilung Jesu* (1913), re-
viewed the proceedings of this " school " and exposed its basic
fallacy: the literature of the Gospels does not provide the proper
and suitable basis for any psychological analysis.

b. *Tendency criticism — the New Tübingen School*

Soon after the appearance of Strauss's *Life of Jesus,* Ferdinand
Christian Baur (1792–1860), Professor of Theology at Tübingen,
came under its influence. Already affected theologically and philosophically by Schleiermacher and Hegel and acquainted with the
historical method of Niebuhr and Ranke and recognizing the
value and the weakness of Strauss's work, Baur set about to establish a new trend in Biblical historical studies *(Das Christenthum
und die christliche Kirche der drei ersten Jahrhunderte,* 1853).
Baur recognized in Strauss the demolition of the traditional faith
in the historical truth of the Gospel records. Strauss, however, had
confined himself to criticism of the history and did not attempt a
literary criticism. Strauss had abandoned the criticism of the documents for a criticism of the stories. Baur intended to go on from
there.

As a historian, Baur felt he must discover the whole connection
of the circumstances out of which a writing arose. However, for
him this meant a schematic frame according to the Hegelian formula of thesis and antithesis, i.e., Judaism and Paulinism. Each
writing had its own " tendency " occasioned by the attitude that
it took toward the problem arising out of the tension between the
two opposite contemporary trends. Among the Synoptic Gospels,
Mark represents the reconciliation between the two opposites —
Matthew (Judaistic) and Luke (Pauline). Mark's omission of the
birth narrative indicates his conciliatory attitude between two opposing parties, referring neither to a natural nor to a supernatural
origin. The story of Jesus' birth appealed to Baur as one that was
characteristic of the process of myth-making in the New Testament and in the ancient world.

Adolf Hilgenfeld (1823–1907), Professor of Theology in Jena,
and influenced by Baur's method, in his *Die Evangelien nach ihrer*

Entstehung und geschichtlichen Bedeutung (1854) thought that everything preceding the genealogy in Luke is nonhistorical and is a preparation for the true Gospel history. He believed, too, that Luke's prehistory extends farther back than Matthew's. He detected an element of controversy in the Lukan narratives, but hastened to add that this element in the record reflects not so much the relation of Jesus himself to John as the relation of the later Christian community to its Johannine rivals. Luke 1:34-35 was interpreted by him to establish Jesus as the Son of God and thus to make him more than the Jewish Messiah, and the Matthaean tradition was understood as the fulfillment of Isa. 7:14. Hilgenfeld interpreted the numerous Old Testament references in Matthew as the Jewish " tendency."

Taking his cue from Baur and others, Gustav Volkmar (1809–1893), Professor of New Testament Criticism and Exegesis at Zürich, made his sole source for the life of Jesus the Second Gospel, Mark. Volkmar had critical support for his theory of the priority of Mark in the " Marcan hypothesis " which was being developed within literary criticism through the writings of Lachmann, Weisse, and Wilke.[23] His chief interest in *Jesus Nazarenus und die erste christliche Zeit mit den beiden ersten Erzählern* (1882) was a systematic investigation of the Synoptic apocalypse in which he formulated the alternative that either Jesus' claim for Messiahship was based on the contemporary political ideal of a Messianic King or Jesus did not put forth any Messianic claims. Volkmar chose the latter alternative. The narratives at the beginning of Luke and Matthew then were viewed by him as doctrinal expressions at the beginning of the second century at a time when Christianity was making a strong appeal both to Jews and Gentiles and within its own ranks was reconciling opposing Petrine and Pauline factions (pp. 29, 34-35).

The most famous and prolific representative of the New Tübingen School was Otto Pfleiderer (1839–1908), Professor of Theology in the University of Berlin. According to him, Baur took the right path between Romantic personalism and social evolutionism. Like Baur, he affirmed that the Gospels give us no historical knowledge of the birth and childhood of Jesus.

Using Mark as his main source, Luke attempted, according to

---

[23] Karl Lachmann (1793–1851), *De ordine narrationum in evangeliis synopticis* in *Theologische Studien und Kritiken* (1835), pp. 570–590; Christian Hermann Weisse (1801–1866), *Die evangelische Geschichte kritisch und philosophisch Bearbeiter* (1838); Christian Gottlob Wilke (1786–1854), *Der Urevangelist* (1838).

Pfleiderer, to satisfy a growing need of the Christian community for information prior to the baptism of Jesus. He calculated to show Jesus' superiority over John. The half miracle of the birth of John is immediately surpassed by the entirely miraculous birth of Jesus. The legend of Jesus' miraculous birth moves the theory of the derivation of his sonship a step earlier in his life to his origin. An older legend placed the origin of Jesus' Messianic Sonship at the descent of the spirit upon him at baptism. The idea of the cause of Jesus' birth without human father and by the Holy Spirit alone was a fortunate choice for Luke in making an appeal to " Heathen-Christians." The term " Son of God " has a double significance: for the Jews — a Messianic-theocratic dignity (Ps. 2) ; for the Gentiles — actual begetting, but transformed from the heathen-mythical notion of a sexual act to the creative power of the Spirit of God. The Old Testament passage Isa. 7:14 is an afterthought used as a proof text to establish an already accepted idea.

Die Entstehung des Christentums is based on his *Das Urchristenthum seine Schriften und Lehren, in geschichtlichen Zusammenhang beschrieben* (2 Aufl., 1902), where these ideas are also treated but with different emphasis and presentation of detail. In his treatment of Luke, most notable is his discussion of the theory of interpolation which took into account the Sinaitic Syriac version of Matt. 1:16. He was sure that the original Lukan narrative did not include v. 34 of ch. 1, and at the time it was added to the narrative the words " as was supposed " were added to ch. 3:23.

Strauss attempted to effect by his mythical interpretation a synthesis between the thesis of the old supernaturalism and the antithesis of rationalistic naturalism. His method was critically unhistorical since he subjected the Gospel history entirely to the Hegelian dialectical procedure. His interpretation of the virgin birth rested on the proposition that myth is the key to the explanation.

The Christ-Myth School changed the " mythical " aspect of his method to the " mythological," whereby Christianity was thought of as a religion subject to the same principles of interpretation as other religions with mythological characteristics. The New Tübingen School adopted Strauss's dialectic and transferred it from the history within the documents to the documents themselves, whereby Christianity was to be interpreted solely in terms of a theological and literary development.

The rationalists employed every critical device at their disposal to prove the nonhistoricity of the birth narratives, and having done so, felt that their interpretative task was complete. They were really only at the beginning. The relationship of the virgin birth pericope to pagan mythology, the place of the concept in the development of early Christian theology, and the textual problems which the extant literary form involved were problems of which the rationalists since Strauss were aware but which none of them carefully investigated and from which all of them drew conclusions suited only to fit their preconceived devices.

Even though Strauss claimed that his mythical interpretation was an alternative for rationalistic interpretation and was, in a sense, a scientific corrective for the older unscientific view and even though Strauss's intention was to have put an end to the kind of rationalism that actually followed him, Strauss must be classified with those who deny the virgin birth on a priori philosophical grounds. His mythical principle was as much a philosophical presupposition as the rationalistic presuppositions of the primacy of reason and the rejection of miracle. Strauss along with his predecessors and successors passed on to the historical and literary critics who followed them the task of making extensive research in areas in which the story of the virgin birth needs careful critical investigation: the historical, theological, and literary background.

Before this development is taken up, it is necessary to trace the conservative reaction of the supernaturalists to the rationalistic naturalism of the nineteenth century. Supernaturalistic theologians for a century following the first quarter of the nineteenth reacted to the whole range of naturalistic philosophical interpretation, justifiably and rigorously defended the place of the virgin birth in the Christian faith, and helped to prepare the way for a historical and intelligent understanding of the story which stands at the portal of the First and Third Gospels.

As the first man originated,
without father,
and without mother,
from that creative agency of God
which spiritualized the dust of the earth,
so did the second man
originate without father,
by that effectual power of the Most High
which spiritualized humanity.

— Johann Peter Lange, *The Life*
of the Lord Jesus Christ

CHAPTER

4

SUPERNATURALISTIC THEOLOGICAL INTERPRETATION

ALL RECENT supernaturalistic interpretation of the virgin birth can be traced to the influence of Strauss. His hand or shadow can be seen wherever supernaturalistic interpreters have given attention to the story of Jesus' origin. The distinguishing features of over a century of supernaturalistic interpretation have been the motivation that it received from the criticism of Strauss and the tenacity by which the historicity of the virgin birth has been maintained. Against whatever objections the rationalists brought forward in denying the virgin birth, the supernaturalists have maintained the validity of the historicity in the literal sense of Jesus' divine origin.

A. THE ORIENTATION OF SUPERNATURALISTIC THEOLOGICAL INTERPRETATION

1. THE POINT OF REFERENCE

The immediate point of reference for supernaturalistic interpreters for the greater part of the nineteenth century was Strauss's *Life of Jesus*. Hermann Olshausen (1796–1839), who from 1822 until 1835 was Professor of Theology at Königsberg and in 1835 occupied the chair of Theology in Erlangen in Bavaria; David Mendel (1789–1850), who was Professor at Berlin; Heinrich A. Ebrard (1818–1888), who was Professor of Theology in the University of Erlangen; and Johann Peter Lange (1802–1882), who was Professor of Divinity in the University of Bonn, all took up the " defense of the Gospel record " against the " negative " criticism of Strauss. Strauss may be credited with having stimulated the discussion that transpired to bring forth an abundance of literature not only on the Gospels and the life of Jesus in general but on the virgin birth as well.

Olshausen's first edition of his *Biblischer Commentar* had been published before Strauss, and was one of the supernaturalists against whom Strauss directed his attack. After the publication of Strauss's *Leben* (1835), Olshausen completely revised his commentary (1837) so as to reply to Strauss. He was sure that Strauss would receive no real following in theological circles and that theologians would soon do to Strauss what Strauss had done to Paulus. It was inevitable, he thought, that scorn would silence Strauss in intellectual, theological, and philosophical circles.

Mendel's *Life of Jesus* (1837) was the first " life " in direct response to Strauss. He shared Olshausen's optimism concerning Strauss's inevitable and sudden fate and felt that the ladder of necessity was unfolded in theological and philosophical rationalism in order that it might be overthrown by Christian truth. The flowering of rationalism in Strauss's mythical theory would accelerate the death of all rationalism, since irrefutable rebuttals, such as his own and that of Tholuck of Halle (*Die Glaubwürdigkeit der evangelischen Geschichte*, 1837), were springing up and would continue to be forthcoming.

Ebrard's purpose was the same. His *Wissenschaftliche Kritik der evangelischen Geschichte* (1841–1842, 2d ed., 1850) was to provide students and ministers with information on the present position and history of the criticism of the Gospels from which they could supply themselves with the necessary weapons for a defense against the attacks of Strauss and Bruno Bauer.

As more and more time elapsed following the publication of Strauss's stormy volume, supernaturalistic interpreters widened the range of the objects of their criticism. The factor of the publisher's purpose was also involved. Lange, for example, wrote his *Life of Jesus* (1844–1847) against the liberal theology of Schleiermacher and the negative critical studies of Strauss and Bruno Bauer. The publishers of the English edition (1872), however, stated that their purpose for issuing the book was to counteract the influence of Hase's *Life of Jesus* (originally published in 1829, reissued in 1854 revised), Schleiermacher's liberal theology, the Christological deficiency of Heinrich Ewald's *Geschichte Christus' und seiner Zeit* (1st ed., 1854; 2d ed., 1857), and particularly Renan's *Vie de Jésus* (1863). Lange's work was published in English as the most complete "Life of Our Lord."

In France it was only natural that Renan's *Vie* should be the immediate cause of conservative reaction. E. de Pressensé (1824–1891) defended the supernaturalistic interpretation of the life of Jesus against Renan in particular and against Strauss in general. Although in his preface to *Jésus-Christ, son temps, sa vie, son oeuvre* (1865) he said that his book did not arise out of any particular circumstances nor did it come in answer to any contemporary work, throughout it is evident that the standpoint of the writing is opposition to the rationalistic interpretation of the aforementioned critics. He was even grateful to Renan for having stirred up interest in what is the most important aspect of the Christian faith, namely, the historical character of Jesus Christ. De Pressensé was convinced that the church could be purified by the fires of conflict.

Supernaturalistic interpretation in Continental Europe culminated toward the close of the nineteenth century in Bernhard Weiss's *Das Leben Jesu* (1882). The great Professor of Theology in Berlin was a liberal Biblical scholar who claimed to be unhappy with both the naturalistic point of view of the old rationalism of Paulus and the new rationalism of Keim and Schenkel and the supernaturalism of Neander (Mendel). The picture of Christ which both supernaturalistic and the rationalistic points of view had obscured each in its own way could be made historically discernible as far as Weiss was concerned only through a study of the condition of the origin of the sacred writings. Although Weiss's median point of view is discernible throughout a large part of his writing, in his treatment of the birth narratives he seems to have adopted a modified form of supernaturalism.

Other significant German supernaturalistic interpretation has appeared in the writings of Paul Schanz (*Commentar über das Evangelium des heiligen Lucas,* 1883), A. Nebe (*Die Kindheitsgeschichte unseres Herrn Jesu Christi nach Matthäus und Lukas,* 1893), Richard Grützmacher (*Die Jungfrauengeburt,* in *Biblische Zeit- und Streitfragen,* II Serie, Heft 5, 1906), Theodor Zahn (*Das Evangelium des Lukas,* 1913), D. A. Schlatter (*Das Evangelium des Lukas,* 1931), and of Karl Bornhäuser (*Die Geburts- und Kindheitsgeschichte Jesu,* 1930).

In the English-speaking world, the supernaturalistic interpretation of the virgin birth found its finest expression in the hands of A. M. Fairbairn, Principal of Airedale College in Bradford, whose *Studies in the Life of Christ* first appeared in 1880 and were originally prepared as a series of Sunday evening discourses while the author was minister in Aberdeen (4th ed., 1885), and James Orr, Professor of Apologetics and Systematic Theology, United Free Church College, Glasgow, whose *The Virgin Birth of Christ* (1907) embodied lectures delivered first at the Fifth Avenue Presbyterian Church in New York City. In America, the best work was done by Louis Matthew Sweet in his *The Birth and Infancy of Jesus Christ* (1906 and 1907) and by John Gresham Machen of Westminster Seminary in his *The Virgin Birth of Christ* (1930).

The starting point of Fairbairn's writing was Strauss's remark in the preface of his *Das Leben Jesu* (1864) that " the critical study of the life of Jesus is the pit into which theology of our age necessarily fell and was destroyed." Fairbairn set out to demonstrate that the exact opposite was true. Like de Pressensé, he felt that even the negative critical study of the life of Christ accomplishes the constructive purpose of renovating and vivifying theology.

The books on the virgin birth by Sweet and Orr were the first full-sized volumes on the subject in English from the conservative or supernaturalistic point of view. They were dependent upon Strauss for supplying the roots of the tree that they were trying to cut down, but by this time — the beginning of the twentieth century — so much more had been written on the virgin birth by liberal scholars in Germany that these conservatives had a new set of sounding boards for their discussions. Numerous volumes and articles written from various rationalistic points of view flooded Europe and stirred up controversy in America. The question now had become, Should the virgin birth be retained in the Christian creed? Sweet was conscious of the unfavorable criticism that the doctrine of the virgin birth had received in Germany in the last decade of the nineteenth century under the influence of Keim, Lobstein, and Harnack, and he was particularly disturbed by the results of a symposium that appeared in the *Biblical World* (Vol. X, pp. 1–30) which concluded that the virgin birth was a compromise between the primitive idea of Messiahship by Davidic descent and the Hellenistic idea of Messiahship by incarnation after pre-existence. Although Sweet claimed that he was defending the virgin birth along exegetical lines and the defense of the virgin birth was chiefly a question of " evidence," he himself accomplished little of what he set out to do. His so-called " defense " was no more than the attempt to reply to the criticisms of the liberal scholars. He failed to establish any real evidence.

Under similar motivation but in much briefer form B. W. Randolph, who was Principal of Ely Theological College, wrote *The Virgin Birth of Our Lord* (1903). Another able, brief discussion similar to Sweet's point of view is J. H. Bernard's chapter on "The Virgin Birth of Christ" in *Studia Sacra* (1917), pp. 17–211).

Orr's lectures and eventual book took as the point of departure Soltau's dictum that an Evangelical Christian at the turn of the century was no longer able to believe in the supernatural origin of Jesus. Soltau had gone so far as to say that all records of the birth are borrowed from later fables and can be traced back in every instance to heathen models, a Christian who affirms the creed at this point makes himself a sharer in the sin against the Holy Spirit, and the church does not have the right to retain in its creed the statement " conceived by the Holy Ghost, born of the Virgin Mary." This whole trend of thinking Orr set out to contradict.

In 1930, Machen had the advantage of looking back over a century of criticism and controversy on the virgin birth. Consequently, his point of reference was no single critic or individual school. He wrote over against the background of a hundred years of criticism and response and tried to make a strong case for the virgin birth from the supernaturalistic point of view. He developed his arguments around a double thesis: the belief in the virgin birth was founded upon a fact (chs. I to XI), and the idea of the virgin birth was a fact (chs. XII to XIV). Machen believed the interpreter was faced with this alternative ultimately: the virgin birth is based upon either fact or error.

2. THE METHODOLOGY

One of the most wholesome consequences of the immediate response to Strauss was the recognition by Olshausen that the proper handling of the birth and infancy narratives necessitated the separate handling of the Matthaean and Lukan accounts. Olshausen conceded to Strauss the fallacy of the old harmonistic view of the Gospels, and, as a result, he took up his discussion of the birth narratives according to the separate documents of Matthew and Luke rather than on the basis of the old harmonistic procedure of trying to establish a single synchronized and chronological order deduced from both accounts. Unlike the rationalists, however, Olshausen insisted that there may be disagreements as to details among the several Gospel writers, but perfect harmony is evident in the Gospel history insofar as essentials are concerned. He spoke of the essential unity of the Scriptures and their unessential disparity.

Ebrard tried valiantly to maintain a harmonistic view of the two narratives and claimed that the harmony was explicable on the basis that both accounts of the miraculous birth of Jesus and the Annunciation of this event bring out the general doctrinal point " Christ is the Son of God." His explanation of the narratives of the Annunciation illustrated how different points of view could be complementary rather than contradictory: Matthew chose the incident of the Annunciation in Joseph's dream because he wished to furnish proof that Jesus was the son of Abraham and David, the seed of Abraham in whom all nations were to be blessed, and the successor to David's throne; the account in Luke, the Annunciation of the birth of Jesus to the woman who was to be his mother, was written for the Gentiles and paid less attention to the theocratical relation than Matthew.

Bernhard Weiss attempted to overcome the harmonistic difficulty by commencing his analysis of the birth and infancy narratives with a discussion and explanation of the apparent diversity between the separate canonical accounts. Weiss accounted for this by assuming that the author of each narrative selected from a storehouse of tradition his own materials that were especially suited to the purpose of his own narrative as a whole. According to Weiss, in no Gospel is a connected description of Jesus' life attempted. This principle applies to the infancy narratives. As a result, Weiss's treatment of the narratives, as a whole, is arranged topically around the central feature, the virgin birth pericopes.

The author of the great conservative French " Life of Jesus," de Pressensé, had learned the same lesson. Rather than allow the interpretation of the virgin birth to become lost in a maze of speculation concerning the harmonization of the facts and the chronology of the two Evangelical accounts, he confined the discussion of the infancy narratives in his *Life* to a discussion of the virgin birth which followed the lines of the essential theological problems that are involved. He argued against the inconsistencies and deficiencies of the naturalistic point of view and for the importance of the virgin birth in relation to the concept of Jesus as the redeemer of the world. His lack of supernaturalistic rigidity was evidenced in his willingness to sacrifice the genealogies to the findings of historical criticism. He agreed with the rationalists that they present notable differences which constitute insoluble contradictions. He disagreed with them, however, that this would in any way effect the validity and historicity of the essential feature of the narrative, the virgin birth, and would not even admit to the rationalists that the artificiality of the genealogies constituted an argument against the fact that both Joseph and Mary are true descendants of David.

The chapter entitled " The Narratives of the Birth and Infancy " in Fairbairn's *Studies in the Life of Christ* (1880) reveals the same advance upon the earlier supernaturalistic harmonistic treatments.[1] In sixteen remarkable pages characterized by a reverent and aesthetic attitude and an acquaintance with the central critical problems, Fairbairn built his chapter upon the sequence of important critical logical points: these narratives are unique in relation to the " parallels " in heathen religions since the Greek mythologies have long ago become incredible but the story of Christ's birth remains credible; the distinction between history and legend is clearly marked " by the reserve of the canonical and the vulgar tattle of the apocryphal Gospels " (p. 31) ; the narratives not only need not be rejected a priori as contrarational but also inexplicable either as ordinary legends or as myths; the narrative in each Gospel is developed according to different points of view — Matthew, Jewish presenting Jesus as Messiah complying with conditions necessary to Messiahship, and Luke, Gentile presenting Jesus in his common brotherhood to man and native sonship to God; the Evangelists agree in representing Christ as the child of the Divine creative energy, finding the cause of his birth in the action of God, Matthew representing this from the Jewish standpoint as a fulfillment of prophecy by the prophetic title " Emmanuel," and Luke denoting the child from the Pauline-Gentile point of view as " the Son of God "; each Evangelist in his own way ratifies the purpose of the other; the affinities either with

---

[1] More recently this was recognized by Alfred Plummer in his commentary in the ICC, " On the Gospel According to St. Luke," 4th ed. (1908) , and in his *An Exegetical Commentary to the Gospel of St. Matthew* (1909) . Plummer resorted to the old view that the difference is to be explained on the basis of the source: Matthew — Joseph; Luke — Mary. As late as 1930, A. T. Robertson *(Word Pictures in the New Testament* [1930]) and J. G. Machen *(op. cit.)* accounted for the diversity in the narratives on the basis of their separate sources — Joseph and Mary.

Old Testament concepts or ideas in Hindu mythologies are in reference to " forms of thought " and do not explain the psychological roots of the belief embodied in the Evangelists' narratives; Matthew's genealogy is the vehicle of prophetic ideas, incorporating the thought of Israel, and Luke's is the vehicle of Pauline ideas, linking Jesus with humanity.

The trio of volumes by Sweet, Orr, and Machen, which were devoted completely to the study of the virgin birth, were developed by their authors along different but strictly logical lines. The " negative " liberal criticism of the preceding century provided the structure for Sweet's analysis. Chapter by chapter, he took up the objections to the supernaturalistic view that had been raised by Keim, Lobstein, Soltau, Harnack, and others. The emphasis of each of these scholars was the pivotal point around which successive chapters revolved. Both Sweet and Orr were trying to make a " case " for the virgin birth, the lines of argument for which were shaped by the unsupernaturalistic interpretation of scholars before them. By its more positive nature, Orr's discussion was superior to Sweet's.

This type of treatment of the virgin birth had its most notable expression in Machen's volume, in which he summarized the whole discussion, not under a half dozen or more headings, but under two: the foundation of the virgin birth upon fact and the virgin birth as a fact even when thought of *as an idea*. Machen's analysis is valuable for bringing into sharp focus the crux of supernaturalistic interpretation; namely, whether or not the virgin birth is a historical fact in the literal sense.

Supernaturalistic interpreters have employed several methodologies: (1) the individual handling of the separate Evangelical accounts (Olshausen), (2) the attempted harmonization of the separate Gospel records (Neander, Ebrard, and Lange), (3) the discussion of the virgin birth pericopes with subsidiary references to other materials in the infancy narratives (B. Weiss, de Pressensé, and Fairbairn), and (4) the argument in defense of the virgin birth against the attacks of liberal criticism, depending on the criticism for the lines along which the argument developed (Sweet, Orr, Machen).

Naturally, the particular methodology was dependent for the most part upon the literary form of each supernaturalistic volume. " Lives of Jesus " were most likely to adopt the harmonistic procedure, whereas volumes devoted solely to the virgin birth were most suitably controlled by some logical scheme of development. It is unfortunate that no one took the cue from Olshausen and devoted an entire book to the discussion of the virgin birth on the basis of a separate exegesis of each Evangelical narrative. Early supernaturalistic interpretation got lost wandering in a forest of harmonistic difficulties. Later supernaturalistic interpretation lost its critical and objective respectability by becoming too greatly obsessed with the desire to reply to " negative " criticism and to adopt a methodology geared to support a point of view which for nearly a hundred years had been obsolete. The supernaturalists' point of reference prevented them from making a positive contribution to the interpretation of the virgin birth, and their methodology stood in the way of their reaching to the heart of the matter.

B. THE THEOLOGICAL PRESUPPOSITIONS OF SUPERNATURALISTIC THEOLOGICAL INTERPRETATION

All supernaturalistic interpretation has been motivated by a priori theological presuppositions on these central issues: (1) a theistic world view, (2) the nature of revelation, and (3) the relation of Christianity to other religions. Definite conclusions on these three subjects before any investigation began predisposed the interpreters to come to their conclusion that the literal historicity of the virgin birth can be affirmed.

1. THE THEISTIC WORLD VIEW

Of the four early German interpreters, Neander (Mendel) made the clearest statement of the difference between supernaturalistic and naturalistic interpretation at the point of the basic world view. At the conclusion of his preface to the third edition of his *Life of Jesus* (1839), he pointed out that the essential differences between himself and Strauss consisted of opposing views of the relation of God to the world, of the personality of the Spirit, of the relation between the here and the hereafter, and of the nature of sin. The struggle was, in Neander's mind, between Christian theism and a system of world and self-deification.

2. THE NATURE OF REVELATION

From this first and basic premise of supernaturalistic interpretation, a definite theistic world view, several other important a priori theological presuppositions were developed. One of these was the supernaturalistic concept of revelation with reference to the virgin birth. As Orr put it, since God is the Creator and Sustainer of the world, the " Cause of all causes, Law of all laws," it is in no way a priori incredible that God should make a new supernatural beginning in the entrance of his Son into humanity. Orr was here revoicing B. Weiss's opinion that the aim of Jesus' appearance was to bring salvation to a lost world, presupposing that humanity had taken an abnormal direction. According to Weiss, the miraculous conception and birth of Jesus is the highest point in a series of divine revelations whose preparations were in the history of Israel. At this point he was in disagreement with Schleiermacher's concept of revelation in which Jesus' appearance is a unique factor in history, but developed entirely according to the known laws of all occurrences.

Many years earlier Mendel had made this same point clear. His interpretation of the miraculous conception of Jesus was based upon his own notion of Christ as a supernatural communication of the divine nature for the moral renewal of man, a new beginning on the scene of human progress. Interpreters further distinguished between two essential aspects of the Christian revelation: the nature of Jesus himself and the nature of the Biblical record.

a. *Revelation and the nature of Jesus*

Supernaturalistic interpretation is indebted to Lange for stressing this basic presupposition: behind the virgin birth is the fact that Christian revelation reached its fulfillment in the incarnate Son of God. Basic to Christianity is the notion that as the incarnate Son of God, Christ should be perfect from his very origin. Christianity, as a new principle, the principle of all improvement, " is the principle of the identity of the eternal Word and human corporeity, of real and ideal life." According to Lange, a completely naturalistic explanation of the life of Jesus with its consequent denial of his miraculous birth is a reincarnation of the old Ebionitism. He was convinced that Ebionitism itself had long since been historically refuted, and it was now perfectly reasonable to accept the supernaturalistic interpretation of the life of Jesus.[2] De Pressensé subsequently insisted that the miraculous birth is in keeping with the framework of history and with the essential nature of Christianity as a revelation of God in Christ.

Because he was one of the closest of all supernaturalistic interpreters historically to the controversy over miracle in the Renaissance and the Enlightenment, it is only natural that Neander (Mendel) stressed the role of miracle in the supernaturalistic concept of revelation. For him, Jesus Christ was above history and the revelation of absolute truth, and miracles were essential elements in that divine revelation; Jesus' *miraculous* conception is demanded a priori; and Christ himself should be thought of as a miracle, and the interpretation of his birth should not be considered apart from this fact (*Das Leben Jesu,* 1850, p. 30).

Lange waxed poetic when he talked about the miraculous element in the Christian revelation. Since the idea of the incarnation of God comes from the very heart of God and as Christ is presented as a new and miraculous life, it is only natural, said he, that a halo of miracles should be formed around this central miracle as " the rays of the rising sun " (*The Life of the Lord Jesus Christ,* Vol. 1, 1872, p. 258). " As the flower must be surrounded by its garland of leaves, and Adam by his paradise, so was the birth of Christ, the bodily manifestation of the Gospels, surrounded by a circle of inspired dispositions and revelations, of reflexes of the Gospels."

The same position was maintained by J. J. Van Oosterzee, Professor of Theology at the University of Utrecht, in Lange's *Theologisch-homiletisches Bibelwerk, Des Neuen Testamentes,* Dritter Theil: *Das Evangelium nach Lukas* (1859).

Olshausen also maintained the absolute possibility of miracles. The laws of nature, he said, are not chains by which the Supreme Lawgiver had bound himself, but the laws of nature are cords that he holds in his own hand and that he can lengthen or shorten as his good pleasure and wisdom dictates. His treatment of the narratives of Jesus' birth was directed to offset two views. One was the view of the Roman and Greek church which transformed Mary into the Queen of Heaven, and the other was the " *Rationalismus Vulgaris* " based on Celsus and developed by Bahrdt and Paulus.

The presupposition of the validity of miracle is also a strong

---

[2] Lange, *op. cit.,* Vol. 1, pp. 257–258. Machen, many years later, insisted that the Ebionite denial of the virgin birth was based upon philosophical or dogmatic presuppositions much more probably than upon genuine historical tradition (*op. cit.,* p. 43).

feature in the writings of Weiss and Orr. The former argued that all objections which may be brought against the miraculous conception testify to the existence of a dogmatic presupposition, a bias against the miraculous. According to him, if the miraculous element in the narratives were denied, the historicity of these traditions would be unthinkable. Here, too, lay the foundation of Orr's approach to the subject. Orr's approach necessitated a supernatural, theistic theology which a priori accepts the concepts of revelation and miracle. Orr noticed that the denial of the virgin birth came largely from those who did not recognize a supernatural element in Christ's life at all, and he insisted that the whole matter could not be discussed with anyone whose mind was made up a priori against miracle.

Others who have stressed the presupposition of miracle have been Alfred Edersheim, for whom miracle was the very essence of thinking about the divine and an essential element in revealed religion (*The Life and Times of Jesus the Messiah*, 1883; American ed., 1943) ; A. T. Robertson, for whom the coming of the Son of God to earth justifies such miraculous manifestation of divine power (*Word Pictures in the New Testament*, 1930) ; and Charles Gore, who scored the credibility of the Biblical miracle of Jesus' origin against the incredibility of pagan extra-Biblical and Christian apocryphal infancy narratives (*Dissertations on Subjects Connected with the Incarnation*, 1895) .

The point at which the difference between the rationalists and supernaturalists was less decisive was the controversy over the relationship of the doctrine of the sinlessness of Jesus to the story of the virgin birth. Schleiermacher and Strauss both had by their exegetical ingenuity tried to establish the lack of connection between the sinlessness of Jesus and the story of Jesus' origin. Both had argued that although the Biblical narrative implies the exclusion of a sinful father, which thereby renders Jesus exempt from sin, nevertheless, exclusion of paternal participation is insufficient grounds upon which to base this assumption. Theologians, they thought, are still left with the problem of sinful inheritance from Mary. In Schleiermacher's and Strauss's judgment, Mary's participation in Jesus' birth renders it impossible for Jesus to be free of the inheritance of impeccability. Supernaturalistic interpretation of this matter was divided in its conclusions concerning the validity of this exegesis.

Among the German supernaturalists who were first to reply to

Strauss, Olshausen and Lange felt that the doctrine of Jesus' sin-lessness was dependent upon the story of the virgin birth, whereas B. Weiss admitted that the doctrines were not inseparably con-nected. In Olshausen's mind, it would have been impossible for anyone who himself had sprung from the sinful human race to heal the ills from which the race suffers. " He, it is true, had to be intimately connected with me, to be of their flesh and of their bones, and yet, at the same time, without sin; for this reason he was not begotten from the sinful seed of man, but Mary was touched by a pure divine fire from Heaven." [3] The whole idea, he said, of Luke 1:35 is that Mary had become a mother without con-nection with man, and that the pure, chaste power of the creative Spirit of God will be the procreative agency. As a result, the ap-pearance of the Redeemer among mankind is reported " as a new and immediate action of divine grace, and the transition of sinful-ness to him from sinful humanity is thus refuted." [4]

Olshausen did not meet Strauss's objection with regard to the inheritance of the sinful strain from Mary. He discussed the ques-tion in the more general context of Jesus' human and divine na-ture and did not even try to explain Strauss's insistence that this implied the possibility of Jesus' inheriting sin from his mother.

Lange, however, from the outset of his discussion of this matter, took notice of Strauss's objection. Behind Strauss's criticism, he insisted, is the fallacious original assumption that the doctrine of the virgin birth was itself not one of the great original facts of Christianity. Lange also insisted that the uniqueness of Christ's origin depended on one's estimation of ordinary generation. No mere son of Joseph could, he said, as the head of mankind, be the Savior of the whole human race. " None but the Son of Mary, con-ceived by the Divine operation, could, as the Son of man, become the spiritual head of humanity." (P. 284.)

Bernhard Weiss was critical of several supernaturalistic inter-preters preceding him who related the sinlessness of Jesus to his manner of generation. He pointed out that nowhere in the New Testament is the sinlessness of Jesus placed in relation to the na-ture of his origin. The metaphysical divine Sonship does not stand or fall with the hypothesis of the miraculous conception. Weiss was not alone among supernaturalists to make this concession to the rationalists.

[3] *Op. cit.*, *Biblical Commentary on the Gospels*, Vol. 1 (1847), p. 47.
[4] *Ibid.*, p. 101.

Frederic Godet (1812–1900), in his *Commentaire sur l'évangile de Saint Luc,* first published in 1869, went along with him. He agreed that the perfect holiness of Jesus does not depend on the miraculous birth, since holiness is an act of volition, not of nature. "The miraculous birth was only the negative condition of the spotless holiness of Jesus." Consequently, Godet discussed the subject in a larger context. The virgin birth, he said, is connected with the perfect holiness of Christ which is the basis of Christology. Denial of the former leads to denial of the latter. The miraculous birth is equally inseparable from the incarnation.

Between the rationalists and the supernaturalists many possibilities have been proposed to explain the relationship between the virgin birth and the " sinlessness of Jesus." Probably the most perceptive comment was made by Alan Richardson, who correctly insisted that the virgin birth is not a rationalization of Christ's sinlessness, " for it is clear that an account that would plausibly break the entrail of sin would have to be much more clever than to leave him connected on even one side of his parentage with the human race and thus so far involved in corrupt human nature " (*A Theological Word Book of the Bible,* 1950, p. 276).

b. *Revelation and the nature of the Biblical record*

Supernaturalists were unanimous in demanding the inseparable connection between the virgin birth and other Christian doctrine or doctrines. It will be seen from the following résumé that supernaturalists presuppose a unity of thought throughout the New Testament. At first the problem was centered in the definition of the historical relationship between the story of the origin of Jesus in Matthew and Luke with other New Testament passages that are suggestive of his origin, but gradually major attention was drawn to the proper connection between the virgin birth and other great Christian doctrines. This unity is demanded on the basis of a systematic doctrinal perspective and everywhere influences the interpretation of the virgin birth with regard to its relation to other formulations of Biblical Christian thought. Furthermore, acceptance of this unity became additional support for the historicity of the virgin birth.

F. W. Macran at the turn of the century made a classic plea for the unity of doctrine.

But it is impossible to regard the various articles of the Christian faith as so many detached statements having no very intimate connection with one another, and as complete in themselves: rather are they to be viewed as portions of one great whole, stones in one grand and massive temple, and the removal of one spoils the symmetry and endangers the security of the whole fabric. (*English Apologetic Theology*, 1905.)

From Olshausen through Machen this development may be traced. Olshausen connected the virgin birth with the Johannine doctrine of the incarnation. According to Lange, neither the death of Christ nor his resurrection can be understood in the full significance apart from the proper interpretation of his birth. Following Olshausen's example, Lange connected the story of the virgin birth with John 1:14, but made even more of its relationship to I Cor. 15:47. For him, both of these passages implied the virgin birth. It was that which was new, that which was miraculous in his origin, that made him the second Man after the first man Adam.

Machen and A. T. Robertson posed unique explanations of the relationship of the virgin birth to the Fourth Gospel. Rather than stress that the Fourth Gospel implies the virgin birth, the former explained that the lack of reference to the virgin birth in John is a warranted omission, since at the time the Fourth Gospel was written the birth of Christ in Bethlehem was a matter of course. The latter offered a novel suggestion: speaking of the author of the Fourth Gospel, " He has taken the *Memra* of the Hebrew, the Logos of the Stoics and Philo, the virgin birth of Jesus in Matthew and Luke, and has put them together in one grand conception on a par with the Jewish idea of Messiah." [5]

M. F. Sadler in *The Gospel According to St. Luke* (4th ed., 1892) described the relation between Luke and John as: Luke 1:34-35 is Scripture's most explicit declaration of the incarnation " on its human side," while its declaration on the divine side is the statement in John 1:14 (p. 23). Frederic W. Farrar pointed out the same fact with regard to the anti-Docetic character of Luke in his *The Gospel According to St. Luke* (Cambridge Greek Text for Schools and Colleges, 1891, p. 82).

Orr's whole discussion of the virgin birth was geared to his presupposition that the virgin birth is an essential part of the Chris-

[5] *Luke the Historian in the Light of Research* (1920), p. 112.

tian faith. Inevitably, he felt, denial of the virgin birth implied denial of the incarnation and the resurrection. He noticed that Meyer, who denied the virgin birth but accepted the incarnation, and Beyschlag, who denied the virgin birth but accepted the resurrection, were rare exceptions.

Canon Box later pointed out that the virgin birth was not the occasion or the cause of the doctrine of the incarnation. He agreed with Bethune-Baker that the virgin birth story symbolizes the whole doctrine of the incarnation (*The Virgin Birth of Christ,* 1916, p. 191). Box and Bethune-Baker described a possible relationship between the two doctrines which Orr had not foreseen. Orr's position, however, was maintained by Anglo-Catholics and Fundamentalists in Britain and America a generation after his time.[6]

According to Orr, Paul's use of " born," " of the seed of David," " spirit of holiness," " with [or " in "] power," " Son of God," " according to the spirit of holiness," are all parallel with and imply Luke's " bring forth a son," " His father David," " Holy Spirit," " Power of the Most High," and " called . . . the son of God " (p. 157). Archbishop Bernard in his *Studia Sacra* (1917, p. 191) noted that such passages as Rom. 1:3 and Gal. 4:4 had been appealed to on both sides of the controversy and are, in any case, not decisive. All Bernard would admit was that Paul may have meant to convey his belief in the Lord's virgin birth. Gore argued that the difference between the expressions concerning Jesus' origin in Paul's letters and the Synoptic records must lie in Paul's " theological " viewpoint as over against the Evangelists' viewpoint as " witnesses." [7]

[6] Bertram Pollock (Bishop of Norwich), *The Virgin's Son,* 2d ed., 1920 (1st ed., 1917).

C. B. Moss (Asst. Priest of St. Bartholomew's, Dublin), *The Virgin Birth,* The Congress Books, No. 5, 1923.

Shirley C. Hughson, *Modernism and the Birth of Christ* (pam.), West Park, New York, 1924.

John Roach Straton (Pastor of Calvary Baptist Church, New York City), *The Virgin Birth — Fact or Fiction?* (the third in a series of Fundamentalist-Modernist debates in Carnegie Hall, March 22, 1924, with Charles Francis Potter, minister of the West Side Unitarian Church, New York City, 1924).

T. F. Royds (Rector of Haughton, Staffs), *The Virgin Birth of Christ* (pam.), No. VIII of *Papers in Modern Churchmanship,* ed. by C. F. Russell (London, 1925).

Walter F. Eagleson, *The Virgin Birth* (pam.), by the Judicial Commission of the Presbyterian Church, Philadelphia (1928).

[7] *Op. cit.,* pp. 10–11. The best discussion of this whole topic is to be found in a criticism of it by Vincent Taylor in his book *The Historical Evidence for the Virgin Birth* (1920). Against Orr, Sweet, Knowling, Gore, and Box he contended that

In Machen's thinking, the virgin birth is inseparably connected with the truthfulness of the Bible, the redemptive work of Christ, and with the resurrection. If the virgin birth is denied, he argued, the supernatural is denied along with the truthfulness of the Bible. " If Christ really rose from the dead, if He really was at all the kind of person that He is represented in the New Testament as being, then there is every reason to think that He was conceived by the Holy Ghost and born of the Virgin Mary " (pp. 268, 387–391).

3. THE RELATION OF CHRISTIANITY TO OTHER RELIGIONS

The uniqueness of Christianity in its relation to the other religions of the world is another basic theological presupposition of all supernaturalistic interpretation. Supernaturalistic interpretation proceeds upon the assumption that Christ's birth had to be different from the birth of other leaders or divine beings because he himself is essentially different, and Christianity itself has no real parallel. On the basis of this line of reasoning, supernaturalistic interpretation has looked askance at Strauss's suggestion of a mythical explanation of the birth narrative and at the whole idea that the story of Jesus' birth may have its analogy in other religions of the world.

Immediately after Strauss, Olshausen had suggested that with regard to purported parallels in the birth of Buddha, Zoroaster, Plato, and others, they were by no means opposed to Biblical history but were, rather, analogous " presentments " of an expected redeemer. " They vouch for the general desire of such a fact, for the longing after it, and hereby for its historical realization." (*Op. cit.*, p. 47.)

Mendel contrasted mythical natural religion and historical revealed religion and related one to the other by saying that the historical elements of the new religion, Christianity, were anticipated in poetic form in the mythical elements of the old religions. Mendel also believed that the presentation in the Gospels of

neither Gal. 4:4; Rom. 1:3; 5:12-21 nor I Cor. 15:47 shows that Paul was acquainted with the virgin birth tradition. By this time too, Taylor thought, the silence of the Fourth Gospel regarding the virgin birth was generally admitted. The only question remaining was the textual problem of John 1:13. Resch, Blass, and Loisy held that this should read " Who was born . . . ," based on readings from Tertullian (*De Carne Christi* 19) , Irenaeus (*Haer.* III. xvii.1, xx.2) , and Justin Martyr (*Dial. c. Try.* 63) . Taylor argued that this reading would lead to a Docetic view of the Person of Christ, against which the Johannine writings earnestly contend.

Joseph and Mary as having other children was in perfect harmony with the Christian view of the sanctity of marriage, and if the miraculous conception had been mythical, the idea of children born later would have been abhorrent to the spirit that originated such a myth.

According to Lange, the heathen had some notion of the miracle of Jesus' birth, since they had some, although obscure, perception of hereditary cause and inherited blessing, that is, of desecrating or consecrating generation. The myths of Hercules and Romulus, Pythagoras and Plato, and others illustrate this fact. These pagan myths were dreams that were types of the Coming One.

Next to the supernaturalistic aspects of the whole life of Jesus, the complete distinction of Jesus and his religion from his own religious environment, as well as from all the other religions of the world, was the most important a priori theological presupposition upon which de Pressensé's analysis of the virgin birth was based. De Pressensé proposed that the truly Christian point of view is completely opposed to the naturalistic theory that Christianity was a product of the ancient world rather than that the religions of the ancient world were part of the preparation for Christianity.

De Pressensé spoke of what he called " a patient work of preparation " that preceded the coming of Christ. This preparation consisted of two parallel lines: (1) in the direct revelation in Judaism and (2) in the free experiment in paganism. The two parallel lines converged in the universal expectation of the world at the time of the birth of Christ. The whole work of preparation for the coming of Christ was to call up before the fallen human race a noble ideal which, as yet, the race by itself was powerless to realize. Although poetry has no more beautiful creation than the scene of the Annunciation by the angel to Mary, this is, nevertheless, in de Pressensé's estimation, by no means a mythical representation. It realistically presents in Christ's coming into the world the divine ideal becoming human reality.

Weiss, Fairbairn, Orr, and Machen all questioned any close relation of the Biblical narrative to non-Jewish sources. The basis for their conclusion lay in their denial of the mythical character of the birth stories. Weiss thought it improbable that anything in Gentile-Christian quarters would find its acceptance in Jewish-Christian circles. Fairbairn thought that the theogonic myths of the Greeks were inconceivable to the Jewish mind. Orr believed that since Greek gods were thought of as being like in form, parts, and passion to mortal men, stories of their origin could not be thought of as being analogous to the Biblical concept. Machen stressed the Jewish character of the birth narrative by speaking of the idea as " a bit of the Old Testament embedded in the midst of the New Testament."

At this point, Alan Hugh McNeile was more specific than the others. He rejected the pagan source theory on the basis that Matthew's stories " are intensely Jewish; the language is Hebraic, and the atmosphere Palestinian." It is true too, he said, that Luke's ideas are not similar to pagan ideas; the goddess is not heavenly but a peasant. Furthermore, pagan ideas could not have gotten into Jewish-Christian circles " if Judaism itself had not previously possessed these or analogous ideas " (quote from and reference to Gunkel in *Zum religionsgeschichtlichen Verständnis des Neuen Testaments,* 1903, pp. 68 ff.). McNeile did not believe that any non-Christian source written or oral had been found that satisfactorily accounts for the Gospel narratives.[8]

One of the oddest consequences that supernaturalists drew from the possible relationship of the Biblical narrative of the virgin birth to pagan parallels was that yielding to the mythical explanation ultimately involves the interpreter in conceding the illegitimacy of Jesus. Weiss, for example, could not admit that the " historical matter of fact " could have been Jesus' paternity by Joseph, since he took Joseph's attitude in the Matthaean narrative as historical. A generation before Weiss, Olshausen had insisted that the ultimate consequence of the mythical explanation was not only the denial of the historicity of the account of Jesus' birth but also the denial that Mary gave birth at all and that Jesus, himself, ever existed.

These supernaturalists were, of course, thinking of the direction that Bahrdt and Venturini and Paulus had taken and anticipating the logic of Bruno Bauer and the Christ-Myth School. As Mendel put it, denial of the birth of Christ contrary to the ordinary laws of nature leads to one of two assumptions: either that the accounts are absolute fables or that some actual fact was the basis of the fabulous conception. This is the paradox on which supernaturalists and naturalists have lined up on opposite sides. It is the breaking up of this naïve set of alternatives that constitutes historical criticism's great contribution to the interpretation of the virgin birth.

---

[8] *The Gospel According to St. Matthew* (1915, 3d reprint, 1949).

Historical criticism — source, form, and textual — has provided other materials that assist in formulating an interpretation of the virgin birth that makes it possible for the interpreter to escape the restrictions imposed by the apparently absolute alternatives proposed by naturalistic and supernaturalistic interpreters.

Out of the milieu created by the rejection of the virgin birth on a priori philosophical grounds (the naturalistic philosophers and Strauss) and the acceptance of the virgin birth on a priori theological grounds, the historical and literary critical study of the virgin birth arose.

The problem of the relationship of the Christian to non-Christian birth narratives which " naturalists " and " supernaturalists " handled so diversely provided the occasion for a whole separate " school " of interpretation of the narrative of Jesus' origin. The scholars of the *religionsgeschichtliche Schule* who dealt with the interpretation of the virgin birth devoted their energies almost exclusively to determining the origin in another religion of the Christian concept of Jesus' nativity. The *religionsgeschichtliche Schule* represents one aspect of a historical approach to the virgin birth that was to emerge into prominence in the nineteenth and twentieth centuries.

*T*he Church salvaged from pagan mysticism a mode of thinking which permitted the abstraction from temporal happenings of universals which manifest themselves repetitively in time; and myths were developed as the best means of sharing the perception of these universals.

— Lynn White, Jr., " Christian Myth and Christian History," in *Journal of the History of Ideas*

COMPARATIVE ANALOGICAL ANALYSIS

In 1796 Charles Dupuis contended that the narrative of Jesus' birth had its origin in the ancient myth of Krishna. Since then, alleged parallels, affinities, and sources for Jesus' origin have been noted by scholars in the literature of Indian, Mesopotamian, Egyptian, Greco-Roman, and Hellenistic traditions. B. Bauer, Drews (and others of the Christ-Myth School), Steinmetzer, Gressmann, Norden, Wendland, Seydel, Pfleiderer, de Bunsen, Cheyne, Gunkel, Jeremias, Fiebig, Petersen, Hartland, Usener, Soltau, Wernel, and a host of their imitators have insisted that the Biblical idea had its origin in a non-Christian religion. Recently Walter E. Bundy referred to this idea with approval: " The idea of a supernatural or virgin birth is pagan, and it must have found its way into the story of Jesus through Gentile-Christian channels." [1]

It is difficult to find a statement in all the literature of historical criticism which is more misleading.

Contemporary writers invariably use only secondary sources to verify such claims. The scholars whose judgment they accept rarely produced or quoted the primary sources. The literature of the old German *religionsgeschichtliche Schule,* which produced this conclusion and which has become the authority for contemporary scholars who wish to perpetuate the notion that the virgin birth in the New Testament has a non-Christian source, is characterized by brief word, phrase, and sentence quotations that have been lifted out of context or incorrectly translated and used to support preconceived theories. Sweeping generalizations based on questionable evidence have become dogmatic conclusions that cannot be substantiated on the basis of careful investigation. The old " history of religions " approach to the problem of the relation of the Biblical idea of virgin birth to non-Christian birth traditions

[1] *Jesus and the First Three Gospels* (1955), p. 11.

was not sufficiently concerned with the precise meaning of " parallel," " source," " similarity," or " analogy." The literature of the world is prolific with narratives of unusual births, but it contains no precise analogy to the virgin birth in Matthew and Luke. Jesus' " virgin birth " is not " pagan." The problem is compounded by the fact that contemporary history of religions experts exercise excellent historical and literary judgment, but none of them has written on the virgin birth.

The scope of the materials that are to be presented and analyzed in this chapter is limited to those non-Christian birth stories that have been proposed as possible sources for the Evangelical tradition. Other stories from around the world such as the story from Tula in ancient Mexico may be of great interest, but their relation to the New Testament is far removed from that of being a possible source for Matthew or Luke. Quetzalcoatl was the teacher of arts, originator of the calendar, and the giver of maize to the peoples of pre-Columbian America. His mother, Chilmalman, conceived when the God All-Father in the form of Citallatonac ("The Morning") breathed on her. Quetzalcoatl was endowed at birth with speech, all knowledge, and all wisdom.[2]

Traditions such as these, however, along with those which will be set forth in this chapter do point to the real nature of the narrative of Jesus' origin. The virgin birth in the New Testament must be understood as part of a universal milieu of mythical birth narratives. It will be seen, however, that even as myth, the virgin birth of Jesus is unique. The true relationship between the myth of Jesus' origin and non-Christian mythical birth narratives is not at the point of the possibility of one being derived from the other. The Christian myth has a message to convey *to* other religions at the point of their common myths of origin of their gods or heroes.

A. BUDDHISTIC TRADITION

Toward the close of the nineteenth century when historians began a serious study of the relationship of Christianity to other religions, several writers tried to prove that the canonical narrative of Jesus' origin was derived from Buddhism. Rudolf Seydel, of the University of Leipzig, in his *Das Evangelium von Jesu in seinen Verhältnissen zu Buddha-Sage und Buddha-Lehre* (1882) and in his *Die Buddha-Legende und das Leben Jesu nach den*

[2] Joseph Campbell, *The Masks of God* (1959), pp. 457, 458.

Evangelien (1884) listed numerous passages from both the canonical Gospels and Buddhistic texts in the attempt to show the correspondence between the two religions. Ernest de Bunsen in *The Angel-Messiah of Buddhists, Essenes, and Christians* (1880) tried to prove that the canonical narrative of Jesus' birth was derived from Buddhism by way of the Essenes. He tried to show that a century before Christ, Buddhist legends were known in Judea. De Bunsen interpreted the Buddhistic record to say that the Buddha was " incarnate by the Holy Ghost of the royal virgin Māyā." He did not hesitate to speak of Gautama as " born of the Virgin Māyā."

Nicholas Notovitch in his *La Vie inconnue de Jésus Christ* (1894) perpetrated a story of his visit to the Lamassary of Himis in Tibet, where he supposedly learned of the " Life of Saint Issa." According to this story taken from scattered Pali texts and arranged by Notovitch into two hundred and forty-four short paragraphs in fourteen chapters, Jesus at the age of thirteen wandered with a caravan of merchants to India to study the laws of the great Buddhas. He spent six years each successively with Jainists, Brāhmins, and Buddhists preaching and studying, from there he journeyed to Persia to preach to the Zoroastrians, and finally he returned at the age of twenty-nine to Jerusalem. The account of the incarnation of Jesus (Issa) is related in chapter IV of Notovitch's fantastic document.

1. And now the time had come, which the Supreme Judge, in his boundless clemency, had chosen to incarnate himself in a human being.
2. And the Eternal Spirit, which dwelt in a state of complete inertness and supreme beatitude, awakened and detached itself from the Eternal Being for an indefinite period,
3. In order to indicate, in assuming the human form, the means of identifying ourselves with the Divinity and of attaining eternal felicity . . .
5. Soon after, a wonderful child was born in the land of Israel; God himself, through the mouth of this child, spoke of nothingness of the body and of the grandeur of the soul.

Since Edgar J. Goodspeed's *Strange New Gospels* (1931) there is no question but that Notovitch's efforts were fraudulent, and since Richard Garbe's *Indien und das Christentum* (1914) there is little reason to suppose that there ever was a direct influence of Buddhist texts upon the New Testament. An examination of the

Buddhistic tradition is valuable, however, for it does reveal the
real relationship that does exist between it and Christianity.

Siddhartha Gautama was born at Kapilavastu of the Śākiya clan
(on the borders of modern Nepal), the son of a Kshatriya chief-
tain Suddhodana and his wife Māyā, daughter of the king of the
neighboring Koliya clan, about 563 B.C.[3] The literature of the
whole course of his life reflects a cult of the life of Buddha.

The oldest accounts of Buddha's ancestry presuppose nothing
abnormal about his birth. In one place he is spoken of as being
wellborn on his mother's and father's side for seven generations
back (Dīgha Nikāya i. 113).[4] Elsewhere when the Buddha referred
to the Lady Māyā as " the mother who gave birth to me," he at the
same time spoke of " King Suddhodana my father " (Buddhavamsa
XXVI).[5]

Early tradition describes conception in terms of the combined
agency of three elements: the father, the mother, and the " genius "
(or being to be born, Gandhabbo[6]). " But if, monks, there is
here a coitus of the parents, and it is the mother's season and the
Gandhabba is present, it is on the conjunction of these three things
that there is conception." [7]

It is obvious that ancient pre-Christian Buddhism knows nothing of the virginity of the mother of Buddha. She is a married
woman who plainly conceives through traditional means. Through
the centuries, however, a tradition of Buddha's unusual birth did
develop. This was in connection with the concept " avatar," according to which Indian tradition described a whole series of incarnations. " Nine avataras of Vishnu have ' descended ' from
time to time, and a tenth, the Kalki-avatara has long been expected." [8] Each avatar indicated a specific manifestation of the

3 Friess and Schneider, Religion in Various Cultures (1932). For the problem of
the date of Buddha's birth, see also Edward Thomas' The Life of Buddha (1927),
n. 1, p. 27.

4 Sonadanda Sutta 5, T. W. Rhys Davids, Dialogues of the Buddha, Part I, Sacred
Books of the Buddhists, Vol. II (1899), p. 146.

5 Bimala Churn Law, Sacred Books of the Buddhists, Vol. IX, The Minor Anthologies of the Pali Canon, Part III (1938), p. 84.

6 Gandhabbo, of Vedic origin, the parent of the first human pair Yama and
Yami, who has mystical power over women and is invoked at marriage as a necessary third party to bring about the transmigration of the soul by entering into
the mother when she was about to receive the germinating seed and so to be
born again.

7 Majjhima-Nikāya, 38 (Mahatanhāsankhayasutta) 266, I. B. Horner, Vol. I
(1954), p. 322.

8 Edward J. Jurji, The Great Religions of the Modern World (1947), p. 87.

Buddha. The stories are filled with unusual and elaborate birth traditions.

In two places in the canonical Pali Scriptures the conception and birth of Buddhas is described in detail: Majjhima-Nikāya, 123 Acchariyabbhutadhammasutta III. 119–124; [9] and Māhapadāna-sutta, Dīgha ii. 12.[10] Both passages elaborate the descent of the future Bodhisatta from the "Tusita body" into the mother's womb, the appearance of the Buddha in the mother as a shining gem, and the accompanying wonders in the natural world.

In the Māhapadāna-sutta, Dīgha ii. 12, the description is of the incarnation of the Vipassi Buddha, who was the first of six to precede Gautama Buddha (Vipassi, Sikhi, Vessabhu, Kakusandha, Konagamana, Kassapa, Gotama). In this description his conception is stated in clear and beautiful prose. " Now Vipassi, brethren, when, as Bodhisat, he ceased to belong to the hosts of the heaven of Delight, descended into his mother's womb mindful and self-possessed."

The core of the Buddhistic tradition is contained in the " noble elephant " legend. At conception the mother Māyā dreamed this dream. " A noble elephant, white as silver or snow, having six tusks, well proportioned trunk and feet, blood-red veins, adamantine firmness of joints, and easy pace, has entered my belly." [11] In preparation for this event the earth was covered with a green carpet, the evils of great heat or cold were absent, and everywhere there was calm and quietness.

Similar and more highly developed tradition is recounted in the *Buddha-Karita of Asvaghosha.* In the opening paragraphs of this, Suddhodana is described as " of the kindred of the sun, anointed to stand at the head of earth's monarchs " (Book I, 9), and Māyā is described as " an effulgence proceeding from his effulgence " and the " most eminent of goddesses to the whole world " (Book I, 15–16). Then is described in brief but vivid detail the birth of Buddha.

Then falling from the host of beings in the Tushita heaven, and illumining the three worlds, the most excellent of Bodhisattvas suddenly entered at a thought into her womb, like the Nâga-king entering the cave of Nandâ.

[9] I. B. Horner (1959), pp. 164–169.

[10] T. W. Rhys Davids, *Dialogues of the Buddha,* Part II, *Sacred Books of the Buddhists,* Vol. III (1910), p. 8.

[11] Lalita Vistara 6, Rajendralala Mitra, *Bibliotheca Indica,* Vol. 2 (1882), p. 94.

Assuming the form of a huge elephant white like Himâlaya, armed with six tusks, with his face perfumed with flowing ichor, he entered the womb of the queen of king Suddhodana, to destroy the evils of the world.

The guardians of the world hastened from heaven to mount watch over the world's one true ruler; thus the moonbeams, though they shine everywhere, are especially bright on Mount Kailâsa.

Mâyâ also, holding him in her womb, like a line of clouds holding a lightning-flash, relieved the people around her from the sufferings of poverty by raining showers of gifts.

Then one day by the king's permission the queen, having a great longing in her mind, went with the inmates of the gynaeceum into the garden Lumbinî.

As the queen supported herself by a bough which hung laden with a weight of flowers, the Bodhisattva suddenly came forth, cleaving open her womb.

At that time the constellation Pushya was auspicious, and from the side of the queen, who was purified by her vow, her son was born for the welfare of the world, without pain and without illness.[12]

. . . As was Aurva's birth from the thigh, and Prithu's from the hand, and Mândhâtri's who was like Indra himself, from the forehead, and Kakshîvat's from the upper end of the arm — thus too was his birth [miraculous].[13]

The most popular legendary account of his birth is in the *Nidānakathā Jātaka,* which accounted for the lives of Buddhas in previous incarnations.[14]

While the Bodhisat was dwelling in the City of Delight, the so-called " Buddha proclamation " took place. At the appropriate time when the deities of ten thousand world systems assembled together and having ascertained which of the then-living beings will become the Buddha, they went to him and besought him in the Heaven of Delight. " O Blessed One, when thou wast fulfilling the Ten Perfections, thou didst not do so from a desire for the glorious state of an archangel — Sakka, or Māra, or Brahma — or

---

12 Zoroaster's mother is described as being ill at the time of his birth.

13 This excerpt is taken from the *Buddha-Karita* Book 1, 19–29, SBE, Vol. XLIX (1894) .

14 Jātaka stories were used as homilies for educational purposes to inculcate moral lessons of Buddhism (F. M. Müller, *Sacred Books of the Buddhists,* Vol. I [1895]) , p. xv) . Buddhistic literature reflects a rapidly growing tradition of Buddha's previous incarnations. Whereas in the Pāli text Māhapadāna-sutta accounted for six previous Buddhas and the Buddhavamsa for twenty-four, the Lalita Vistara listed fifty-four, and the later Mahāvastu has more than a hundred.

of a mighty king upon earth; thou wast fulfilling them with the hope of reaching Omniscience for the sake of the Salvation of mankind! Now has the moment come, O Blessed One, for thy Buddahood; now has the time, O Blessed One, arrived! " Thereupon the " Great Being " reflected on five important points: the time of his advent; the continent and country where he should appear; the tribe in which he should be born; the mother who should bear him; and the time when her life should be complete. Having determined the Time, Continent, District, Tribe, and Mother, Buddha said, " The time has arrived, O Blessed Ones, for me to become a Buddha." Here follows a full account of how at the midsummer festival in Kapilavastu on the seventh day before the full moon Mahā Māyā arose early and bathed in perfume water and having observed several ceremonies entered her beautiful chamber and lying on her royal couch fell asleep and dreamed.

The four archangels, the Guardians of the world, lifting her up in her couch, carried her to the Himālaya mountains, and placing her under the Great Sāla-tree . . . stood respectfully aside. Their queens then came toward her, and taking her to the lake of Anotatta, bathed her to free her from human stains; and dressed her in heavenly garments; and anointed her with perfumes; and decked her with heavenly flowers. Not far from there is the Silver Hill, within which is a golden mansion; in it they spread a heavenly couch, with its head towards the East, and on it they laid her down. Then the future Buddha, who had become a superb white elephant, and was wandering on the Golden Hill, not far from there, descended thence, and ascending the Silver Hill, approached her from the North. Holding in his silvery trunk a white lotus flower, and uttering a far-reaching cry, he entered the golden mansion, and thrice doing obeisance to his mother's couch, he gently struck her right side, and seemed to enter her womb.

When Māyā awoke from her sleep, she related her dream to the Rāja, who summoned sixty-four eminent Brāhmans and asked from them an interpretation of Māyā's dream.

The Brahmans said, " Be not anxious, O king! your queen has conceived: and the fruit of her womb will be a man-child; it will not be a woman-child. You will have a son. And he, if he adopts a householder's life, will become a king, a Universal Monarch; but if, leaving his home, he adopt the religious life, he will become a Buddha, who will remove from the world the veils of ignorance and sin."

Then is described how at the moment of the Buddha's conception the constituent elements of the ten thousand world systems quaked, and the Thirty-two Good Omens were made manifest. The blind received their sight, the deaf heard, the dumb spoke with each other, the crooked became straight, the lame walked, prisoners were freed from their bonds and chains, in each hell the fire was extinguished, hungry ghosts ate and drank, wild animals ceased to be afraid, the sick were restored, all men began to speak kindly, horses neighed and elephants trumpeted gently, musical instruments played without players, bracelets and ornaments jingled by themselves, all the heavens became clear, everyone felt a soft cool breeze, rain fell out of season, water welled up through the ground, birds forsook their flight, rivers ceased to flow, waters of the ocean became fresh, lotuses covered the earth, all flowers on land and sea blossomed, and trees were covered with appropriate bloom.

Following this is a brief description of how the mother and son were watched over by the four angels and the statement of the necessity of the mother's early death. " But as the womb in which a future Buddha has dwelt, like a sacred relic shrine, can never be occupied by another; the mother of the Bodisat, seven days after his birth, died, and was reborn in the City of Delight."

And queen Mahā Māyā, when she too had thus cherished the Bodisat in her womb, like oil in a vessel, for ten months, felt herself far gone with child: and wishing to go to her family home she spake to King Suddhodana, and said, " O King! I wish to go to Devadaha, to the city of my people."

Thereupon he had the road from Kapilavastu to Devadaha made plain and decorated it with arches of trees, waterpots, flags and banners, and he seated the queen in a golden palanquin carried by a thousand attendants. Between the two towns the great retinue came upon the Lumbinī grove, which was decorated in a manner suggesting the banqueting hall of a mighty king.

The queen beholding it was filled with the desire of besporting herself in the sal-tree grove; and the attendants, carrying the queen, entered the wood. When she came to the monarch sal-tree of the glade, she wanted to take hold of a branch of it, and the branch bending down, like a reed heated by steam, approached within reach of her hand. Stretching out her hand she took hold of the branch, and then her pains came upon her. The people drawing a curtain round her retired. Standing, and holding the branch of the sal-tree, she was delivered.

That very moment the four pure-minded Mahā Brahma angels came there bringing a golden net; and receiving the future Buddha on that net, they placed him before his mother, saying, " Be joyful, O Lady! a mighty son is born to thee! "

Now other living things, when they leave their mother's womb, leave it smeared with offensive and impure matter. Not so a Bodisat. The future Buddha left his mother's womb like a preacher descending from a pulpit or a man from a ladder, erect, stretching out his hands and feet, unsoiled by any impurities from contact with his mother's womb, pure and fair, and shining like a gem placed on fine muslin of Benares. But though this was so, two showers of water came down from heaven in honour of them and refreshed the Bodisat and his mother.

Then is described how at his birth he took seven great steps and at the seventh he shouted, " I am the chief of the world," how he at birth held in his hand some medicine that became for him the drug by which he later healed the sick and blind and deaf, how at birth he wished to give a gift but was presented one himself by his mother, and how lastly he sang the song of victory.[15]

An elaborate and detailed version of Buddha's conception and birth is related in the Mahāvastu. The Mahāvastu records practically all the history, quasi history, and legend pertaining to Buddha. In this his supramundane characteristics are graphically brought out, and the supreme qualities of Māyā are emphasized.

Bodhisattvas enter the womb of a mother who observes the fasts, who is outstanding among women, who is joyful, distinguished, holding no intercourse with what is mean, who is gracious, pure of body, and tender of passion, is of good birth and family, comely, beautiful, renowned, tall and well proportioned, and accomplished and who is in the prime of life, learned, wise, mindful, self-possessed, in all ways right-minded and perfect, the very best of women.[16]

Having conceived, the Great Brahmā speaks:

The woman who in her dream has seen the sun from the sky enter her womb will give birth to one who is the woman's jewel, her husband's treasure. He will be a mighty universal king.

The woman who in her dream has seen the moon from the sky enter her womb will give birth to a son who is both man and deva. He

15 Following this is the narrative of the " Buddhist Simeon," and the description of the name-giving ceremony. The entire descriptions of the narrative above and quotations are taken from *Buddhist Birth Stories or Jātaka Tales*, T. W. Rhys Davids, Vol. I (1880), pp. 58 ff.

16 *Sacred Books of the Buddhists*, Vol. XVIII. *The Mahāvastu*, Vol. 2, J. J. Jones (1952), p. 8.

will be a noble universal king. The woman who in her dream has seen a white elephant enter her womb will give birth to a being as select as the elephant is among animals. He will be a Buddha who knows the Good and the True.

The queen is asked, "Whom do you bear?" and she replies, "A universal king."

"I bear a universal ruler, a choice man, a valiant king, who illumines my womb with his golden beauty,[17] and is endowed with the marks of excellence."

But the devas in the sky acclaimed him with the title of "Exalted One," saying, "He will become a Buddha, not a universal king." And Great Brahmā recited this verse:

You bear one who is an elephant among men, the best of treasures, the destroyer of the force and violence of intoxication, the dispeller of dark and murky folly, the storehouse of good qualities, the possessor of boundless wealth, a royal seer, whose chariot wheel knows no obstacle, whose radiance is deathless.

The queen replied:

"As passion and malice no longer have sway over me who has conceived the seed of the king of men, there is no doubt that he will be of such splendour as you say."

Then follows a superlative and florid description of the pregnant mother and the details of the birth of her son. The delivery of the son was to take place in the Lumbinī grove.

Quickly make ready Lumbinī's grove by clearing it of grass, litter and leaves. Make it a mass of fair and fragrant flowers, and make it sweetly smelling with the scented water. . . .

When Māyā, the Conqueror's mother, surrounded by her friends, enters the fair grove, she rides on in her gay chariot, a queen like the consort of an immortal, knowing the rule of joy.

She, coming to it in play, leant with her arm on a branch of the wavy-leafed fig-tree, and playfully stretched herself at the moment of giving birth to the Glorious One. . . .

"And the Bobhisattva, mindful and thoughtful, issues from his mother's right side without doing her any harm." "Again, because of the Bodhisattva's power, immediately after the Sugata was born, the mother of the Bodhisattva was without hurt or scar. The womb of the Bodhisattva's mother was unscathed and at ease."

[17] "His golden beauty" is reminiscent of the Vedic hymn "To an Unknown God": "In the beginning there arose the Golden Child; soon as born, he alone was the lord of all that is. He established the earth and this heaven." (SBE, Vol. XXXII, p. 1.)

Immediately after the Bodhisattva was born five-hundred Śākyan young men with Sundarananda at their head, five hundred maidens with Yaśodharā at their head, five-hundred men-servants with Chandaka at their head, five-hundred horses with Kaṇṭhaka at their head, five-hundred elephants with the young elephant Candana at their head, and five-hundred stores of treasure appeared. Five-hundred kings sent messengers to greet him. . . .

King Suddhodana gave orders to his ministers, saying, " Now lead the child, who is the strength of the Śākyans, to the temple to worship at the feet of the goddess Abhayā."

. . . Against his will the Hero, the great Saviour of the world, the Teacher of kings entered the shrine. But when they would have him salute the goddess with his head, it was his feet that he put forward.

Then the goddess Abhayā said, " It is not fitting that he should worship me. If he should make obeisance to anyone, that one's head would assuredly be split in seven."

. . . When the chief of all the world was born, all the king's affairs prospered. Hence, he who was the boon of men was named Sarvārthasiddha.[18]

This is followed by a vivid description of his entrance into his father's palace, and the tale of his birth concludes:

He has feet with level tread.
He has designs of wheels on the soles of his feet.
He has long toes and fingers.
He has broad and projecting heels.
He has sharply arched feet.
His legs are like the antelope's.
His body is divinely straight.
He can touch his knees with his hands when standing erect.
His male organ is encased in a sheath.
His body is proportioned like the banyan-tree.
His hands and feet are soft and tender.
His hands and feet are webbed.
His body is perfectly formed.
The down of his body grows in single hairs, one to each pore.
The down of his body grows straight upwards.
He has smooth skin.
He has a [   ] skin.
He has the gait of a swan.
There is no hollow between his shoulder-blades.
His body has the seven convex surfaces.

18 " Successful in all things."

He has an excellent sense of taste.
His skin is the colour of gold.
He has the bust of a lion.
He has regular teeth.
His eye-teeth are perfectly white.
His bust is equally rounded.
His tongue is long and slender.
His voice is like that of Brahmā.
His eyes are blue.
His eyelashes are like a cow's.
Between his eyebrows he has a hairy mole.
His head is shaped like a royal turban.
Such is the Saviour with the thirty-two marks of excellence.[19]

If these references are not enough to discourage objectively minded analogy hunters, the textual problem at least ought to caution scholars against advocating the theory that the narratives of Jesus' birth in Matthew and in Luke were derived from Buddhistic tales. Although in his article on " Buddhism " in the *Encyclopædia Britannica* (11th ed.), Rhys Davids states that the canonical Pali texts received their present form before the fourth century B.C., both the Lalita Vistara and the Jātaka tales form a great composite, the growth of centuries; and according to Hopkins, the oldest extant text of Jātaka dates from A.D. 500.[20] Windisch, Götz, and Faber all dated the Nidānakatha, the Mahāvastu, and the Lalita Vistara all between A.D. 77 and 500. J. J. Jones described the Mahāvastu as a compilation that may have originated in the fourth century A.D.[21] Thomas did not think there is any reason to date even the canonical Pali texts before the Lalita Vistara, since the legendary and probably the traditional matter in both the Pali and the Sanskrit texts come from earlier commentaries, and there is no way in which to determine the date of any part of either.

The tremendous complexity of the problem of dates of the material in the texts has not prevented scholars, however, from making strong assertions concerning the relation of the Buddhistic birth stories to the evangelical narratives. Seydel, G. A. van den

[19] *Sacred Books of the Buddhists*, Vol. XVIII, *The Mahāvastu*, Vol. 2, J. J. Jones (1952). An almost identical account of Dīpamkara Buddha, under whom the Gotama made his resolution to win enlightenment, is in *The Mahāvastu*, Jones, *Sacred Books of the Buddhists*, Vol. I, xvi (1949).

[20] Edward W. Hopkins, *India Old and New* (1901), p. 186.

[21] *Op. cit.*, p. xi.

Bergh van Eysinga (*Indische Einflüsse auf evangelische Erzählungen,* 1904, 1909), and Edmunds have all advocated the theory that the New Testament has borrowed Buddhistic ideas. Ernest Windisch presented a strong argument against this theory (*Buddha's Geburt,* 1908).

Christianity could not have borrowed from Buddhism the idea of the virgin birth. The texts above show clearly that the Buddhistic idea did not state or imply virginity on the part of the mother and conception as the responsibility of any divine being. There do exist, however, two possible analogies: the idea of a supernatural birth and something similar to Immaculate Conception.

Scholars generally have overlooked the place in which an affinity between Christian and Buddhistic birth tales is apparent. The correct relationship was pointed out by Richard Garbe in his *Indien und das Christentum* (1914), which fortunately is now available in English as *India and Christendom* (1959). Garbe was justifiably critical of the history of religions experts who tried to demonstrate that there is an affinity between Buddhistic and New Testament narratives. He was convinced, however, that there was a direct relationship between Buddhistic legends and the apocryphal Gospels. Unfortunately Garbe did not have very much to say about the relationship between the birth traditions. Since he was dealing with the whole problem of the relationship between Buddhism and Christianity, he devoted a minimum of space to the problem of the birth narratives.

There is an obvious parallel between Buddhistic and Christian birth traditions at the point of the Christian apocryphal legends. This may be seen by comparing the material that has been outlined in this chapter with the literature that has been set before the reader in Chapter 2. In both traditions the child to be born chooses his mother beforehand; the mother is supreme among women; the White Elephant or White Bird (reference to Mary's conception in Hanna) is the symbol of conception, and the gem is the analogy for the unborn child (in Māyā a shining stone, in Hannâ a white pearl); the term is ten months; wonders occur throughout the natural world; the infant is brilliant as the sun and pure and undefiled at birth; he announces at birth who he is; and the newborn child is received immediately with royal pomp and ceremony.

At some points the analogies are striking but not as precise. In Buddhism the ideas of Gotama's pre-existent activity and purity at birth are much more highly developed than in the Christian stories. The same is true for the "manifestations in nature." In the *Nidānakathā Jātaka,* for example, "musical instruments played without players, bracelets and ornaments jingled by themselves." In Buddhism the perfection of Māyā's body is described in much greater detail than in the analogous story of Mary. In the Buddhistic tale the perfection of the several members of Gotama's body are stressed and enumerated. In the Christian tradition Mary is the object of this concern, and the prodigious characteristics of the infant are ascribed to Mary rather than to Jesus. Whereas in the stories of Buddha the description of the gem is always confined to Buddha and to his prenatal state, in the Christian legend the pearl is passed on from Adam from the beginning and is applied to Mary.

The story of the virgin birth in the New Testament should not be drawn into the question of the relationship between Buddhistic and Christian birth narratives. If there is a bridge between the Christian and Buddhistic tales, it is at the point of Christian apocryphal traditions. Properly speaking, the only possible clear analogy is between Buddhism and Old Roman Catholicism. A comparison may be made between the portrait of Jesus in the apocryphal Gospels and the Buddhistic birth narratives. The closest affinity exists between the apocryphal portrait of Mary and the Buddhistic Gotama.

B. KRISHNA TRADITION; ASSYRO-BABYLONIAN, ZOROASTRIAN, AND MITHRAIC AFFINITIES

Although the "analogies" between the virgin birth in the New Testament and birth traditions in other religions have not been as close as those in Buddhism, spokesmen have arisen to advocate that the Christian birth narrative was derived from one of several other possible sources: the Krishna tradition, Assyro-Babylonian literature, Zoroastrianism, and Mithraism.

1. KRISHNA TRADITION

The myth of Krishna elaborates how the divine Vishnu himself descended into the womb of Devaki and was born as her son, i.e., Krishna. The Hindu *Vishnu Purana* related: "Devaki bore in her womb the lotus-eyed deity. . . . No person could bear to gaze upon Devaki, from the light that invested her, and those who contemplated her radiance felt their minds disturbed." [22] Note the reference to " the light." In the Mahāvastu, Māyā refers to the one " who illumines my womb with his golden beauty." This tradition is reminiscent of the Vedic hymn " To an Unknown God." " In the beginning there arose the Golden Child, as soon as born, he alone was the lord of all that is." F. M. Müller explained that " Golden Child " literally refers to " the golden germ of child " and is an attempt at naming the sun.[23]

In the myth of Krishna the deity is not only the effective agent in conception. He is also the offspring. " The divine Vishnu himself, the root of the vast universal tree, inscrutable by the understandings of all gods, demons, sages, and men, past, present, or to come, adored by Brahma and all the deities, he who is without beginning, middle, or end, being moved to relieve the earth of her load, descended into the womb of Devaki, and was born as her son, Vasudeva, i.e., Chrishna." [24]

The same criticism that was made of the alleged Buddhistic parallels can be made of the supposed background for the Christian idea in the story of Krishna. The analogy is not precise, and how one tradition may have borrowed from the other cannot be demonstrated.

2. ASSYRO-BABYLONIAN AFFINITIES

The inscriptions and literature of Assyria and Babylonia are not without suggestion that some sort of parallel may exist between the myths of these countries and the stories in Christian literature.

A building inscription speaking of Tukulti-Urta II (890–884 B.C.) tells how the gods created him in the womb of his mother.

The great [gods,] who carry out decrees [who decide fate], gloriously [?], Tukulti-Urta, the exalted prince, [they have created] [in] the womb of my mother . . . my [lowly (?)] birth to a lordly birth [they changed].[25]

Another building inscription describes the activity of the goddess of procreation at the conception of Sennacherib (705–681 B.C.) .

[22] Thomas William Doane, *Bible Myths* (1883) , p. 114.
[23] SBE, Vol. XXXII (1891) , pp. 1, 6.
[24] Doane, *op. cit.,* p. 114.
[25] Daniel David Luckenbill, *Ancient Records of Assyria and Babylonia* (1926) , Vol. I, ¶ 427. 3 (No. 91) .

The queen of the gods, the goddess of procreation, looked upon me with favor [while I was still] in the womb of my mother who bore me, and watched over my conception, while Ea provided a spacious womb, and granted [me] keen understanding, the equal of Master Adapa's.[26]

In addition to this, an inscription on the " Temple of the New Year's Feast " speaks of " Assur, the god, my begetter." [27]

On one of the cylinder texts (col. I, lines 1 ff.) Ashurbanipal (668–626 B.C.) is described as the offspring of the gods. " ' I [am] Assurbanipal, offspring [creature] of Assur and Bēlit, the oldest prince of the royal harem, whose name Assur and Sin ' " (¶ 765).

Later, however, he spoke of Esarhaddon as " the father who begot me " (¶ 766).

Behind these ideas lie the ancient Sumerian and Akkadian and Babylonian mythologies. The tradition shows that there was great concern for the procreative affairs of the gods. The " Paradise Myth of Enki and Ninhursag " describes how Enki successively impregnated the goddess Ninhursag, Nimnu, the daughter by this union, Ninkurra, the offspring of this one, and so on until he had impregnated his wife, daughter, granddaughter and great-grand-daughter (ANET, pp. 37 ff.).

The " Creation of Man by the Mother Goddess," whose theme is the creation of man out of clay mixed with the flesh and blood of a slain god, describes Mami: " Thou art the mother-womb, the one who creates mankind " (ANET, p. 99).

The earth, as a divine power, is Nin-tu, " the lady who gives birth." Reliefs show her as a woman suckling a child with other children tucked away under her dress and peeping out wherever they can. She is the " mother of all children." She is Ninmah, " the exalted queen," " queen of the gods," " queen of kings and lords." [28]

Ugaritic literature is also highly suggestive of a mother goddess. One of the most expressive texts reads:

> After this goes Puissant Baal,
> Also goes the Maiden Anath.
> As they do homage to Lady Asherah of the
> Sea,

[26] Luckenbill, Vol. 2, ¶ 407.

[27] Ibid., ¶ 446.

[28] Henri and H. A. Frankfort, *The Intellectual Adventure of Ancient Man* (1946), p. 145.

> Obeisance to the Progenitress of the Gods,
> Quoth Lady Asherah of the Sea:
> " Why do ye homage to Lady Asherah of
> the Sea,
> Obeisance to the Progenitress of the
> Gods?
> Have ye done homage to Bull El Benign,
> Or obeisance to the Creator of Crea-
> tures? "
> Quoth the Maiden Anath:
> " We do homage to [th]ee, Lady Asherah of
> the Sea,
> [Obei]sance to the Progenitress of the
> Gods."
> (II. AB. iii, lines 24–35, ANET, p. 132.)

Two pieces of tablet (IV. AB and RS 319) describe Baal's pursuit of the Maiden [29] Anath. After he has overtaken her, a brief
encounter follows, she conceives and bears an offspring which she
with great joy presents to Baal.

> And so she goes up to Arar,
> Up to Arar and Zaphon.
> In the pleasance, the Mount of Possession,
> She cries aloud to Baal:
> " Receive, Baal, godly tidings,
> Yea receive, O Son of Dagon:
> A wild-ox is [born] to Baal,
> A buffalo to Rider of Clouds."
> Puissant Baal rejoices.
> (IV. AB. iii, lines 30–38, ANET, p. 142.)

In an Akkadian ritual text that dates to the Seleucid period, but
that depicts what is probably a traditional rite, the urigallu priest
of the Temple Ekua is described as entering into the presence of
the god Bel and the goddess Beltiya and reciting a prayer according to a prescribed ritual. Having recited a prayer to Bel, he must
then recite the following to Beltiya:

> My merciful Lady — My Lady, be calm!
> . . .

---

[29] " Maiden " reads " Virgin " in the translation by Cyrus Gordon in the Loves
and Wars of Baal and Anat (1943).

Planet Venus, who shines brilliantly
[among] the stars, whose name is My
Lady,
The star Ban, who fells the mighty, whose
name is My Lady.

. . .

The star Baltesha, the star of *sensuousness,*
whose name is My Lady.

. . .

The star Eru, who creates sperm, whose
name is My Lady,
The star Ninmah, who makes a gift of life,
whose name is My Lady,
My Lady, her name is My Lady. Is not her
name My Lady?

(ANET, p. 333.)

The exaltation of the goddess deity is a dominant theme in Sumero-Akkadian literature. The " Hymn to Ishtar " (ca. 1600 B.C.) brings out a vivid picture of the feminine deity. In this she is described as the perfect woman, the " queen of women," queen among the gods.[30]

One of the most important references in Assyrian-Babylonian literature is " The Legend of Sargon." In it, Sargon of Agade is represented as having been born of a poor mother in secret and as not knowing his father.

Sargon, the mighty king, king of Agade,
am I.
My mother was a *changeling,*[31] my father I
knew not.
The brother[s] of my father *loved* the hills.

[30] ANET, p. 383. Similar references in " Prayer of Lamentation to Ishtar," pp. 383 ff.

[31] " Enitu," which Jeremias in *Das alte T. im Lichte des a. Orients* (1904), p. 205, translated " vestal-mother." A similar tale appears in the Indian epic the *Mahābhārata* (Third Division, Vana Parva, ch. 307). The lady Kuntī has conceived by Sūrya, the Sun. Immediately after the birth of the child Karna, he is placed in a waterproof wickerwork basket, pillowed and sheeted, and the basket is set on the waters of the river Asva, and is borne on its course to the Ganges. There the beautiful lady Rādhā, who has no son, sees it drifting down the stream. After the waves bring the basket to the bank, the babe is discovered and accepted as a gift from the gods. The boy is reared by Rādhā and her husband in their own home. (J. Estlin Carpenter, in *Studies in the History of Religions* [1912], " Buddhist and Christian Parallels: the Mythological Background," p. 70; *Mahābharata,* ed. by Manmatha Nath Dutt, Vol. 1 [1895].)

> My city is Azupiranu, which is situated on
> the banks of the Euphrates.
> My *changeling* mother conceived me, in
> secret she bore me.
> She set me in a basket of rushes, with bi-
> tumen she sealed my lid.[32]

Here, however, the meaning of " changeling " (Akk. enītum) is
uncertain, and this passage lacks reference to the instrumentality
of deity. It then is no real parallel to the idea of the virgin birth
in the New Testament.

In the Akkadian " Creation Epic " the advocates of the relation
of the Biblical virgin birth to Babylonian sources found the most
likely parallel. In it is described the birth of Marduk.

Ea, having overheard the plan of the primordial deities to destroy the other gods, deceived Apsu and Mummu and put them to
death. " Ea, his triumph over his enemies secured, in his sacred
chamber in profound peace he rested." (ANET, p. 61, lines 74–
75.) Then he took over the place which Apsu had used for his cult.

> Ea and Damkina, his wife, dwelled [there]
> in splendor.
> In the chamber of fates, the abode of
> destinies,
> A god was engendered, most potent and
> wisest of gods.
> In the heart of Apsu was Marduk created,
> In the heart of holy Apsu was Marduk
> created.
> He who begot him was Ea, his father;
> She who conceived him was Damkina, his
> mother.
> The breast of goddesses he did suck.
> The nurse that nursed him filled him with
> awesomeness.
> Alluring was his figure, sparkling the lift of
> his eyes.
> Lordly was his gait, commanding from of
> old.
> When Ea saw him, the father who begot
> him,
> He exulted and glowed, his heart filled with
> gladness.

[32] ANET, p. 119. The copy of this dates about the eighth century B.C. Sargon
of Agade is ca. 3800 B.C.

He rendered him perfect and endowed him
with a double godhead.
Greatly exalted was he above them, exceed-
ing throughout.
. . .
" My little son, my little son!
My son, the Sun! Sun of the heavens! "
Clothed with the halo of ten gods, he was
strong to the utmost,
As their [awe] some flashes were heaped
upon him.
(ANET, p. 62, lines 77–104.)

The emphasis of the Assyrian and Babylonian tradition of the
mother goddess and the general concurrence of incidents between
purely mythological figures portrays ideas of origin on a level foreign to New Testament thought. Assyrian and Babylonian references to origins demonstrate that the procreative concept was
deified, mythologized, and expressed in two ways. First, in the idea
of relationships between gods and goddesses resulting in other gods
and goddesses, such as Ea and Damkina assisted by Apsu giving
birth to Marduk, and Enki and Ninhursag generating Nimnu.
Secondly, we find the idea of procreative deities, either male or female, playing a part in the birth of other deities or great personages, such as the Ugaritic tradition of Lady Asherah, " the Pro-
genitress of the gods "; Mami, " the Mother-womb, the one who
creates mankind "; Father Nanna, the " begetter of gods and
men "; the Assyrian traditions that Tukulti-Urta was created by
the gods in the womb of his mother, and that Sennacherib's birth
was assisted by Ea, who provided a " spacious womb," and Assur,
" the god, my begetter "; and the North Arabian myth of the
mother goddess who was responsible for Dusares. The Assyrian
and Babylonian traditions were extremely flexible in the descriptions of conception; but nowhere is there anything precisely analogous to the incidents in Matthew and in Luke.

3. ZOROASTRIAN AFFINITIES

The conclusion is similar when we compare Jesus' origin with
stories from Zoroastrianism. The Biblical idea is one of direct operation of divine power, whereas the Zoroastrian idea is one in
which the divine factor assists in the preservation of Zoroaster's

seed. Moreover, the myth of Zoroaster's origin specifically describes the conjugal relations of his parents.

The Avesta and the Pahlavi texts both include the tradition that the " kingly glory " is handed onward from ruler to ruler and from saint to saint for the purpose of illuminating ultimately the soul of the Zarathushtra (Zoroaster). It is ordained in heaven, according to the tradition, that the Glory shall be combined with the Guardian Spirit and the Material Body so as to produce the wonderful child from this threefold union.

The descent of the Glory is described in three distinct and separate stages. First the Glory descends from the presence of Aūharmazd, then passes through heaven down to earth, and finally enters the house where the future Zarathushtra's mother herself is about to be born. It unites itself with her and abides in her until she reaches the age of fifteen when she gives birth to Zarathushtra. Meanwhile the archangels Vohūman and Ashavahisht convey to earth the Guardian Spirit, bearing it in the stem of the Hōm-plant. Finally the Substantial Nature or Material Body which completes the triad is miraculously combined with a special mixture of milk and water and Hōm, and the parents of the future prophet drink it. Despite the efforts of demons to prevent conception by three times uttering scurrilous remarks to the parents Pōrūshāspō and Dūkdāub as they are having intercourse, the conception takes place. The birth is attended by marvels, and evil forces continue to be at work to destroy the infant.

Here the " Herod-figure " appears as Dūrāsrōbō. This malicious creature, a renowned wizard, visited the newborn child at his father's own invitation for the purpose of inspecting the marvelous creature. He, however, determined to cause his death, even by so bewitching the father Pōrūshāspō that he desired the death of his own son. Meanwhile the mother is watching over him, but in spite of her alertness, four separate attempts are made at his life. Dūrāsrōbō kindled a huge fire, and although it burned fiercely throughout the night where Zarathushtra was, it did not burn him, and at dawn his mother snatched him unscathed from the flames. Dūrāsrōbō also persuaded Pōrūshāspō to place Zarathushtra upon a narrow path along which many oxen would come and trample him to death, but a kindly old ox came along and blocked the path of the onrushing oxen until at dawn the mother came along and snatched him from the path. Then Zarathushtra was placed at a drinking pool where horses would come and trample him. Again he was saved in similar fashion. Finally he was placed in a wolf's den with slaughtered cubs with the intent that the enraged wolf would mangle Zarathushtra in revenge. But the wolf was struck dumb by sacred beings and the babe was suckled by a sheep until his mother found him (Dk. VII. iii. 4 ff.) .

There is no textual evidence either to support Cheyne's statement that the Zoroastrian Saoshyant (Savior) " was born of a Virgin." [33] Cheyne made that assertion on the basis of the following passage from the " Bundahish " (xxxii. 8) :

This, too one knows, that three sons of Zaratūst, namely Hūshēdar, Hushēdarmāh, and Sōshyans, were from Hvōv; as it says, that Zaratūst went near unto Hvōv three times, and each time the seed went to the ground; the angel Nēryōsang received the brilliance and strength of that seed, delivered it with care to the angel Anāhīd, and in time will blend it with a mother.[34]

Elsewhere the tradition explains that a maid, Eredatfedri, bathing in Lake Kāsava, will conceive by that seed and bring forth the Savior Saoshyant; moreover, his two forerunners, Ukhshyat-ereta and Ukhshyat-nemah, will be born in the same way to Srūtat-fedhri and Vanghu-fedhri.[35]

Chapter viii of Book VII describes the end of the millennium of Zarathushtra and the arrival of Aūshēdar, the descendant of Zarathushtra. In it is the story of the conception of Shemigabu, who is Aūshēdar's mother.

Then, when thirty winters of the tenth century are unelapsed [that is, thirty winters *are* remaining] a maiden, who is Shemig-abū walks up to the water; she that is the mother of that famous Aūshēdar, and her former lineage is from Vōhūrōkō-i Frahānyān in the family of Īsadvāstar, the son of Zaratūst *that* is brought forth by Arang. Then she sits in that water *and* drinks *it,* and she kindles in a high degree those germs which were the third *of* the last that the righteous Zaratūst was dropping forth originally, and they introduce that son whose name is the Developer *of* Righteousness. Though she is fifteen years old, the girl [kanīg] *has* not before that associated with men; nor afterwards, when she becomes pregnant, *has she done so* before the time when she gives birth. (55–57.)

When he is thirty years of age, the sun stands still in the zenith of the sky for the duration of ten days and ten nights (Dk. VII.

[33] Thomas K. Cheyne, *Bible Problems* (1904) , pp. 200–201.
[34] SBE, Vol. V, Pahlavi Texts, Part I (1880) , p. 144.
[35] SBE, Vol. XXIII (1883) ; Farvardīn Yast XX, n. 2, p. 195.

viii, 58). A similar description of Aūshēdar's son Aūshēdar-māh through the maiden Gobak-abu follows in chapter ix of Book VII.

In the story of the birth of Zoroaster himself it is difficult to find any analogy to the idea of Jesus' birth. Clemen has pointed out how incomprehensible it is to compare the Biblical conception by the direct operation of divine power with the Zoroastrian idea in which the divine factor only assists in the preservation of Zoroaster's seed.[36]

4. MITHRAIC AFFINITIES

The Persian Mithra was among the most ancient and most honored gods of Roman paganism. His name appeared in the Persian Avesta and in the Indian Vedas. The relation of the Persian Mithra to the more ancient Indian is obscure, since the Vedic references to him are obscure.[37] " Fundamentally, he was the god of light, invoked together with Heaven under the name of Varuna, even as in the Persian system Mithra was associated with Ahura." [38] In Persian thought Mithra was represented as the genius of heavenly light and as the guardian of truth and the preserver of good faith. Yet he was terrible, for he was the implacable foe of all evil in his efforts to maintain the creation of Mazda. After the Chaldean conquest, Mithraism learned astrology from the Chaldeans and continued thereafter as an astronomical religion. In the Hellenistic period it took on final modifications which gave it the definitive form it maintained through the imperial period. Cumont vividly pictured it in terms of the luxuriant vegetation of Hellenistic art that grew out of the Mazdean substratum and the thick sediment of Chaldean astrology and the rich alluvial deposits of belief local in Asia Minor.[39] By the middle of the first century A.D., Mithraism had become familiar to Rome and Italy.

Unfortunately the legend of Mithra has been lost, but it can be reconstructed relatively well from bas-reliefs. Cumont gives an account.

The light bursting from the heavens, which were conceived as a solid vault, became, in the mythology of the Magi, Mithra born from the rock. The tradition ran that the " Generative Rock," of which a standing image was worshipped in the temples, had given birth to Mithra

---

[36] *Primitive Christianity and Its Non-Jewish Sources* (1912), p. 294.

[37] Franz Cumont, *The Mysteries of Mithra* (1903), p. 1.

[38] Harold R. Willoughby, *Pagan Regeneration* (1929), p. 143.

[39] *Textes et Monuments figurés relatifs aux Mystères de Mithra*, I, 34 ff.

on the banks of a river, under the shade of a sacred tree, and that shepherds alone, ensconced in a neighboring mountain, had witnessed the miracle of his entrance into the world. They had seen him issue forth from the rocky mass, his head adorned with a Phrygian cap, armed with a knife, and carrying a torch that had illuminated the somber depths below. Worshipfully the shepherds drew near, offering the divine infant the first fruits of their flock and their harvests. But the young hero was naked and exposed to the winds that blew with violence: he had concealed himself in the branches of the fig-tree, and detaching the fruit from the tree with the aid of his knife, he ate of it, and stripping it of its leaves he made himself garments. Thus equipped for battle, he was able henceforward to measure his strength with the other powers that peopled the marvellous world into which he had entered. For although the shepherds were pasturing their flocks when he was born, all these things came to pass before there were men on earth.[40]

Justin Martyr in *Dial. cum Trypho* 70 alluded to Mithra's birth from a rock, and the *Protevangelium Jacobi* states that Jesus was born in a cave. These references are significant for showing that the Mithraic tradition was known in the Christian world and that it was associated with apocryphal tradition. It is possible that Luke's story of the shepherds has its background in the Mithraic legend, but this is the sole point of contact between the two accounts. The apocryphal reference is an instance of how traditions outside Christianity influenced later Christian traditions. The most obvious contact between the two religions came many years later when the Christian celebration of the birth of Christ was made to coincide with the Mithraic celebration of the new birth of the Sun (*Natalis invicti*) at the termination of the winter solstice on December 25. This is all evidence, not of the mythological origin and nature of Christianity, but of the influence of one religion upon the other.

C. EGYPTIAN TRADITION

Several historians, Cheyne, Petersen, and Norden, placed special emphasis on the relation which the idea of the virgin birth in

[40] *The Mysteries of Mithra*, pp. 130–132. Ancient tradition alludes to his birth as the result of the incestuous intercourse of Ahura-Mazda with his own mother, but it also gives reference to his origin from a common mortal. Justin Martyr in *Dial. cum Trypho* lxx. 1 says that the followers of Mithra are initiated " in a place to which they give the designation of a cave " in imitation of our Lord's birth in a cave (Lxxviii. 5 sq.). Cf. *Protevangelium Jacobi* 18–19, 21.

the Gospels supposedly has with ancient Egyptian religious ideas. In the story of the birth of Horus and in the idea of the divinity of kings (pharaohs) great resemblance is thought to be found.

1. THE DOCTRINE OF PARTHENOGENESIS IN THE TRADITION ABOUT THE GODDESS NEITH (NET)

E. A. Wallis Budge in *The Gods of the Egyptians* (Vol. 2, 1904, p. 220) tells us that the doctrine of parthenogenesis [41] was well known in Egypt in connection with the goddess Neith of Saïs centuries before the birth of Christ; and along with the belief in the conception of Horus by Isis through the power given her by Thoth which is coeval with the beginnings of history in Egypt, we have the impression that the idea was firmly established in Egyptian religious thought.

Net was one of the oldest of all the Egyptian goddesses. Her most famous sanctuary was at Saïs, the capital of the fifth nome of Lower Egypt. In the IVth Dynasty she was thought to be at once the mother and the daughter of the Sun-god Rā, and she possessed the power to conceive and bring forth the new Sun-god daily by means of the divine and magical formulas with which she was provided.[42] An inscription described a conversation between Cambyses when he came to Egypt and Utchat-Ḥeru, a high priest of Net, in which the latter " told him that it was Net, the mighty mother, who had given birth to Rā, that she was the first to give birth to anything, and that she had done so when nothing else had been born, and that she had never herself been born." [43]

In Upper Egypt, Net was chiefly worshiped at Seni, the Latopolis of the Greeks. Here she was identified with Nebutt, and others, and was represented with the head of a lioness painted green, with the titles: " Father of fathers, and Mother of mothers," and " Net-Menḥit, the great lady, lady of the south, the great cow who gave

[41] For a discussion of " partheno-genesis " itself as a scientific phenomenon in its relation to the interpretation of the Christian idea of virgin birth see: A. T. Robertson, *Luke the Historian in the Light of Research* (1920) ; C. A. Briggs, an article in *The American Journal of Theology*, April, 1908; T. J. Thorburn, *A Critical Examination of the Evidences for the Doctrine of the Virgin Birth* (1908) , Appendix G.

Thorburn cautioned that " partheno-genesis " has been observed only in the lower forms of life. Briggs pointed out that a parthenogenesistic explanation of the virgin birth is an indirect denial of conception by the Holy Spirit alone. Robertson, nevertheless, insisted that science cannot set aside the virgin birth of Christ because of the evidence of " virgin birth " in the lower forms of life.

[42] Budge, Vol. 1, pp. 450 ff.

[43] *Ibid.*, p. 458.

birth to the sun, who made the germ of gods and men, the mother of Rā, who raised up Tem in primeval time, who existed when nothing else had being, and who created that which exists after she had come into being." [44]

In Thebes, Net, as the mother and wife of Amen-Rā, was known as Ament. Under the name of Ament-Rā she is seen suckling Horus, and she also appears as a ram-headed goddess wearing the atef crown. Ament is styled " the Cow, the great lady, who fashioned the company of the gods, the mother of Rā, who gave birth to Horus " (p. 465).

2. The Legend of the Birth of Horus

Numerous forms of Horus are mentioned in Egyptian texts. Horus, the son of Isis, is the fourteenth listed by Budge. He is Heru-sa Ast, sa-Asar, " Horus, son of Isis, son of Osiris." In general he represented the rising sun and in this respect was comparable to the Greek Apollo. A hymn on an ostracon found in the tomb of Ramesses IX reads " Beautiful is thine [awakening] O Horus, who voyageth over the sky. . . . The fire-child with glittering rays, dispelling darkness and gloom. Child increasing in stature [?] . . . The vessel pursueth its course in the waters of Neserser. . . . The two daughters of the Nile shatter for thee the dragon." [45]

In the *Hymn to Osiris*,[46] Isis is described searching for the body of the dead Osiris. Having found him by means of the magical use of certain words given her by Thoth, she restored her husband to life, was united with him, and conceived Horus. " She stirred up from his state of inactivity him whose heart was still, she drew from him his seed, she made an heir, she suckled the babe in solitariness, and the place wherein she reared him is unknown, and his hand is

---

[44] P. 463. Modern primitives, the Shilluk, relate: " In the beginning was Jo-ok the Great Creator, and he created a great white cow who came up out of the Nile and was called Deung Adok. The white cow gave birth to a man-child whom she nursed and named Kola." See Adolf Erman's *The Literature of the Ancient Egyptians* (1927), p. 115.

[45] Erman, *The Literature of the Ancient Egyptians*, p. 302. For the tradition of the birth of the sun deity three generations before Horus, see Erman's *A Handbook of Egyptian Religion* (1907), p. 26. " According to some a lotus flower sprang out of the primeval waters on which sat the young sun god as a child. In *Eshumnēn*, however, tradition told of a mound in the waters of Desdes, and of an egg laid in a nest there, from which the sun god was hatched in the same way as the waterfowl of Egyptian marshes."

[46] For reconstruction of the tale " Isis and Osiris," see James H. Breasted, *Development of Religion and Thought in Ancient Egypt*, pp. 18 ff.

mighty with the house of Seb. The company of the gods rejoice and are glad at the coming of Horus, the son of Osiris." [47]

After this, Isis was persecuted by Set, held prisoner with Horus in a house but helped to escape by Thoth, and set out on a journey with the protection of seven scorpions (which probably represent the seven stars of the constellation Canis Major, in which the stars of Isis and Sothis were situated). After wandering through several cities and into a great swamp, she left Horus alone one day. In her absence he was stung by a scorpion. When she found him, he was lying on the ground, foaming at the mouth and rigid in his muscles and limbs. At the advice of her sister Nephtys, who came with Serqet the scorpion goddess to assist her, she cried to heaven for help and was heard by Rā. Thereupon Thoth came down with words of power and raised Horus to life and health. Soon after this, Horus set out to avenge the death of his father.

Horus fought with Set for three days, and when Isis seemed to assist Set, Horus cut off her head. Thoth, however, by means of his words of power restored the slain mother by transforming the head into the head of a cow and affixing it to the body of Isis.[48]

It is difficult to see how these stories form the background for the idea of virgin birth in the New Testament. Nor is it easy to see how the accompanying incidents are relevant in bringing out the relationship between the Egyptian and Christian traditions. Budge has correctly pointed out that the only possible relationship is on the grounds of an analogy with the apocryphal narratives of Jesus and Mary.

There is little doubt that in her character of the loving and protecting mother she appealed strongly to the imagination of all the Eastern peoples among whom her cult came, and that the pictures and sculptures wherein she is represented in the act of suckling her child Horus formed the foundation for the Christian figures and paintings of the Madonna and the Child. Several of the incidents of the wanderings of the Virgin and the Child in Egypt as recorded in the Apocryphal Gospels reflect scenes in the life of Isis as described in the texts found on the Metternich Stele, and many of the attributes of Isis, the God-mother, the mother of Horus, and of Neith, the goddess of Saïs, are identical with those of Mary the Mother of Christ. The writers of the Apocryphal Gospels intended to pay additional honour to Mary the Virgin by ascribing to her the attributes which up to the time of the advent of Christianity they had regarded as the peculiar property of

[47] Budge, *op. cit.*, Vol. 2, p. 150.
[48] *Ibid.*, Vol. 1, pp. 487–489.

Isis and Neith and other great indigenous goddesses, and if the parallels between the mythological history of Isis and Horus and the history of Mary and the Child be considered, it is difficult to see how they could possibly avoid perceiving in the teaching of Christianity reflections of the best and most spiritual doctrines of the Egyptian religion.[49]

This is the only basis upon which the Egyptian and Christian traditions ought to be compared.

3. THE LEGEND OF THE GOD RE GENERATING WITH THE WIFE OF A PRIEST

Norden stressed the importance of the Egyptian legend of the god Re generating with the wife of a priest as a primary motif over against which the Gospel narrative is set. This explains, said he, how Mary can be the wife of Joseph and the bride of God at the same time.[50]

Nothing is known of the origin and beginnings of the worship of Re at Heliopolis, but it is quite certain that under the Vth Dynasty, about 3350 B.C., the priests of Re had settled there and had obtained great power. The Westcar Papyrus indicates that User-ka-f, the first king of the Vth Dynasty, was the high priest of Re and that he was the first to add " son of the Sun " to the titles of the Egyptian monarchs. This was adopted by every succeeding king of Egypt. The Westcar Papyrus tells how User-ka-f and his two immediate successors, Sahu-Ra and Kakaa, were the sons of the god Re by Ruddadt, the wife of a priest of the god Re of Sakhabu. " All chronological tradition affirms that Rā had once ruled Egypt, and it is a remarkable fact that every possessor of the throne of Egypt was proved by some means or other to have the blood of Rā flowing in his veins, or to hold it because he was connected with Rā by marriage." [51] The newborn child was regarded as a god incarnate, and later with appropriate ceremonies he was presented to Re or Amen-Re, in his temple, where the god accepted it and acknowledged it to be his child.[52]

49 *Ibid.*, Vol. 2, p. 220.

50 *Die Geburt des Kindes*, pp. 81–82.

51 Budge, *op. cit.*, Vol. 1, p. 329. The Westcar Papyrus (see Erman, *Die Märchen des Papyrus Westcar* [1890]) , is from 700 to 1,000 years later than the birth of the three kings which it narrates. Breasted, *Ancient Records of Egypt* (1906) , Vol. 2, p. 76.

52 *Ibid.*, p. 330. Cf. G. Maspero, *The Dawn of Civilization* (1894) , p. 259.

Lineal descent from Re was claimed by the kings of Egypt, and in the strictest sense their title " Son of Re " indicated that the king was immediately and physically the offspring of the god and a mortal mother. " It is probable that this interpretation was pressed at first only by kings whose claims to the throne through their mortal parents were questionable." [53]

Through the years many literary versions developed out of this theme and finally took stereotyped form in a series of reliefs and inscriptions on the Der el-Bahri temple which tell about the birth of Queen Hatshepsut and the inscriptions at Luxor which tell about Amenhotep III.

Since the story of Hatshepsut has been defaced by the erasures of Thutmose III, and similar treatment has befallen those of Amon by Amenhotep IV, it is necessary to employ both stories in order to obtain one connected tale.

Breasted has pointed out that the inscriptions are nearly identical, and the scenes of Hatshepsut even picture her as a boy. This, said Breasted, indicates the stereotyped form of the legend. Later kings adopted the same scenes, and even in Ptolemaic times these incidents of the divine birth of the king were depicted in the temple reliefs. The most notable example in late times was the similar representation of Alexander the Great in order that he might gain the proper recognition in Egypt as the god's son. Only in this way could he become the legitimate king of Egypt.[54]

The inscription opens with Amon (Re) prophesying the birth of Hatshepsut with the promise of great power. An interview between Amon and Thoth follows in which Thoth mentions that Queen Ahmose's husband is an old man, and that while his majesty is away is the time to go to her. In the next scene Amon and Queen Ahmose are seated facing each other and the god extends to her the symbols of life. Amon-Re " made his form like the majesty of this husband, the king Okheperkere [Thutmose I]. He found her asleep in the beauty of her palace. . . . He went to her immediately, *coivit cum ea*, he imposed his desire upon her, he caused that she should see him in his form of a god."

Then the Queen exclaimed, " It is splendid to see thy front; thou hast united my majesty with thy favors, thy dew is in all my limbs." Then Amon did all that he desired with her.

In his next utterance Amon spoke her name and declared that

53 Breasted, *Ancient Records of Egypt*, p. 76.
54 *Ibid.*, p. 77.

she shall exercise kingship in the whole land. Next he called
on the aid of the god Khnum, who created man, and beseeched
him to fashion in the Queen a daughter " whom I have begotten."
The next scene pictures the god Khnum at work at a potter's
wheel fashioning the daughter with assistance from the goddess
Heket.

The next scene, which depicts a conversation between Thoth
and the Queen, is almost completely destroyed. The scene of the
birth follows.

The queen sits enthroned in the middle of the upper row, holding the
child; before her are four female divinities, acting as midwives and
extending their arms for the child.

Other divinities attend and perform various functions. In the
Luxor tale the child is then presented to the father by Hathor who
in turn extends the child to Re who rejoiced at the sight of his
newborn child. The scene following depicts Queen Ahmose on a
couch supported by a goddess with the child being suckled by two
Hathor cows.

Other scenes portray the coronation of kingship among the gods,
the purification (in which the child has water poured over her
head as she stands between Amon and Khonsu), the presentation
of the child to all the other gods, and the journey of the child to
the north.[55]

Herodotus is responsible for our knowledge of the general as-
similation of this theme in both Babylonian and Egyptian traditions. Describing Babylonia he said:

On the topmost tower there is a spacious temple, and inside the temple
stands a couch of unusual size, richly adorned with a golden table by
its side. There is no statue of any kind set up in the place, nor is the
chamber occupied on any nights by any one but a single native woman,
who as the Chaldaeans, the priests of this god, affirm is chosen for himself by the deity out of all the women of the land. . . .

They also declare — but I for my part do not credit it — that the god
comes down in person into this chamber, and sleeps upon the couch.
This is like the story told by the Egyptians of what takes place in their

Ibid., pp. 78–90. ANET, contains numerous references to the kings who claimed
divine sonship. Thut-mose III, pp. 238–239; Thutmose IV, p. 449; Amen-hotep II,
p. 246; Amen-hotep III, p. 376; Amen-hotep IV, p. 370; Seti I, p. 253; Ramses II,
p. 253; Ramses III, p. 262.

city of Thebes where a woman always passes the night in the temple of the Theban Jupiter. In each case the woman is said to be debarred of all intercourse with men.[56]

4. THE DIVINITY OF EGYPTIAN KINGS

By means of this tradition the pharaoh was elevated to the position of divinity. The Memphis and Karnak Stelae have references to Amen-hotep II as " the God-Ruler-of-Heliopolis." Similar inscriptions were preserved on the Amada and Elephantine Stelae (ANET, pp. 245–247).

It is not clear that in Egyptian tradition the pharaoh was thought of solely as the offspring of a divinity and a human mother. A building inscription of Amen-hotep III himself has Amon-Re say of Amen-hotep III:

> My son, of my body, my beloved, Neb-
> maat-Re,
> My living image, whom my body created,
> Whom Mut, Mistress of Ishru in Thebes,
> the Lady of Nine Bows, bore to me,
> And [she] nursed thee as the Sole Lord of
> the people —
> My heart is very joyful when I see thy
> beauty.
>
> (ANET, p. 376.)

The inscription of " The Divine Nomination of an Ethiopian King," which dates ca. 600 B.C., but which is similar in setting to the times of Amen-hotep's predecessor Thut-mose III (father of

---

[56] *The History of Herodotus,* Vol. 1 (1875), chs. 181 and 182, pp. 247–248.

Josephus tells a story based on the same theme. Early in the Christian era a woman named Paulina was desired by Decius Mundus, who persuaded the priests at the temple of Isis at Rome to collaborate with him to trick Paulina into taking her place in the temple with the expectancy of spending the night with the god Anubis, to whom she had succumbed; whereupon she was greatly distressed and told her husband, who in turn notified the emperor Tiberius. Tiberius had the priests crucified, demolished the temple of Isis, had the statue of Isis thrown into the Tiber, and banished Mundus. Josephus told this story to illustrate " a sad calamity" which put the Jews to disorder in Rome at the time when Pilate was creating calumnies among the Jews in Jerusalem. *Antiquities of the Jews* III. 4.

Strabo's version of this (9th c. A.D.) : At Thebes in ancient times a beautiful girl of noble family and tender years was regularly dedicated at the temple of the god Zeus. She prostituted herself with any man according to her fancy until she reached the age of puberty. She was then mourned for as dead and replaced (xvii. I. 46) . Hartland, *Primitive Paternity,* Vol. 2 (1910), p. 264.

Amen-hotep II), speaks of the new king as the " Son of Amon, and the Child of Mut, Lady of Heaven, the Son of Re." The inscription adds Amon-Re speaking: " His father was my son, the Son of Re: [*Inle-Amon*] the triumphant. His mother is the King's sister, King's mother, Mistress of Cush, and Daughter of Re " (ANET, p. 448).

The parentage of a pharaoh may have been described in terms of divine father and human mother or divine father and divine mother.

All of this tradition must be understood in the light of what may be called the ancient " mystery of procreation." Even at the time of the Pharaoh Amen-hotep IV, who broke the established religion of Egypt and instituted the worship of Aton (the sun disc as the source of life), divinity was made responsible for all procreative processes. " The Hymn to Aton " has,

> Creator of seed in women,
> Thou who makest fluid into man,
> Who maintainest the son in the womb of
>   his mother,
> Who soothest him with that which stills his
>   weeping,
> Thou nurse [even] in the womb,
> Thou givest breath to sustain all that he has
>   made:
> When he descends from the womb to
>   *breathe*
> On the day when he is born,
> Thou openest his mouth completely,
> Thou suppliest his necessities.
>   (ANET, p. 370.)

In Egyptian thought, the natural act of procreation was understood as an act of god. This applied not only to kings but to everyone else as well. In the case of pharaohs this myth was made into the form of a special legend that was designed to keep both the priests and the pharaohs in power. Actually the origin of kings was no more divine than that of the laity. What was special was the particular legend with all its attending incidents which applied only to kings.

Basic to Egyptian ancient tradition was the belief that Re was the fecundating principle of life other than human. The opening stanza of " A Hymn to Amon-Re " illustrates this, where he is described as the one who made mankind, beasts and cattle, trees and herbage (ANET, pp. 365 ff.) .

Egyptian thought is extremely more complex and crude than Biblical. A clear analogy to the virgin birth of the New Testament is not to be found in Egyptian traditions.

D. GRECO–ROMAN AND HELLENISTIC AFFINITIES

Greco-Roman and Hellenistic " influences " is another theory equally difficult to demonstrate from textual evidence. The legend of Perseus (in which his mother conceived him by Jupiter when he visited her in a golden shower) ; stories of the generation of gods and goddesses by other gods and goddesses (such as the traditions of the birth of Apollo by Zeus and Leto, of Theseus by Zeus and Maia, of Dionysus by Zeus and Semele, of Dionysus Zagreus by Zeus and Persephone, and of Persephone by Zeus and Demeter) ; legends of the birth of gods by generation of a god with a mortal woman (such as the birth of Hercules by the union of Zeus and Alcmena and that of Pan by Hermes with a shepherdess) ; tales of the birth of heroes through the union of a god with a mortal (such as Ion by Apollo and Creusa, Romulus by Mars and Aemila, Asclepius by Apollo and Coronis, and Helen by Zeus and Leda) ; and stories of the birth of emperors (such as the legend of Augustus' generation by a serpent-god and Atia, and his coming to be known as the " son of Apollo ") — all these have been cited as the resource from which the Biblical idea of the virgin birth has been drawn. None of these ideas is at all comparable to the Biblical formula.

The publication of *The Legend of Perseus,* by Edwin Sidney Hartland, popularized the theory that the Evangelical infancy narratives are derived from Greco-Roman sources. The Greek myth of the divine and virginal origin of Perseus is outlined by him, and the story in its various derivatives in ancient and modern folklore is set forth in great detail.[57]

For consideration of the phenomena of supernatural birth around the world, one should consult Hartland's books. He produced scores of illustrations: the virgin of the Tupis of Brazil who was fertilized by means of a mysterious fish, the Chinese maiden who bathed in a certain pool and later found on the skirt of her

[57] Two volumes. Vol. 1, *The Supernatural Birth* (1894) .

raiment a red fruit and ate it and became pregnant, the Finnish woman who is impregnated by a vapor bath of the breath of horses and bears a child and cradles it in a manger, the Mongolian tale of the khan's daughter who swallowed a stone and became pregnant, the Peruvian goddess who ate of the fruit of the luoma tree which had been used to disguise the semen of Uiracocha and was immediately impregnated and later demanded to know which of the gods was the father of her child, and the Siamese virgin who conceived by the prolific rays of the sun.

These incidents and scores of others represent chiefly universal superstition concerning means of pregnancy. Popular and common superstitions concerning magical formulas for becoming pregnant by many peoples were transposed into legends concerning both gods and men. Water, flowers, stones, nuts, fish, berries, fruit, and scores of other things were believed by different peoples to produce the proper conditions for conception. The traditions are also steeped in the ignorance of peoples concerning the place of the origin of pregnancy. The stories tell of conception occurring at the navel, on top of the head, at the thigh, through the fingers, on the hand, and various parts of the anatomy. Hartland's book *Primitive Paternity, The Myth of Supernatural Birth in Relation to the History of the Family* (2 vols., 1909) makes this obvious. His final chapter on " Physiological Ignorance " makes this clear. Therefore, reference to all these tales as " virgin birth " is misleading. These traditions form no real part of the problem of analogy.

Hermann Usener (*Religionsgeschichtliche Untersuchungen*, I, 1911, pp. 70 ff.; *Das Weihnachtsfest*, 1911) and Wilhelm Soltau (*Die Geburtsgeschichte Jesus Christi*, 1902) were champions of the theory that the idea of the virgin birth in the New Testament relied upon Greek parallels. Their theory has been criticized mainly by Harnack (*Dogmengeschichte*, 1914), Richard Grützmacher (*Die Jungfrauengeburt*, in *Biblische Zeit- und Streitfragen*, 1906), and Alan Hugh McNeile (*The Gospel According to St. Matthew*, 1915).

Since there has been so much discussion among historians about the relationship of the virgin birth in Matthew and Luke to Greek parallels, and so many references have been brought into the discussion, it is necessary to review and analyze carefully the literature in question and observe the nature of the births that it conveys.

1. THE BIRTH OF THE GODS

The literature is rich in the tradition of birth among the gods. The basic legend, according to Hartland, is that of Perseus, whose mother conceived him by Jupiter when he visited her in a golden shower (cf. Ovid, *Metamorphoses*, Book IV). There are many others also.

Hesiod in his " The Origin of the World and the Birth of the Gods " [58] describes how out of Chaos were born Erebus and Night, Aether and Day, Heaven and High Mountains, the Sea and Oceanos, and others including Hyperion, Iapetos, Theia, and Rhea, Themis, and Phoebe.

Ancient Greek religion has many other vivid descriptions of birth among the gods which indicate the Greek background for the term " Son of God." Homer's " Hymn to Apollo " [59] describes the birth of Apollo as the result of the union of Zeus and Leto. Leto for nine days and nights was continually pierced with sharp pangs of childbirth. The whole scene stressed the difficulty of her delivery along with her great desire to give birth to her noble son. Finally " around a palm tree she cast her arms, and set her knees on the soft meadow, while the earth beneath smiled, and forth leaped the babe to light, and all the Goddesses raised a cry. Then, great Phoebus, the Goddesses washed thee in fair water, holy and purely, and wound thee in white swaddling bands, delicate, new woven, with a golden girdle round thee." Then the child was suckled with nectar and sweet ambrosia and immediately pronounced, " Mine be the dear lyre and bended bow, and I will utter to men the unerring counsel of Zeus."

Hermes was the offspring of Zeus and Maia. " But when the mind of great Zeus was fulfilled, and over *her* the tenth moon stood in the sky, the babe was born to light, and all was made manifest; yea, then she bore a child of many a wile and cunning counsel. . . . Born in the dawn, by midday well he harped, and in the evening stole the cattle of Apollo . . . on that fourth day of the month wherein lady Maia bore him." (HH, pp. 134 ff.) Special note is made that " when he leaped from the immortal knees of his mother, he lay not long in the sacred cradle."

The setting of this birth is in a cave, and after a brief excursion outside, Hermes returns to his cradle. " Quickly to his cradle came

[58] In *Greek Religious Thought*, F. M. Cornford (1923), pp. 19–20.
[59] Andrew Lang, *The Homeric Hymns* (1899), pp. 103 ff.

glorious Hermes and wrapped the swaddling bands [60] about his shoulders, like a witless babe, playing with the wrapper about his knees."

Helios was also a child of Zeus by " dark-eyed Euryphaessa." Another of his names was " the son of Earth and starry Heaven." Helios was called both the son of Zeus and the son of Hyperion (HH, p. 248).

The Homeric " To Pan " describes the origin of Pan as a child of Hermes. It tells how he fell in love with a shepherdess, married her, and how she bore him a son.

From his birth he was a marvel to behold, goat-footed, two-horned, a loud speaker, sweet laughter. Then the nurse leaped up and fled when she saw his wild face and bearded chin. But him did boon Hermes straightway take in his hands and bear, and gladly did he rejoice at heart. Swiftly to the dwellings of the Gods went he, bearing the babe hidden in the thick skins of mountain hares; there sat he down by Zeus and the other Immortals, and showed his child, and all the Immortals were glad at heart, and chiefly the Bacchic Dionysus. Pan they called the babe to name: because he made glad the hearts of all of them. (HH, p. 232.)

Tradition had it also that Semele bore Dionysus to Zeus (in two Hymns to Dionysus, HH, pp. 217, 255). In Euripides' " The Bacchae " the same idea is formulated.

> Behold, God's Son is come unto this land
> Of Thebes, even I, Dionysus, whom the
>   brand
> Of heaven's hot splendor lit to life, when
>   she
> Who bore me, Cadmus' daughter Semele,
> Died here. So, changed in shape from God
>   to man,
> I walk again by Dirce's streams and scan
> Ismenus' shore.
>   (CGD, Vol. 2, p. 227.)

The tradition was that Semele, the daughter of the Theban Cadmus, was once loved by Zeus and asked the god to come to her in his complete majesty. Zeus appeared to her in a flash of lightning

---

[60] Reference to " swaddling " clothes is also in Apollodorus' " Library " i, I, which is derived from Hesiod. He tells how " Rhea wrapped a stone in swaddling clothes and gave it to Cronus to swallow, as if it were the new-born child." Cornford, *op. cit.*, p. 21.

by which she was consumed. Before she died, however, she gave birth prematurely, and the life of the child was spared by Zeus himself, who opened his own flesh, enclosed and fostered the infant, and in the due course of time brought forth the god by a mysterious second birth.

> 'Tis all his word,
> This tale of Dionysus; how that same
> Babe that was blasted by the lightning
> flame
> With his dead mother, for that mother's lie,
> Was re-conceived, born perfect from the
> thigh of Zeus, and now is God! [61]

This second birth was an important factor in the worship of Dionysus. He was an earth deity. He was *dithyrambus,* " he who entered life by a double door." This son of earth and sky functioned as the personification of vegetable life. " As such he was a yearly divinity, who came and went with the seasons." The Bacchic rites celebrated his going to bed in winter and his rising in the summer. In popular phases of worship he was both the god of vegetation in general and the vine god in particular. The sheer physical intoxication from the drinking of wine was the essence of the Dionysian religion. The orgiastic character of this religion was also brought out in the " feast of raw flesh " (Cornford, pp. 68–70, 76) . For his worshipers, Dionysus was " Iacchos, Bromios, Lord, God of God born! " (Euripides, " The Bacchae," CGD, p. 253.)

Heracles and Orpheus were also sons of the gods. Homer styled Heracles " the son of Zeus " (HH, p. 226) . Sophocles' " The Trachinae " (CGD, Vol. 1, p. 456) opens with reference to him as the " glorious son of Zeus and Alcmena." Epictetus insisted on the divine sonship of Heracles, regarding Zeus not only as father of Heracles but as the father of men (III. 24) . Apollodorus' " Library " I. iii, 2 preserves the tradition that " Calliope [the Muse] bore to Oeagrus or, nominally, to Apollo . . . Orpheus " (Cornford, p. 54) .

Important to Orphic theology was the myth of Dionysus Zagreus which is preserved in Clement of Alexandria's *Protrepticus* ii. 14 ff. According to his version of the myth, Persephone bore to Zeus a son who had the form of a bull.

This divine son was Dionysus Zagreus, or " the hunter." He was the favorite of his father, and Zeus destined him to become the ruler of

[61] *Ibid.,* p. 235.

the universe. Even while he was a child, the father of gods and men entrusted him with thunderbolts and allowed him to sit on his throne. But the malignant Titans, stung by jealousy and urged on by the vengeful Hera, sought the young child's life. . . . The Titans succeeded in luring him away. . . . Having gained possession of the divine child, the Titans savagely tore him to pieces, and cooked and ate the pieces. Athena, however, preserved the heart of Zagreus and carried it away to Zeus who, in his anger, blasted the savage Titans with his thunderbolts. Clement omitted one item of the myth which formed an interesting connection with the Theban legend of Dionysus. Zeus, having received the heart of Zagreus from Athena, swallowed it. So when Semele bore Dionysus to Zeus the new god was but Zagreus reborn.

From the ashes of the blasted Titans, the Orphic said, man was created. But these Titans had already consumed the god Dionysus, and their ashes contained the vitality of a divine being. Hence man by his very constitution was believed to be a compound of two natures, one Dionysian and immortal, the other Titanic and mortal. (Cornford, pp. 95–96.)

Among the traditions of the origin of the gods, at least two notable deviations from the usual theme are prominent, i.e., the stories of Athena and Aphrodite. Athena's birth, which is without the mother factor, is described in Aeschylus' " The Eumenides."

> This too I answer; mark a soothfast word
> Not the true parent is the woman's womb
> That bears the child; she doth but nurse the
> seed
> New-sown: the male is parent; she for him,
> As stranger for a stranger, hoards the germ
> Of life, unless the god its promise blight.
> And proof hereof before you will I set.
> Birth may from fathers, without mothers,
> be:
> See at your side a witness of the same,
> Athena, daughter of Olympian Zeus,
> Never within the darkness of the womb
> Fostered nor fashioned, but a bud more
> bright
> Than any goddess in her breast might bear.[62]

[62] CGD, Vol. 1, p. 294. Part of a speech by Apollo. See Homer's " Hymn to Athene," for the tradition of her origin. " Her did Zeus the counsellor himself beget from his holy head, all armed for war in shining golden mail, while in awe did the other Gods behold it " (HH, p. 242) .

The other is the legend of Aphrodite's love for a mortal man, the shepherd Anchises, which may be found in *The Homeric Hymns* ("Aphrodite," pp. 166 ff.). In Aeschylus' *Seven Against Thebes* (CGD, Vol. 1, p. 2) she was "mother and queen of our race." The predominant theme in which Aphrodite plays a vital role is the mating of gods with goddesses and gods with mortal women. These unions produce other gods or mythological figures.

2. THE BIRTH OF HEROES

Euripides' " Ion " opens with a speech by Mercury in which he attests his birth by Maia and Jove. In this speech Mercury described how Erechtheus, a king, had a daughter Creusa, who was secretly seduced by Apollo.

> Her growing burden, to her sire unknown
> [Such was the pleasure of the god], she bore,
> Till in her secret chamber to a son
> The rolling months gave birth: to the same
>   cave,
> Where by the enamour'd god she was com-
>   press'd,
> Creusa bore the infant; there for death
> Exposed him in a well-compacted ark
> Of circular form, observant of the customs
> Drawn from her great progenitors, and
>   chief
> From Erichthonius, who from the Attic
>   earth
> Deriv'd his origin: to him as guards
> Minerva gave two dragons, and in charge
> Consign'd him to the daughters of Aglau-
>   ros:
> This rite to the Erechthidae hence remains,
> Mid serpents wreathed in ductile gold to
>   nurse
> Their children. What of ornament she had
> She hung around her son, and left him thus
> To perish.

This describes the circumstances of Ion's birth. The child, however, was rescued by Phoebus and brought up in the temple at Delphi and later returned victorious to his native land. (CGD, Vol. 1, pp. 1121 ff.)

The drama treats the theme of Creusa's mourning her lost child and Ion's loneliness for his unknown mother. They are finally united when a priestess gives him the ark in which he was originally placed and uses it to make himself known to his mother.

Creusa

Childless no more, no more alone, my house
Now shines with festive joy; my realms now
 own
A lord; Erechtheus blooms again; no more
His high-traced lineage sees night darken-
 ing round
But glories in the sun's refulgent beams.

Ion

Now let my father, since he's present here,
Be partner of the joy which I have given
 you.

Creusa

What says my son?

Ion

Such, such as I am proved.

Creusa

What mean those words? Far other is thy
 birth.

Thereupon Creusa reveals how she conceived Ion by Phoebus, and later convinced by a revelation by Minerva that the whole story is true, they all proceed to Athens to assume his paternal throne.

Plutarch records in his *Lives* (Vol. 1, p. 2) how Theseus and Romulus were both born out of wedlock and of uncertain parentage and at the same time had the reputation of being sprung from the gods. Theseus' grandfather Pittheus was responsible for the story that Theseus was the child of Neptune in order to conceal the fact of his true lineage as the son of Pittheus' daughter Aethra and Aegeus (pp. 3 ff.).

Tradition accounted for the origin of Romulus in several ways. Some stories told how Romulus and his brother, Remus, were sons of Aeneas and Dexithea. Other stories told how they were sons of Roma and Latinus. The story of his divine origin has it that Aemila, the daughter of Aeneas and Lavinia, had him by the god Mars. Plutarch related additional details of how Tarchetius consulted an oracle and received the answer that a virgin should give herself to an apparition (earlier in his own house a strange vision, a male figure that arose out of a hearth and stayed there for many days, appeared to him) and that a son should be born to her. Thereupon Tarchetius ordered one of his daughters to carry out the wishes of the oracle, but she, overcome with personal indignation, sent her handmaid in her place. Tarchetius, hearing of this, ordered them imprisoned, and only the intercession of the goddess Vesta prevented his murdering them. When two sons were finally delivered by the maiden, Tarchetius ordered one Teratius to destroy them, but he instead carried them to the riverside, where a wolf suckled them and birds fed them, until a cowherd came along and rescued them (pp. 40–41).

A variation of the Romulus and Remus legend has them as the unexpected and undesired offspring of a vestal, who was supposed to live forever in a single and maiden life. Only the intercession of her sister spared her from death at the hands of her father, the King Amulius. When the boys were born, Amulius commanded one Paustulus to get rid of them. He, however, placed them in a basket near the river. Rising waters wafted the basket away. When they finally settled on land, a she wolf nursed them and a woodpecker fed and watched them. Since the woodpecker and the she wolf were creatures esteemed holy to the god Mars, the word of their mother that Mars was the progenitor readily came to be accepted. Plutarch adds that the others thought the real explanation was that Amulius, dressed in armor, was mistaken by Ilia for Mars.

Several other heroes, Asclepius, Helen, and Oedipus, ought to be mentioned.

Homer's brief " Hymn to Asclepius " attributes Asclepius' origin to the god Apollo and the daughter of King Phlegyas.

> Of the healer of diseases, Asclepius, I
> begin to sing, the son of Apollo, whom
> fair Coronis bore in the Dotian plan, the
> daughter of King Phlegyas; a great joy to
> men was her son, and the soother of evil
> pains.
> Even so do thou hail, O Prince, I pray thee
> in my song.
>
> (HH, p. 220.)

Pausanias described Phlegyas as " the greatest soldier of his time." While on a journey to the Peloponnesus, accompanied by his daughter, she revealed to him what she had before kept secret, that she was with child by Apollo. She bore the child in the country of the Epidaurians, where she exposed him on the mountain called Nipple, which in more ancient times was named Myrtium.[63]

Asclepius became the most popular of the hero gods of Greece. He was the divine patron of the healing art. His cult met the need of the belief that religion was concerned with sickness and disease. Disease was attributed in ancient times to the wrath of a justly angry god or to infection by a malignant demon. In either case his sanctuaries throughout the Greco-Roman world became so famous that in gratitude to this hero god for his beneficence there was a spontaneous movement to make him a god of the first rank and identify him with Zeus himself. Asclepius was " the one who leads and controls all things, the savior of the whole world, and the guardian of mortals." [64]

The illustrious Helen of Troy was worshiped as a heroine in several parts of the ancient world during the early historical epoch. The tradition developed by Stesichorus, a Greek poet of the early sixth century B.C., maintained that not Helen, but only a phantom, went with Paris to Troy, and the Greeks and Trojans fought for ten years over a delusion. Meanwhile the real Helen had been transported by the gods to Egypt, where she remained under the protection of Proteus, the king of Egypt. The setting of Euripides' " Helen " is dependent upon this tradition. The drama opens with Helen describing what she knows of her legendary birth.

For a legend tells how Zeus winged his way to my mother Leda's breast, in the semblance of a bird, even a swan, and thus as he fled from an eagle's pursuit, achieved by guile his amorous purpose, if this tale be true. (CGD, Vol. 2, p. 7.)

The words of the chorus (1133 ff.) clarify the meaning of " semblance of a bird." " Thou Helen art the daughter of Zeus; for thy sire was the bird that nestled in Leda's bosom." Actually Helen thought she was hatched from an egg, but the way of expressing it in a way that would be becoming to a demigoddess was to attribute the birth to Zeus, the sky out of which the bird had come. A similar legend is recorded of the Egyptian Osiris (a syncretistic tradition). An inscription over a grave of Osiris at Nyasa in Arabia says: " My father is Kronos. . . . I am the oldest son of

---

63 " Description Graeciae " II, 26, 3-5, in " Testimonies " of *Asclepius*, E. J. and Ludwig Edelstein (1945).

64 Willoughby, *op. cit.*, p. 23, quoting Aelius Aristides *Oratio*, 6.

Kronos, and as a germ out of a beautiful egg was I born." [65]

Later Helen philosophized.

Good friends, to what a fate am I united? Did not my mother bear me to be a monster to the world? For no woman, Hellene or barbarian, gives birth to babes in eggs enclosed, as they say Leda bare me to Zeus. My life and all I do is one miracle, partly owing to Hera and partly is my beauty to blame. (CGD, Vol. 2, p. 14.)

As the drama went on, Menelaus, her husband, referred to her as " the begotten child of Zeus " and as " the daughter of Zeus and Leda." Homeric tradition had labeled Menelaus himself " Son of Zeus " (*Odyssey* iv. 561).

The Greeks also used the theory of semidivine origin to describe Oedipus' birth. In Sophocles' " Oedipus the King " the chorus sings.

Who was it, my son, who of the race whose years are many that bore thee in wedlock with Pan, the mountain-roaming father? Or was it a bride of Loxias that bore thee? For dear to him are all the upland pastures. Or perchance 'twas Cyllene's Lord, or the Bacchants' god, dweller on the hill-tops, that received thee, a new-born joy, from one of the Nymphs of Helicon, with whom he most doth sport. (CGD, Vol. 1, p. 404.)

In the opening speech of Euripides' " The Phoenissae," Jocasta, Oedipus' mother, reveals how Oedipus came into being.

Men called me Jocasta, for so my father named me, and I am married to Laius. Now when he was still childless after being wedded to me a long time, he went and questioned Phoebus, craving moreover that our love might be crowned with sons born to his house. But the God said, " King of Thebes for horses famed! seek not to beget children against the will of heaven; for if thou beget a son, that child will slay thee, and all thy house shall wade in blood." But he, yielding to his lust in a drunken fit, begat a son of me, and when his babe was born, conscious of his sin and of god's warning, he gave the child to shepherds to expose in Hera's meadow on mount Cithaeron, after piercing his ankles with iron spikes; whence it was that Hellas named him Oedipus. But the keepers of the horses of Polybus finding him took him home and laid him in the arms of their mistress. So she suckled the child that I had borne and persuaded her husband she was its mother. (CGD, Vol. 2, p. 171.)

She then briefly summarizes the chief incidents in Oedipus' life: his later encounter with his father, not recognizing him, killing

[65] Erman, *A Handbook of Egyptian Religion* (1907).

him and soon chosen as the new husband of the widowed queen, his own mother; how he had two sons and daughters by Jocasta; and how upon learning that she who was his wife was also his mother, blinded himself in a fit of agonized fury. It is clear from this passage that Oedipus is considered to be the offspring of Laius and Jocasta. The same is obvious in Sophocles' " Oedipus the King" (CGD, Vol. 1, p. 409). The two passages indicate that in the Greek mind the thoughts of divine and human paternal participation in conception were not mutually exclusive.

This phenomenon may be illustrated further in the tradition of the origin of Plato. In Diogenes Laërtius' *Lives of the Philosophers* (1853, p. 113), Plato is the son of Ariston and his wife Perictione. However, the same passage suggests that Apollo was the progenitor. Conybeare relates how Plutarch in his " Convivial Disputations " tells how Ariston saw a vision in a dream and heard a voice forbid him to approach or touch his wife for ten months. After citing an old Greek poet to the effect that the currents of winds impregnate hen birds, he continues as follows:

I see nothing absurd in the supposition that God, instead of approaching women in human wise, touches them to finer issues with other modes of contact, and so fills the mortal with divine offspring. The myth is not of my making, for the Egyptians say that Apis was thus conceived through touch and contact of Selene the moon. The fact of the intercourse of a male god with mortal women is conceded by all, but it is not believed that mortal man can occasion pregnancy and birth in a goddess, because the stuff of which gods are made is air and spirit and certain forms of warmth and moisture. (*Myth, Magic, and Morals*, p. 195.)

3. The Theory of Hellenistic Influence

During the Hellenistic age the religious ideas of various cultures were mixed, and it is out of this syncretism that some scholars thought that the Biblical virgin birth arose. Norden believed that the virgin motif mystically interpreted arises out of the Greco-Egyptian priest doctrine (in which Re generates with the wife of a priest), and what seems contradictory in the Biblical narrative, that Mary is the wife of Joseph and yet the bride of God, is to be explained on the basis of this extra-Biblical motif which was current in the Hellenistic age. He believed that the Biblical tradition combined the Greco-Egyptian idea of a married woman giving birth as the result of contact with a god with the Hellenistic virgin motif.[66] The traditional association of this motif with temple prostitution makes it hardly likely that the Biblical idea was rooted in this Hellenistic concept.

Alexander, the Ptolemies, and the Caesars were said by some scholars to have been " virgin born " and the stories of their origins are said to have been the source for the Gospel tradition. This is not likely, although an aura of great wonder did surround the stories of their origin.

Alexander the Great journeyed to the Oasis of Amen in order that he might be recognized as the god's son and thus become a legitimate and recognized king of Egypt. Inscriptions show that he and the Ptolemies after him had the incidents of their birth regularly depicted in temple reliefs.[67] With the stories of the origin of the Caesars the characteristics of the stories are transformed somewhat and accord with what Norden calls the Hellenistic virgin motif. Evidence shows, however, that Alexander must have had a double tradition of origin. It is recorded that " Alexander the Great and Augustus are deemed to have been conceived of a serpent god, and they claimed between them Phoebus and Jupiter as their progenitors." [68]

Suetonius' *The Lives of the Caesars*, Book II, chapter 94, gives us the account of Augustus' birth which he says he derived from the " theologumena " of Asclepias of Mendes. He summarizes the legend after he noted what Julius Marathus had said a few months before Augustus was born. A portent was observed at Rome which gave warning that nature was pregnant with a king for the Roman people. " Thereupon the senate in consternation decreed that no male child born that year should be reared; but those whose wives were with child saw to it that the decree was not filed in the treasury, since each one appropriated the prediction to his own family."

Then he narrated what he had learned from Asclepias.

When Atia had come in the middle of the night to the solemn service of Apollo, she had her litter set down in the temple and fell asleep, while the rest of the matrons also slept. On a sudden a serpent glided up to her and shortly went away. When she awoke, she purified her-

[66] Eduard Norden, *Die Geburt des Kindes* (1924), pp. 81–82.

[67] Breasted, *Ancient Records of Egypt*, Vol. 2, p. 77.

[68] Sidonius Apollinaris, " Carmina " II, 121, *Testimonies* 289 in *Asclepius*, E. J. and Ludwig Edelstein (1945).

self, as if after the embraces of her husband, and at once there appeared
on her body a mark in colors like a serpent, and she could never get
rid of it; so that presently she ceased ever to go to the public baths. In
the tenth month after that Augustus was born and was therefore regarded as the son of Apollo. Atia too, before she gave him birth,
dreamed that her vitals were borne up to the stars and spread over the
whole extent of land and sea, while Octavius dreamed that the sun
rose from Atia's womb.[69]

Suetonius learned from Gaius Drusus that when Augustus was
still an infant, he was placed by his nurse at evening in his cradle
on the ground floor. The next morning he disappeared. Later he
was found lying on a lofty tower with his face toward the rising
sun. Quintus Catulus dreamed that he saw the boy in the lap of
Jupiter of the Capitol and that when he ordered that he be removed, the god warned him to desist, " declaring that the boy was
being reared to be the saviour of his country. When Catulus next
day met Augustus, whom he had never seen before, he looked at
him in great surprise and said that he was very like the boy of
whom he had dreamed " (*Suetonius*, Vol. 1, p. 269).

Pliny in his *Natural History* associates Augustus with the comet
as an object of worship.

The only place in the whole world where a comet is the object of
worship is a temple at Rome. His late Majesty Augustus had deemed
this comet very propitious to himself; as it had appeared at the beginning of his rule, at some games which, not long after the decease of
his father Caesar, as a member of the college founded by him he was
celebrating in honour of Mother Venus. In fact he made public the
joy that it gave him in these words: " On the very days of my Games a
comet was visible for seven days in the northern part of the sky. It was
rising about an hour before sunset, and was a bright star, visible from
all lands. The common people believed that this star signified the soul
of Caesar received among the spirits of the immortal gods, and on this
account the emblem of a star was added to the bust of Caesar that we
shortly afterwards dedicated in the forum. (Book II. xxiii. 93–94.) [70]

Suetonius tells how Augustus visited the studio of the astrologer
Theogenes. Augustus was reticent to reveal the time of his birth

---

[69] *Suetonius*, Vol. 1 (1924), p. 265. Soltau gives two quotations from the " Inscription from Priene " which refer to the greatness of the day on which the
theiotatou Caesar was born, and to the birthday of this god as the beginning of
glad tidings for the world. (*Die Geburtsgeschichte Jesu Christi*, pp. 34–35.)

[70] *Pliny*, the elder. Vol. 1 (1938), p. 237.

for fear that he might be found less eminent than his companion Agrippa with whom he had come to the astrologer. " When he at last gave it unwillingly and hesitatingly, and only after many urgent requests, Theogenes sprang up and threw himself at his feet. From that time on Augustus had such faith in his destiny, that he made his horoscope public and issued a silver coin stamped with the constellation Capricornus, under which he was born." The passage continues:

As he was entering the city on his return from Apollenia after Caesar's death, though the heaven was clear and cloudless, a circle like a rainbow suddenly formed around the sun's disc, and straightway the tomb of Caesar's daughter Julia was struck by lightning. Again, as he was taking the auspices in his first counselship, twelve vultures appeared to him, as to Romulus, and when he slew the victims, the livers within all of them were found to be double at the lower end, while all those who were skilled in such matters unanimously declared to be an omen of a great and happy future.[71]

The Emperor Augustus was praised as the Savior of the world. " He deserved it, for he had liberated the provinces from the oppressions of greedy Roman officials and the sufferings of war and given them peace and happiness." The idea of Savior was not unique or original with Augustus himself. Before him the same title was given Seleucid and other Hellenistic kings. Throughout this period there were frequent longings for a savior from the present troubles.[72]

The most specific expression of this hope is made by Virgil in his " Fourth Eclogue." This Eclogue is remarkable in showing how widespread was the idea of a savior who should come to bring peace on earth and restore the golden age. The poem is definitely dated. It is dedicated to Pollio, who was one of the great influential men at the time of the civil wars and had been Virgil's patron and friend. At the time of his consulate in 40 B.C., the political situation was greatly improved, for it seemed that at last peace would be established. The hero of the poem is a child born or to be born in this auspicious year (714) who is gradually to perfect the restoration then beginning.[73]

[71] II. xcv, op. cit., p. 273.
[72] Martin P. Nilsson, The Historical Hellenistic Background of the New Testament (1941), pp. 28–29.
[73] Paul Carus, Virgil's Prophecy on the Saviour's Birth (1918), pp. 5 ff. The Open Court Publishing Co., La Salle, Illinois.

The new era that is to come is in fulfillment of an older oracle.

> Now comes the era described
>   in the verse of the Sybil of Cumae
> From the beginning is started again
>   the great order of ages,
> Now does the virgin return,[74]
>   the Saturnian Kingdom appeareth;
> Now from the heavens on high
>   is descending a new generation.

The birth of an infant marks the turning point

> Bless him, the infant with whom
>   discontinues the era of iron;
> Bless him with whom will arise
>   the new race that is gloriously golden,
> Bless, chaste Lucina, the boy;
>   now reigneth thy brother Apollo.

Then follows a brief description of the new age under the consulship of Pollio in which crime will be abolished and the earth will be free from terror.[75] After this the attention is returned to the child whose birth will usher in this era.

> First will the earth without culture,
>   dear boy, bring thee gifts for thy child-
>   hood,
> Vines of green ivy, and ladygloves
>   lovely with wonderful fragrance;
> Mixed with the cheerful acanthus
>   will grow Colocasian lilies.
> Yea, at the cradle for thee,
>   there shall blossom the sweetest flowers;
> Goats will return by themselves
>   to our homesteads with udders distended,
> Nor any longer our cattle
>   shall fear huge terrible lions.

[74] See the *Sibylline Oracles*, Book V, 206–212, a composition of later date which contains a similar idea: " And Capricorn . . . and Taurus among the Twins encircles the mid-heaven, when the Virgin ascending and the Sun fastening the girdle round his forehead dominates the whole firmament."

[75] The *Sibylline Oracles*, III, 371 ff.: " Blessed shall the man and woman be who lives to see that time, as are they who dwell in the isles of the blest; for law and justice shall come from the starry heaven upon men, and with them wise concord, best of all gifts for mortals, and love and faith and hospitable ways; but lawlessness, blame, envy, anger and madness shall depart."

> Then will the serpent die out,
>   and the herbs disappear that bear poison,
> While the Assyrian spikenard
>   will thrive in the most bountiful plenty.

The poet then dwells on the increasing bounties of nature: the growth of grapes upon briars and brambles and the dripping of honey from oak trees, and other wonders expressing reversal of the normal course of nature. In the midst of this description the role of the child is more clearly defined.

> But that boy will partake of the life of the
>   gods,
> he will meet them,
> Meet all the heroes; and he
>   will in turn by the gods be beholden.
> Over a pacified world will he rule
>   patriarchic in virtue.

The whole world awaits the arrival of this illustrious infant.

> Deign to accept — for the time is fulfilled —
>   the illustrious honors,
> Thou, O loved offspring of gods,
>   O son of great Jove, the Almighty.
> See how the world toward thee
>   with its ponderous mass is inclining.
> See all the countries, the tracts of the sea,
>   and the depths of the heaven,
> See how they hail the arrival,
>   they all, of the age that is coming.

The poet's next words express the sentiment which is reminiscent of the Biblical Simeon.

> Oh that my life for the future
>   would last but sufficiently longer,
> Also my spirit, that I thy glory
>   might praise in my verses.

He then boasts that in his rejoicing he would excel Orpheus, Linus, and Pan in singing. The poem ends with a picture of the child in his mother's arms.

> Show, little boy, by thy smile
>   that already thou knowest thy mother

Who for thy sake hath endured
　　ten months of solicitous trouble.
Smile, little infant! on Thee
　　have not yet been smiling thy parents,
Nor hast thou dined with the gods,
　　nor been wedded as yet to a goddess.

A similar hope of a coming age of blessedness is expressed in
Virgil's " Aeneid."

Yonder behold thy hero, the promised
　　prince, upon whom
Often thy hopes have dwelt, Augustus Cae-
　　sar, by birth
Kin to the godlike dead, who a golden age
　　upon earth
Comes to renew where once o'er Latium
　　Saturn reigned,
Holding remote Garamantes and India's
　　tribes enchained.[76]

(Book VI, 791 ff.)

Martin Dibelius' theory for the explanation of the relationship
between Buddhistic and Christian traditions must be taken into
account in order to acquire an understanding of the real relationship between the Christian tradition and non-Christian narratives.
The many points of agreement between Buddha legends and the
stories about Jesus, he said, arise not from " borrowing " or from
the phenomenon of one serving as the " source " of the other, but
from the " law of biographical analogy." [77] Even though events
generally parallel to and vaguely similar to the Biblical mother-

[76] Full recognition of the relationship of this tradition to the narratives of
Jesus' birth and infancy has been made by Norden in his *Die Geburt des Kindes*
and by Gottfried Erdmann in his *Die Vorgeschichten des Lukas- und Matthäus
Evangeliums und Vergils vierte Ekloge* (1932). The latter is the more systematic
and developed of the two. According to Erdmann, the Simeon motif was the point
of contact between the Biblical infancy narratives and the Hellenistic tradition of an
Augustan golden age. He, however, traced the tradition through the *Sibylline
Oracles* back to passages in the Old Testament. The Septuagint of Gen. 46:30 was
the Old Testament basis of the Simeon motif which in III, 371 ff. of the *Sibylline
Oracles* was united with a tradition whose root was in Isa. 52:7 ff. Both the author
of Lukan birth tradition and Virgil's *Eklogue* IV, 53–59, drew independently upon
this tradition in the *Sibylline Oracles*. A reference in Luke 2:35 can also be traced
to the *Sibylline Oracles* III, 316 (" For a sword shall pass through the midst of
thee.").

[77] *Die Formgeschichte des Evangeliums* (1933), p. 196.

and-child motif, conception, birth, attendant disturbances in nature, threat of adversity, and visitation to the temple can be found nearly in whole or in part in other religions, direct contact of one religious tradition with the other is not necessarily implied. Similar stories exist in various cultures because of the universal cultural and racial tendency to describe the life of a hero similarly.

In the days in which Jesus was born it was customary for the life of a great man or hero to be embellished with birth narratives. This was true in both Gentile and Jewish circles.[78] This continued to be true in many primitive cultures. The explanation of the growth of such traditions by the law of biographical analogy (Dibelius) and by the laws of development out of racial psychological consciousness (Berguer [79]) makes it possible to account for both the similarity and diversity between Christian and non-Christian traditions without resorting to the inadequate theory of " borrowing " or " source."

Insight into the psychological aspects of the relationships between apparently parallel mythical narratives has been given by Carl Jung in his concept of mythical archetypes and by Otto Rank, who correctly observed that the general unanimity of these myths may be accounted for in the " very general traits of the human psyche rather than in primary community or migration." Rank also pointed out the ultimate connection between myth and dreams and the ultimate source of all myths, the imaginative faculty of humanity at large (*The Myth of the Birth of the Hero*, 1959, pp. 7–10).

What is common between Christian and " pagan " traditions is the idea of miraculous birth. In this sense they are parallel or analogous. There is a striking difference, however, between the Christian and non-Christian traditions. The Christian formula is unique. The idea that it contains — divine conception and human birth without anthropomorphism, sensuality, or suggestions of moral irregularity — is to be found nowhere in the literature of the world outside the canonical Biblical narratives. Rather than being an idea borrowed from other traditions, it is original with

---

[78] See *Some Hellenistic Elements in Primitive Christianity*, Wilfred L. Knox (1944), for a list of Jewish miraculous birth stories of Noah, Abraham, Isaac, Moses, Samuel, Samson (pp. 22–25). See also Enslin in JBL (LIX, p. 328) for a discussion of E. R. Goodenough's reference in *By Light, Light* (pp. 153–166) to the idea in Hellenistic Judaism of Isaac's mystic marriage with the ever-virgin Sophia.

[79] Georges Bergeur, *Quelques traits de la Vie de Jésus au point de vue psychologique et psychanalytique* (1920).

Christianity. The Christian story of miraculous birth reflects primitive Christian belief: faith in one God who is mighty in his creative power, belief in the supreme worth and dignity of man, belief in the imperative of the moral life, and the conviction that the nature and person of Jesus should be described in language which is descriptive of both the divine and the human.

The Christian story of the virgin birth is as different from pagan "analogies" as monotheism is from polytheism, as different as Biblical ideas of the relationship between God and man are from the mythological activities of gods in human affairs, and as different as the polygamous and incestuous pagan society was from the Christian teaching on morals and marriage. Primitive Christianity as opposed to Gentile thought (Greek, Roman, Egyptian, Babylonian, and Persian) believed in marriage as over against asceticism and monogamy as over against polygamy.[80] Over against early Catholic Christianity (as reflected in apocryphal tradition) and Buddhistic thought, it believed that sex in itself was not sinful and that moral order could result from the human process of birth. Furthermore, primitive Christianity did not project its hope for a new society into the life of the gods, i.e., into suprahuman speculation. Its hope for humanity lay in reflection on him who was the first in a new order within society.

Real significance lies in the fact that in the most general connotation of miraculous or extraordinary birth, Jesus' virgin birth was analogous to non-Christian traditions, but in its precise content and form it was in no way analogous to them. Because extraordinary birth was a universal theme, the early Christians had a point of contact with the ancient world, and because of the unique content and form of the Christian birth narrative, the Christians had a distinctive message to convey to Jewish and pagan society. In the Christian formula of conception by the Spirit and birth from a woman, Christianity's estimation of its Savior and its view of man were conveyed to the world. In this truth lay redemptive power.

The virgin birth is of fundamental and primary importance both to the Christian and to the non-Christian world. It is an exalted concept of God's action in the life of man, and is an idea that all men need to know.

[80] Herein lies the real reason for the resistance of Islam to the Biblical virgin birth tradition. Islam sanctioned polygamy.

The stories told by the primitive Christians in connection with the birth of Christ are of importance for christological thought because they are indicative of the high valuation which these believers placed upon the person of Christ and their conviction that he was not to be explained solely in terms of human perfection — God was supremely and specially involved in the life of their Lord.

— W. Norman Pittenger, *The Word Incarnate*

CHAPTER

6

HISTORICAL AND LITERARY ANALYSIS

WHILE THE STUDY of the virgin birth by the *religionsgeschichtliche Schule* was demonstrating the true literary classification of the Biblical narratives, other serious historians were taking up important questions that had been raised by the rationalists, Strauss, and his successors which had to do with the immediate context of the virgin birth pericopes. Two figures, Philo Judaeus and John the Baptist; two Biblical texts, Isa. 7:14 and Ps. 2:7; primitive Christology; the experience of the early Christian community; and the integrity of the canonical texts commanded great interest.

A. PHILO JUDAEUS

A number of scholars have seen in Philo of Alexandria in Egypt the connecting link between Greek thought and the New Testament world. Conybeare, Norden, Warschauer, Dibelius, Worcester, and Kirsopp and Silva Lake [1] have recognized in Philo a close affinity with Christian ideas. The question of the relationship of Philonic ideas to the canonical birth narratives is one which is in need of careful critical inquiry.

In the second half of the Hellenistic period, Jews were scattered throughout the civilized countries of the Mediterranean world. The *Sibylline Oracles* explained this dispersion of the Jews as a punishment. Philo (*Against Flaccus* 7) explained it as the result of the immense population of Jews which made it impossible for any one land to contain them all. Even before the conquests of Alexander the Great, there were foreign settlements of Jews in Mesopotamia, Egypt, and in Persia. The northern settlements of

[1] *An Introduction to the New Testament* (1937), p. 14.

Jews were the result of forcible deportations under Nebuchadnez-
zar. Those in Egypt, however, were voluntary, and were found
there as early as the sixth century before Christ. A Jewish colony
flourished at Elephantine from the fifth century onward. The most
important settlement was the one made by Alexander the Great at
Alexandria. Up until the time of Caligula (A.D. 37–41), the Jews
in Alexandria enjoyed a considerable degree of autonomy even
though they did not possess the full Alexandrian citizenship.[2] In
this situation, it is unthinkable that there would not be an inter-
change of ideas between Judaism and Greek thought. During this
period the influence of the Greek environment created a growth
of a Hellenized Judaism which was favorable to Greek philosophy.
" It would seem likely that wherever Judaism came into contact
with Hellenistic or Graeco-Oriental influences it allowed itself to
be more or less penetrated by them and in turn reacted upon
them." [3]

Philo Judaeus was born about 15 B.C., and died about A.D. 50.
He was primarily a philosopher, but since most of his thirty-eight
works are either parts of a commentary on the Pentateuch, or essays on selected topics in the Pentateuch, he necessarily deals with
Biblical history. In Philo may be recognized a mixture of Greek
and Judaistic thought which is especially evident in his interpretation of the births of Israel's heroes.

Philo plainly speaks of divine paternity in the case of the unusual conception of those whom he terms " Children of Promise."
In chapter xxiii of *De mutatione nominum* is an elaboration of the
significance of Isaac's birth. Immediately following the change of
Sarai's name to Sarah came the promise of the birth of Isaac.

"I will give thee a child from her." . . . First, then, the giver of anything in the proper sense of the word must necessarily give something
which belongs to himself, and if this is so Isaac must be not the man
Isaac but the Isaac whose name is that of the best of the good emotions,
joy, the Isaac who is the laughter of the heart, a son of God, who gives
him as a means to soothe and cheer truly peaceful souls. It were a
monstrous thing that one should be a husband, and another the parent,
parent therefore of bastards born in adultery, and yet Moses writes of
God as the husband of the virtue-loving mind when he says, " The
Lord seeing that Leah was hated opened her womb " [Gen. xxix. 31],

---

[2] Robert H. Pfeiffer, *History of New Testament Times* (1949), pp. 166 ff.
[3] Guignebert, *The Jewish World in the Time of Jesus* (1939), p. 252.

for moved by pity and compassion for the virtue hated by our mortal race and for the soul that loves virtue he sends barrenness . . . to the nature which loves excellence and opens the fountain of happy parentage by granting her welfare in childbirth. And Tamar too; she bore within her womb the divine seed, but had not seen the sower. . . . But she closely scanned the symbols and tokens, and judging in her heart that these were the gifts of no mortal she cried aloud, " To whomsoever these belong, he it is by whom I am with child." (Gen. xxxviii. 25.)

In this passage, Philo does not hesitate to call Isaac a " son of God " on account of God's part in the procreative process. The beginning of chapter xxiv of the same work makes it clear that God himself is the begetter. " So, too, the wisdom which as in motherhood brought forth the nature of the self-taught declares that God had begotten it. . . . He formed, He wrought, He begot, Isaac." In his tract *De Abrahamo*, Philo made Isaac the offspring of Abraham and Sarah. Having described how Abraham had a child by Sarah's handmaid, he added: " But long afterwards the wedded pair, who had despaired of the procreation of children, had a son of their own, a reward for their high excellence, a gift from God the bountiful, surpassing all their hopes " (ch. xliii) . For Philo, human paternity was not inconsistent with divine paternity.

It appears that Philo's emphasis on divine paternity comes at the point where he allegorizes the passage upon which he is commenting. A passage in *De Migratione Abrahami* indicates that for Philo, Isaac's birth had a spiritual significance, and it was the origin of this " side " of his make-up that was traced directly to God. " How the soul bore it she does not know; it is a Divine growth; and when it appeared she that seemed to have given birth to it acknowledges her ignorance of the good thing that had occurred." (Ch. xxv.) The divine impregnation of Tamar is also to be understood in the sense of her particular virtue, and demonstrates that divine impregnation is an allegorical means of describing the origin of one who is virtuous (*Quod Deus Immutabilis Sit*, ch. xxviii) .

A passage concerning Moses from *De Cherubim* (ch. xiii) clarifies what Philo meant by divine impregnation.

Thus then must the sacred instruction begin. Man and woman, male and female of the human race, in the course of nature come together to hold intercourse for the procreation of children. But virtues whose offspring are so many and so perfect may not have to do with mortal man, yet if they receive not seed of generation from another they will never themselves conceive. Who then is he that sows in them the good seed save the Father of all, that is God unbegotten and begetter of all things? He then sows, but the fruit of His sowing, the fruit which is His own, He bestows as a gift. For God begets nothing for Himself, for He is in want of nothing, but all for him who needs to receive. I will give as a warrant for my words one that none can dispute, Moses the holiest of men. For he shows us Sarah conceiving at the time when God visited her in her solitude [Gen. xxi. 1], but when she brings forth it is not to the Author of her visitation, but to him who seeks to win wisdom, whose name is Abraham.

And even clearer is Moses' teaching of Leah, that God opened her womb [Gen. xxix. 31]. Now to open the womb belongs to the husband. Yet when she conceived she brought forth not to God [for He is in Himself all-sufficing for Himself], but to him who endures toil to gain the good, even Jacob. Thus virtue receives the divine seed from the Creator, but brings forth to one of her own lovers, who is preferred above all others who seek her favour. Again Isaac the all-wise besought God, and through the power of Him who was thus besought Steadfastness or Rebecca became pregnant [Gen. xxv. 21]. And without supplication or entreaty did Moses, when he took Zipporah the winged and soaring virtue, find her pregnant through no mortal agency. (Ex. ii. 22.)

It is clear from this passage that Philo makes use of the allegorical method to account for the particular virtues of the offspring of the patriarchs. Another passage in *De Cherubim* demonstrates that Philo's idea of divine paternal participation in so far as its relation to the human mother was concerned was only in terms of a spiritual or allegorical way of thinking. The relationship of God to the virginity of the woman is in terms only of what Philo calls the " soul."

For it is meet that God should hold converse with the truly virgin nature that which is undefiled and free from impure touch; but it is the opposite with us. For the union of human beings that is made for the procreation of children, turns virgins into women. But when God begins to consort with the soul, He makes what before was a woman into a virgin again, for He takes away the degenerate and emasculate passions which unmanned it and plants instead the native growth of unpolluted virtues. Thus He will not talk with Sarah till she has ceased from all that is after the manner of women [Gen. xviii. 11], and is ranked once more as a pure virgin. XV. Again even a virgin soul may perchance be dishonoured through the defilement of licentious passions. Therefore the oracle makes itself safe by speaking of God as the husband not of a virgin, for a virgin is liable to change and death, but of virginity, the idea which is unchangeable and eternal. . . . It is meet and right therefore that God the uncreated, the unchanging, should sow the ideas of the immortal and virgin virtues in virginity which changes not into the form of a woman.

Both Norden and Worcester quoted a passage from Plutarch and linked it with Philo. On Plutarch's *Numa* 4, Worcester says: " The Egyptians teach that it is not impossible that God cohabit with a mortal woman in a supernatural manner: the Spirit approaches her and begets in her germs of the future being." [4] Worcester agreed with Norden that this passage " bears an unmistakable relation to the oft-repeated statement of Philo that God descends to the wombs of mortal women, who conceive and bear children through His co-operation. In Plutarch, no allusion is made to the woman's virginity, whereas Philo describes these favored ones as possessing a nature ' unstained, untouched, pure,' and though the mothers of these children of promise were married women, yet Philo declares that they were restored to their virginity by their contact with God." [5] The incongruity here is that Norden and Worcester had in mind physical virginity, whereas Philo was talking about qualities of the soul. It is also not correct to say, as Worcester did, that Philo speaks often of how God descends to the wombs of mortal women, who conceive and bear children through his co-operation, or, to use Norden's words, " *Gott steigt in den Schoss sterblicher Frauen hinab, um mit ihnen zu zeugen.*" [6] Nor is the allegorical nature of Philo's description in keeping with the Egyptian conception of the relationship between the god and a mortal woman. It was for the purpose of explaining the virtues and abstract qualities of important personages that Philo employed the allegorical method, and his use of the language of " divine impregnation " must be understood as part of this method.

[4] Cf. Norden (*op. cit.*, p. 77) and Worcester (*op. cit.*, p. 153) on Plutarch's statement in *Isis and Osiris* 36 that " The Egyptians call the Spirit [*pneuma*] Zeus [Amon]." Also a prayer in an Egyptian magic papyrus: " Thou art the Spirit [*pneuma*] of Amon." Also see reference to " The Holy Spirit of God " and Amon as " the breath " or " life-giving breath of God," quoted by Norden from Wessely, *Archics der Wien. Akad.* (1880), p. 120, and Reitzenstein, *Mysterien-religionen*, p. 160, and W. Spiegelburg, *Aegypt-Z*, XLIX (1911), p. 128.

[5] Worcester, *op. cit.*, p. 154.

[6] Norden, *op. cit.*, p. 78.

Worcester and Barton noticed that in Philo the ideas of human parentage and the impregnation of the mother by God are not mutually exclusive. Because of this association of ideas, it is possible that the Matthaean and Lukan narratives do not deny human parentage; morever, whenever Joseph is spoken of as the father of Jesus, this is not a contradiction, but perfectly in keeping with Hellenistic Judaistic tradition. What is incorrect is the idea that Philo is speaking about " virgin birth " and in doing so supplies us with a parallel to the Gospels in Hellenistic Judaism. What the Philonic tradition really implies, and implies only, is that the narratives in the New Testament may be interpreted thus: Jesus is the true son of Mary and Joseph; his divine conception stands for and accounts for the outstanding quality of his character. Kirsopp and Silva Lake came close to saying this. " It is possible to regard Jesus as the son of Joseph, given to him miraculously by the spirit of God through his wife." [7] They, however, like all who noticed the Philonic " analogy " missed the real significance of Philo's interpretation.

As in the pagan world divine begetting explained the mystery of procreation, so in Hellenistic Judaism divine procreation solved the problem of the origin of superior virtues. In each sense, a person of unique fame could be considered a child or son of God.

Barton has suggested that Apollos was the intermediary between Philo and the Christian community. He wrote a series of papers for the *Journal of Biblical Literature* entitled " Some Influences of Apollos in the New Testament." The first of these, in Volume XLIII (1924), pp. 207–223), concerned Apollo's influence on the birth narratives.

In the Acts of the Apostles, Apollos is described as eloquent, fervent of spirit, mighty in the Scriptures. Originally, he was a disciple or follower of John the Baptist, but was converted to Christianity by Priscilla and Aquila. In I Corinthians, Paul alluded to him as a colleague with whom he was not completely in accord on all religious views and teachings. It is clear that Apollos was known for having been both at Ephesus and at Corinth. It is evident, too, that Apollos was philosophically minded, and it is difficult to presume how coming from Alexandria he could have avoided contact with Philo. Apollos probably arrived in Ephesus in A.D. 53, and thus had sufficient time for influencing Christian tradition with his own particular mode of thinking.

7 Lake, *op. cit.*, p. 14.

B. JOHN THE BAPTIST

The suggestion that Apollos was associated with the Baptist movement and the fact that the narratives of Jesus' and John's infancy stand side by side in the Third Gospel commit the historian to an inquiry into the relationship between Jesus and John. Historical criticism can demonstrate that the proper background for the form of the Lukan infancy narratives is the historical relationship between originally separate Baptist and Christian movements in Palestine.

Recent attempts have been made to change the historical picture of John the Baptist radically by the use of later sources. Robert Eisler in *The Messiah Jesus and John the Baptist* (1931), pp. 223–226) introduced the theory that a biographical account of the Baptist composed by one of his disciples was used by Josephus in his " Capture of Jerusalem " as known from the " Slavonic " version of Josephus' *Wars of the Jews*. R. Reitzenstein in *"Das mandäische Buch des Herrn der Grösse und die Evangelienüberlieferung"* (*Sitzungsberichte der Heidelberger Akademie der Wissenschaften*, 1919, Abhandlung 12) introduced the literature of the Baptist sect of later Mesopotamia, the Mandaeans, as a means of understanding the portrait of John. Carl Kraeling, (*John the Baptist*, 1951) evaluated Eisler's and Reitzenstein's hypotheses. Kraeling has justly noted that neither yields new information which is more valuable than that already contained in the Gospel narratives.

Although the roots of Mandaean literature are difficult to trace and its precise relationship to the earlier John the Baptist movement almost impossible to ascertain, it is of great interest because of the continuance of its movement up to the present day. A small sect survives in Iraq and Iran and is famous for its metal work and practice of magic. They are sometimes called " St. John-the-Baptist Christians." [8]

Harnack, Dibelius, and Kraeling all agree that the narratives of John's infancy had their origin in Baptist circles and indicate a historical relationship between John and Jesus which is to be ascertained only on critical analysis of the sources. According to Harnack, the story of John's infancy is very ancient and must have originated in the circle of the disciples of John. Originally the story

[8] Cyrus Gordon, *The Living Past* (1941); C. R. Bowen, *Studies in the New Testament* (1936).

of the Baptist and that of Jesus were separate. The passage Luke
1:39-45, 56, binds together the two entirely independent stories
and makes John " the preparer of the way for the coming of Jah-
weh the Saviour." [9]

Dibelius' form-critical analysis accounted for the story of the
Baptist as arising out of the Jewish worship of John, that is, out
of the Baptist movement.[10] " The autonomy and significance of
John in the Infancy Narrative demands that the story arose in Baptist circles, and as an early Baptist narrative it requires careful consideration in any discussion of John's antecedents." [11] Also on the
basis of form criticism, H. L. MacNeill believed that Luke 1:5 to
2:40 was the first attempt to link the Baptist and the Christian
movements. He thought that certain passages such as John 1:1-18;
3:22 f.; 4:1 f.; Acts 18:24 f.; 19:1 f. indicate that John the Baptist
was considered to be the Messiah by many of his disciples, and his
movement continued long after his death. At the time when the
two traditions were united, the prestige of John still stood very
high in the Christian community.

Kraeling described the Baptist movement as occurring in Judea
with its background in rural priestly circles. He concluded that
the historical nucleus of the infancy narrative of John comes from
this Baptist movement.[12]

The possibility of this historical phenomenon may be ascertained by examining information found in the Synoptic Gospels
and in the Fourth Gospel.[13] The Matthaean material is given in
ch. 3:1-17 (John's early ministry and the baptism of Jesus), ch.
9:14 (the disciples of John), ch. 11:2-19 (John's question concerning the Christ together with the reference to Elijah in vs. 7-15),
ch. 14:1-12 (John and Herod), ch. 17:9-13 (John as Elijah), and
ch. 21:25 (the question whether or not John's baptism was from
heaven).

---

[9] *The Date of the Acts* (1911), p. 154.

[10] *Jungfrauensohn und Krippenkind* (1932), pp. 5, 10.

[11] Kraeling, *op. cit.*, p. 18.

[12] *Ibid.*, pp. 23, 165.

[13] For Kraeling's analytical procedure, see the chapter on " John the Baptist and
Jesus." In his opinion, very little, if any, historical value may be derived from any
of the episodes except the baptism. Even the latter, however, presents historical difficulties (pp. 130–131). For indications in the New Testament outside the Gospels
for evidences of a Baptist movement, Kraeling pointed to the probable explanation
of Paul's reference in Gal. 1:22 (the churches of Judea) in relationship to Acts
1:15; 2:41 and 4:4; 6:7. The simplest solution to the enigma of the great company
of the converted is that large numbers of Baptist disciples entered into, or were
counted as members of, Christian fellowship (p. 172).

The material in Mark is distributed as follows: ch. 1:1-11 (John's early ministry and the baptism of Jesus), ch. 1:14 (John's arrest), ch. 6:14-29 (John and Herod), ch. 8:28 (the question whether or not Jesus was John), and ch. 11:30 (the question whether or not the baptism of John was from heaven).

The Third Gospel records the material concerning John in ch. 1:5-80 (birth stories), ch. 3:1-21 (John's early ministry, John's imprisonment, the baptism of Jesus), ch. 7:18-20 (John's question concerning the Christ), ch. 9:7-9 (John and Herod), ch. 9:18-19 (the question whether or not Jesus was John), and ch. 11:1 (the fact that the disciples of John pray). The Fourth Gospel presents the story of John's early ministry in ch. 1:19-34 and the story of the independent baptisms of or by Jesus and John in ch. 3:22-24. (See also ch. 4:2.)

Even a hasty reading of these references indicates certain facts that stand out. First of all, only Luke records the story of the Annunciation and the birth of John. We notice, too, that Luke's order of the next events differs from the other Synoptics. Luke has the baptism of Jesus by John coming after John's imprisonment, whereas Mark has the baptism before the imprisonment and Matthew omits reference to the imprisonment altogether. Matthew gives the question of the disciples' fasting, an incident omitted by both Mark and Luke. John's question about the Christ found in Matthew and Luke is omitted by Mark. Only Matthew gives the discussion of John as Elijah, and Luke omits the question concerning whether or not the baptism of John was from heaven, a question which both Matthew and Mark include in their accounts. The Fourth Gospel is conspicuous for its omission of all incidents following the episode of the baptism.

Within the accounts themselves are other factors that are worthy of mention. Matthew 11:12, "From the days of John the Baptist until now," seems to indicate an interval of time between the ministries of John and Jesus which does not harmonize with the references in Luke 1:26, "And in the sixth month the angel Gabriel was sent from God," and Luke 1:36, "And this is the sixth month with her." [14] The Lukan reference seems to imply a short lapse of time

[14] Kraeling noted that this story, based on the assumption that Mary and Elizabeth are blood relatives, endows Jesus from his mother's side with any advantage of Aaronic descent that John could boast, making him, as a descendant both of David and Aaron, the natural fulfillment of national hopes for deliverance. "The story is a product of the struggle between Christian and Baptist loyalties, an effort of the Christian disciples to show the superiority of their Master." *Op. cit.*, p. 126.

between the birth of John and the birth of Jesus. If this is the case, it is difficult to understand the Matthaean reference which seems to imply a lapse of considerable time between John's ministry and the beginning of Jesus'. If their births were so close together, the advent of their individual ministries would have been nearly simultaneous or one began his ministry several years later in life than the other. In any case, an established Baptist movement, based on John's own ministry, must be presumed to have taken place before the advent of Jesus' ministry. This is clear from the New Testament record. The implication of Matt. 11:12, together with the facts just mentioned, is that if Jesus were about thirty years of age when he began his ministry (the usual presumption), John must have been considerably younger than thirty when he began his, or if John were of the usual age of thirty at the commencement of his own ministry, Jesus must have been considerably older than the age usually ascribed to him when he began his. Rather than furnishing historical chronological data, Luke 1:26 and 36 are evidences of the attempt to subordinate the ministries of John and Jesus. The six months' interval is a legendary expression of close subordination. It is one of the links by which the two originally separate infancy traditions were joined.

The Lukan narrative assigns the Magnificat (ch. 1:46-55) to Mary. A few variant readings of Luke 1:34,[15] however, give " Elizabeth " instead of " Mary," which makes the following verses refer originally to John rather than to Jesus. Harnack's suggestion that the Magnificat really did belong originally to the Baptist tradition has found acceptance by many scholars.[16] The place of Mary in the accepted text may indicate the attempt by the early church to decrease some of the honor that tradition had ascribed to John.

The accounts of John's early ministry show another interesting point. Mark's quotation from Malachi (LXX) has been changed (Mark 1:2; Mal. 3:1). Malachi reads: " *prosopou mou.*" As it appears in Mark, it reads: " *prosopou sou.*" By changing the personal pronoun from the first person to the second, the author of

---

[15] A few MSS. of Latin Gospels, a, b, 1. See Nestle's *Greek New Testament.* See also MacNeill, " *The Sitz im Leben* of Luke 1:5 to 2:20," JBL, Vol. LXV, June, 1946, p. 124 and J. H. Bernard, *op. cit.,* pp. 212 ff.

[16] " Das Magnificat der Elisabet nebst einigen Bemerkungen zu Luk. 1 und 2," *Sitzungsberichte der kgl. preuss. Akademie der Wissenschaften zu Berlin* (1900), pp. 538–556. Cf. Kraeling, *op. cit.,* pp. 169, 208.

Hugh J. Schonfield, who tried to reconstruct the Nativity of John, included the Magnificat in the Johannine narrative. The *Lost " Book of the Nativity of John "* (1929), p. 42.

the Second Gospel effected the subordination of John to Jesus.

The stories of the baptism also are interesting. Matthew says, " *This* is my beloved son," [17] whereas Mark and Luke say, " Thou art my beloved son." In the latter, the theophany is addressed to Jesus. In the former, it is addressed to John and to the others standing by. Furthermore, the order of events in Luke is different, as mentioned above, and no reference is made to Jesus' baptism *by* John. Most interesting, however, is the fact that the Fourth Gospel records the baptism incident but in a totally different way. It leaves out Jesus' baptism by John. Instead, it records the fact that Jesus and his disciples baptized (John 3:22-24, but cf. John 4:2) , and that John was also baptizing. Here the baptism story presents Jesus' baptism as parallel with John's, whereas in the Synoptic account Jesus is obviously subordinate to John. This may indicate that the Johannine account should not be considered to be parallel with the accounts of the baptism in the Synoptics. It may have an entirely different point of reference. However, the association that the Fourth Gospel makes between the incident of baptism and the imprisonment of John seems to indicate that the account of the baptism in the Fourth Gospel is parallel to the Synoptic accounts but is an attempt to give still another interpretation to the same event. Furthermore, it may be that neither the Synoptics nor the Fourth Gospel gives the complete or precise record of what actually happened historically between John and Jesus. Possibly each account is one aspect of a whole period in the life of Jesus when he really was baptized by John and then proceeded to carry on his own baptizing activities, all within a relatively short period of time.

Against the judgments of Morton Enslin, who did not believe that any historical relationship existed between Jesus and John (*Christian Beginnings*, 1938, p. 151), and Klausner, who maintained that Jesus was baptized by John, but that John had no personal acquaintance with Jesus, nor did he recognize Jesus' Messiahship (*Jesus of Nazareth*, 1925, p. 249), the conclusion may be drawn that the Synoptics record the early phase of the " baptist event," and the Fourth Gospel records the last phase of the development in the relations between John and Jesus. The choice of materials, therefore, from whatever sources were available was determined by the particular purpose of each individual Evangelical writer. Nevertheless, the very choice of materials indicates a pur-

[17] " Thou art " is given as a variant reading.

pose of the writer of the Fourth Gospel (and even of Luke) that was motivated by something other than an interest in the actual facts. He wanted to establish a definite relationship between Jesus and John in the minds of the people according to what it ought to have been and not according to what it actually was. Or it may have been that he did not so much try to change the facts of what happened historically as he tried to clear up some misunderstanding concerning the relationship between Jesus and John which he could do only by a careful choice of the facts and by the way in which he related them.

The material in the Synoptics and in the Fourth Gospel reflects a tension between the disciples of Jesus and the disciples of John in the days of the early church. There is no historical certainty in the accounts. Details vary. Legendary characteristics are prevalent, and the apologetic motives of the writers stand out. The Synoptics, by means of the forerunner theory and the Fourth Gospel with the Lamb of God motif, made deliberate attempts to subordinate John to Jesus by demonstrating without question that John provided the proper preparation for the historical Jesus and that Jesus, himself, was truly the Christ.

Underlying the Gospels is the presupposition that Jesus was the Messiah. Much of the material set forth in them is in defense of that presupposition as over against the claim of the Baptists that John and not Jesus was the Messiah. The accounts may be understood as deliberately designed to settle the question of the relationship between the two in a manner that was favorable to the Messianic status of Jesus. The Christians, therefore, interpreted John as the forerunner of Jesus and gave John a position subordinate to our Lord. This interpretation was made sometime after the historical relationship between John and Jesus at a time when the Baptists, as well as the Christians, were fighting to maintain their religious prestige.

After Jesus had begun his ministry and had attracted a following and after John had noticed this, it is probable that John thought that Jesus was the Messiah and may have asked, "Art thou the Christ or do we look for another?" Furthermore, John himself may have consciously taken a position subordinate to Jesus, whereas following his sudden death, his followers were not inclined to do the same. John, himself, probably thought that Jesus was the Messiah even though at times he may have questioned this. However, the loyalty by which his own followers were bound to him was never completely severed. They were devoted to his teaching and practice. After his death, they wished to continue it and did. Later when both the Baptist and the Christian parties had developed and had gotten farther away from their historical founders, the traditions no longer retained historical clarity. The interpretation, however, that the Christians gave to the whole situation was in general correct. The historical errors came at the point of details in the tradition and not at the point of interpretation of the tradition.

The infancy narratives in the Third Gospel are designed to subordinate John to Jesus, to show that from their very birth and prenatal stage there was a recognizable supremacy of Jesus over the Baptist. Knowledge of the Baptist-Christian controversy and how it was handled by the author of the Third Gospel not only provides an understanding of the sources of the Lukan narratives and the background over against which the narratives are set, but it also brings out another notable use to which the narrative of the virgin birth was put by the author of the Lukan story; namely, to demonstrate the superiority of Jesus over John.

The question of what light the Dead Sea scrolls cast on the relationship between John and Jesus is answered by W. H. Brownlee in his article in *Interpretation,* 9 (1955) , on " John the Baptist in the New Light of Ancient Scrolls," which appeared in 1957 in K. Stendahl's volume on *The Scrolls and the New Testament.* " Nothing in the Qumran Scrolls can shed any light on this question." (P. 53.) Brownlee's article may be referred to profitably for the light which the scrolls do cast on the background of such concepts as " the wilderness," " Make straight the way of the Lord," " repent," and " the Holy Spirit and with fire."

Most significant was Brownlee's pointing out that in the Qumran community the concepts of servant and child had been united. The Suffering Servant motif was one of wide application among the Qumran Covenanters. " It was applied to the community as a whole, to a special group of twelve or fifteen men who actually (or ideally) headed the society, to the Teacher of Righteousness, and probably also to the Messiahs of Aaron and Israel." Brownlee believed too that *The Thanksgiving Psalm* V (iii. 6–15) united the servant and child motifs, the " pregnant one " being the community as a whole with whom the author of the hymn identifies himself as its corporate head. Also, " the suffering of the one destined to be the Davidic Messiah is in connection with the suffering of the corporate Servant of the Lord." (P. 51.)

Here then the " servant " gives birth to the " child."

> I am in distress
> like a woman in travail with her firstborn,
> when her pangs come,
> and grievous pain on her birth-stool,
> causing torture in the crucible of the preg-
>   nant one;
> for sons have come to the waves of death,
> and she who conceived a man suffers in her
>   pains;
> for in the waves of death she gives birth to
>   a man-child;
> with pains of Sheol he bursts forth
> from the crucible of the pregnant one,
> a wonderful counselor with his power;
> yes, a man comes forth from the waves.
> (*The Dead Sea Scrolls*, Burrows, 1955,
> p. 403.)

C. PRIMITIVE CHRISTOLOGY

1. HARNACK'S THEORY OF THE RELATIONSHIP OF THE VIRGIN BIRTH TO ISAIAH 7:14

Harnack advocated that the idea of the virgin birth had its origin among the Hellenistic Jews of Palestine (*Date of Acts*, p. 147). He traced the origin of the idea of the virgin birth of Jesus to the practice of the early Christians by which they applied the Jewish allegoristic and haggadic method of exposition to the Old Testament. This practice was part of the pattern of a growing Christology. The impression that Jesus made was the occasion for the interpretation of many passages in the Old Testament in a sense that was foreign to them. James Moffatt, referring to Matt., chs. 1 and 2, said, " It is a piece of early Christian midrashic narrative, drawn up in order to show how the various incidents and features of the nativity were a fulfillment of Old Testament prophecy " (*An Introduction to the Literature of the New Testament*, 1915, p. 250). Alfred Loisy in *La Naissance du Christianisme* (1933) said that Matthew's legend has the form of a Jewish haggadic collection. Matthew, chs. 1 and 2, is presented by Harnack as a good example of this practice, and in the same sense too,

he said, Luke, chs. 1 and 2, is in the spirit of the Old Testament
(*Date of Acts,* p. 156). By means of this type of interpretation, the
belief that Jesus was born of a virgin springs from Isa. 7:14. This
was Harnack's line of reasoning. Guignebert, however, argued that
even had the idea of the belief in the virgin birth arisen from the
misinterpretation of the supposedly prophetic passage in Isa. 7:14
(Guignebert denied that this is a Messianic prophecy), the idea
would be nevertheless Greek, since the interpretation in question
is " according to the Greek text of the Septuagint " (*Jesus,* ET,
p. 122).

For a full discussion of the relationship between Isa. 7:14 and
Matt. 1:23, one should read Crawford Howell Toy's *Quotations in
the New Testament* (1884, pp. 1–4), Thomas James Thorburn's
*A Critical Examination of the Evidences for the Doctrine of the
Virgin Birth* (1908, Appendix E, pp. 144–148), George A. Bar-
ton's *Studies in New Testament Christianity* (1928, p. 11), and
Charles Cutler Torrey's *Documents of the Primitive Church*
(1941, pp. 48–49).

Much of the discussion of Isa. 7:14 revolved around the various
uses and translations of *parthenos.* The Greek Versions of Aquila
and Symmachus and Theodotion have *neanis* (young woman) instead of *parthenos* (virgin). Gesenius and Fürst support this reading as the older. Toy pointed out that in Exodus, Psalms, and
Song of Songs of the LXX, *almah* is *neanis.* Toy, Thorburn, and
Barton agree that the Hebrew *'a-lm̄ah* means a young woman,
whether married or unmarried. Torrey cautioned against too
much stress on what the word ought to mean. The important question, he said, is " what the Jews in the first century ordinarily supposed the word to mean in this particular passage, and as to this
the evidence seems clear." Torrey insisted that the Greek word is
not a mistranslation and this interpretation of Isa. 7:14 was not
only the most natural and most impressive interpretation, it was
also the usual one (p. 49). Barton thought that *parthenos* not only
is a mistranslation of the Hebrew but also was itself misinter-
preted. In Homer, he said, *parthenos* was applied to a young married woman (*Iliad,* Book II, 514). Because it was probably used
in this sense in the Koinē dialect of Egypt, the translators of the
LXX translated *almah* by it. In Attic Greek, *parthenos* meant an
unmarried young woman, and was apparently so employed in the
dialect of the Koinē known to the Evangelist.

Harnack left no doubt concerning the significance of his analy-

sis of the birth narratives. " We know nothing of Jesus' history for
the first thirty years of his life " (*Das Wesen des Christentums*) .[18]
Harnack's views on the infancy narratives are developed most completely at the conclusion of his *The Date of the Acts and of the
Synoptic Gospels* (New Testament Studies IV, 1911) . He included
the infancy narratives of both Matthew and Luke among a whole
series of " primitive legends of Christendom " which were all of
Palestinian origin, dating before A.D. 60. " No one can maintain
that these traditions cannot have taken their present form until
after the destruction of Jerusalem, or at least until after the year
A.D. 60. Neither can it be proved that they bear the trace of foreign, extra-Palestinian influence " (pp. 140–141) .

The virgin birth of Jesus in Matthew is, therefore, in Harnack's
estimation, a combination of two traditions, the conviction that
Jesus was born of the Holy Spirit with the reinterpretation of the
passage in Isaiah. " But the conviction that our Lord was born of
the Holy Spirit did not, according to Jewish ideas, involve the exclusion of an earthly father any more than of an earthly mother,
although ' ruah ' is feminine. Hence one may, indeed must, cher-
ish very serious doubts as to whether the idea of the Virgin Birth
would have ever made its appearance on Jewish soil *if it had not
been for Isaiah vii. 14.*" (P. 145.)

2. Johannes Weiss's Theory of the Relationship of the Virgin Birth to Psalm 2:7 and the Development of Adoptionist Christology

Johannes Weiss (1863–1914) sketched the development of the
tradition that led to the narratives of Jesus' birth along similar
lines. The idea of the birth of Jesus took shape in the development
of Christology in early Jewish-Christian circles in Palestine. He
detected in Acts 2:36 the earliest Christology in the New Testament. Jesus became Messiah through his exaltation. This is adoptionist Christology, implying that Jesus was not originally Messiah,
or Son of God, but he first *became* such by a definite act of God.
This idea has its analogy to the primitive Semitic idea which is
referred to in Ps. 2:7, " Thou art my Son, this day have I begotten
thee," and according to which the king is a Son of God by adoption on the day he ascends his throne. In Paul this idea took on a

[18] *What Is Christianity?*, lectures delivered in the University of Berlin during
the winter term 1899–1900 (ET, 2d rev. ed., 1901) .

different meaning. In Rom. 1:3 ff., he states that Jesus " was declared Son of God with power after the resurrection from the dead." Weiss said that here were combined two originally independent ideas: Paul's idea of the Son of God who was such from the beginning of all things, and the idea of the primitive community that Jesus after his resurrection was exalted " to be Son of God with power." The older idea, derived from the Palestinian community, is consistent in representing Jesus as a man, before his exaltation (Acts 2:22) .[19] In primitive Christian thought Jesus was spoken of as " of the seed of David." This idea naturally predicated a human, family descent. At this time the idea of a supernatural birth was unknown both to Paul and to the early Christians. Paul's reference in Gal. 4:4 to " born of a woman " signifies normal human birth. The genealogies in both Matthew and Luke indicate that the idea of supernatural birth was foreign to early Christians. The authors of Matthew and Luke, each in his own way, adapted the genealogies to suit their own specific individual needs, Luke by inserting the words " being the son [as was supposed] of Joseph," and Matthew by altering the conclusion of the genealogy. The old Syriac translation preserves the earlier form of the text.

Weiss was sure that originally Jewish-Christian opinion had regarded Jesus as the Son of Joseph. Through the development of the adoptionist Christology a Jewish-Christian author had come to advocate the virgin birth of Jesus by the Spirit, but in this respect, neither the author of this idea nor the early Jewish-Christians who accepted it can be identified with the Ebionite Jewish-Christians, who throughout their history maintained the human origin of Jesus.

3. Lobstein's Attempt to Maintain the Religious Value of the Virgin Birth

As early as 1890, Paul Lobstein, who was Professor of Dogmatics in the University of Strasbourg, developed the thesis that proper explanation of the source of the idea of the virgin birth is to be found rather than in heathen myths, in the development of early Christian Christology. His treatment of the narratives brought out that they were none the less legendary; however, unlike Harnack and Johannes Weiss, he did not relegate the narratives to obscu-

[19] *Das Urchristentum* (1914; ET, 1937, Vol. 1) , pp. 118–119.

rity, but insisted that even though they were legendary they were of great importance.

The occasion for his investigation was his feeling for the inadequacy of the positions of those who determine that the narratives of Jesus' birth do not belong strictly to the realm of history and then proceed either to ignore or to disparage their significance. Lobstein directed his investigation with equal vigor against those who maintained the conservative traditional view of the historicity of the virgin birth against all the results of historical research.

Lobstein proposed that the idea of the physical generation of the Son of God developed out of the early Christian consciousness which was closely akin to the religion of Israel.

If the faith of Israel invested the ancestors and heroes of the nation with a privilege which at the outset set a divine seal upon them, is it surprising that the Christian consciousness, absolutely convinced of the divine nature of the work and inspiration of Christ, should have attempted to explain the birth and nature of the Messiah by a greater miracle than any which had presided over the origin of the most famous prophets? Being greater than those who *received* the Holy Spirit from their earliest infancy, he was *conceived* by the Holy Spirit; His life proceeds directly from the life of God himself; His entire personality is an immediate creation of the divine activity; the primitive and essential relationship which unites Jesus to God is not only a bond of spiritual sonship, it embraces the life of the body no less than that of the soul: the divine sonship of Jesus is a physical filiation.[20]

On this basis Lobstein saw the miraculous birth of Christ as the material expression of an experience of the Christian consciousness which had been brought into contact with the person and work of Jesus. The supernatural birth of Jesus is then an explanatory formula that attempts to solve the Christological problem of accounting for the divine character of the work and person of Jesus. In quest of new arguments to support this theory, the early Christian consciousness discovered that the prophetic passage in Isa. 7:14 could be made to apply to the new faith. The Alexandrian Version, which rendered *almah* by *parthenos,* paved the way for the religious construction adopted by the Evangelist

[20] *The Virgin Birth of Christ,* trans. from the French (1890) and revised German (1896) editions, 1903. German edition *Die Lehre von der übernatürlichen Geburt Christi* (Zweite stark vermehrte Auflage, 1896), pp. 71–72.

(pp. 74–75). Lobstein, therefore, would disagree with Harnack's view that the virgin birth originated out of a mistranslation of Isa. 7:14. He would say instead that the virgin birth originated out of the Christian consciousness, and the text from Isaiah was one of several that the Christian community later used to support and convey its belief.

Lobstein used the term " myth " to classify the nativity narrative, but he warned that this designation in no way lessens the meaning or significance of the incident which is being described. " Myth, no less than history, can serve as a means and channel of revelation from above, and some of the profoundest conceptions of the Old and New Testaments have found their way to hearts and consciences in the garb of symbols containing immortal and divine truths." (P. 128.) When, however, this idea is transformed into a dogma, the tradition of the miraculous birth marks the first stage in the doctrinal evolution which ends in a purely material conception of the divinity of Christ and of the incarnation. This official doctrine actually lowers the notion of the Savior's divinity in the material and physical sphere and does away with his full and real humanity (pp. 95, 106 ff.).

D. FORM CRITICISM. THE THEORY OF THE ORIGIN OF THE VIRGIN BIRTH AS THE PRODUCT OF THE CHRISTIAN COMMUNITY

The most systematic presentation of the view that the idea of the virgin birth is to be found in the development of the religious consciousness of the primitive Christian community is to be found in the investigations of the advocates of the *formgeschichte Schule*. Viewing primitive Christianity from the standpoint of form criticism brings the history of that period under two principal procedures: an analysis of the literary type of the Evangelical narratives, and an analysis of the motives and factors within the primitive Christian community which produced the narratives.

1. Dibelius' Criticism of the Birth Narratives

The most definitive work on the birth narratives according to the form-critical method has been done by Martin Dibelius. His findings are elaborated in his *Die Formgeschichte des Evangeliums*

(1st ed., 1919; 2d revised ed., 1933), *Jungfrauensohn und Krip-penkind* (1932), and in *Jesus* (1st ed., 1939; 2d ed., 1949; ET, 1949).

a. *Their proper relationship to mythology*

Dibelius rendered great service to our understanding of the birth narratives by carefully defining and distinguishing between myth and legend. According to his analysis, the story of Jesus is not of mythological origin for the oldest witnesses, for the process of the transformation of the Gospel tradition from oral to written form, viz., the paradigms, do not tell of a mythological hero. Furthermore, a thoroughgoing mythological treatment of the life of Jesus would formulate his descent upon the earth, his death, and his liberation from death by resurrection and return to heaven. The most important events of his life for a mythological presentation would be the commencement of his work. In this life of Jesus, the thoroughgoing mythical formulation has not been carried out.

Dibelius substantiated his position by arguing that the story of Jesus lacks a mythological presentation of the descent of Christ upon the earth. The stories of the shepherds and Simeon bear witness to the greatness and announce the future of the child already born, but a description of the way in which God became man is lacking. Luke 1:26-38 tells nothing of true mythological event in terms of the divine eternity of the child in the body of the Virgin. Although this story rests upon the theologumenon of Hellenistic Judaism, it avoids every kind of presentation shaped mythologically. It is not a mythological event which takes place. It is legendary. The only narratives in the Gospels which really describe a mythological event, i.e., a many-sided interaction between mythological but not human persons, are the stories of the baptism, temptation, and the transfiguration.

Dibelius' views may be summarized as follows: The narratives of Jesus' birth perform the function intended of legends. They tell the story of a saintly man in whose works and faith interest is taken. The absence of them in Mark proves that they did not belong to the common ancient treasure of tradition of the church. The different quality of the narratives in Matthew and in Luke shows that an early tradition was not available, and the birth narratives do not belong to the content of the earliest proclamation of the Christian gospel. The beginning of the gospel was Mark 1:1 (*Jesus,* 1949, p. 50).

b. *The proper relationship of the virgin birth pericopes to the other legends of the infancy*

Dibelius developed his ideas of the relationship of the birth pericopes to the surrounding legends in this way: The earliest tradition designated Jesus as " Son " or " descendant " of David (Rom. 1:3; Mark 10:47). Jesus himself seems to have set little store by descent from David (Mark 12:37). It is quite possible, however, that in certain circles of the primitive Christian community there was interest in Jesus' origin, with the subsequent effort to determine his pedigree, i.e., the ancestry of Joseph. The genealogical tables in Matthew and in Luke bear witness to this. They remained in the Bible even though the belief in the virgin birth of Jesus renders the ancestry of Joseph unimportant. The story of Jesus' birth in Luke, ch. 2, even preserves the tradition of Davidic descent of Jesus' ancestors. It is also quite possible that the story of the Annunciation in Luke 1:26-38 aimed originally to attribute Davidic descent to Mary.

Dibelius also described how the grandsons of Jude, a brother of Jesus, are supposed to have declared in the reign of Domitian that they were from David's family (Eusebius, *Church History* iii. 20), and since the Jews were careful about preserving their tradition as to their ancestors, it is a natural supposition that the family of Jesus also may have had such information. But even if Jesus actually was of Davidic descent, and the purpose of Mark 12:37 was in no way opposed to kinship with David, Jesus' pure Jewish descent is not thereby assured, nor is a Galilean origin excluded. The Gospels describe Jesus as living in Nazareth until his public appearance and as being called a Nazarene or Nazorean. The term " Nazorean " is connected by the Evangelists with Nazareth in Galilee. Jesus is regarded, therefore, as a Galilean. Even if his family, regardless of whether it was of Davidic origin or not, had settled in Galilee some generations earlier, a doubt as to his pure Jewish character would still be permissible (*Jesus,* p. 36).

The prophecy of the virgin birth in Luke 1:34-35, Dibelius thought, must be regarded as an essential element in the whole legend of the Virgin and not as a later addition of some sort, since the first Annunciation of the birth (ch. 1:31) depends verbally on

Isa. 7:14, and this passage itself in Greek Judaism was understood to refer to a virgin's son.

Besides the classification as to the " Form " of the nativity narratives as " Legends " and analyzing them as originally independent stories, along with demonstrating how the use of these stories in the early church are best understood in the context of a developing Christology, form criticism has emphasized the place which these narratives have had in the broader context in the primitive Christian community.

Form critics generally paid little attention to the problem of the source of the virgin birth idea; Dibelius, however, in *Jungfrauensohn und Krippenkind*, (1932) discussed fully the matter of the Gentile, Hellenistic, and Jewish parallels to the miraculous birth, along the same lines pursued by the *religionsgeschichtliche Schule*. Although Dibelius, like experts of the *religionsgeschichtliche Schule*, overemphasized the importance of possible parallels to the Biblical idea in a pagan source, Dibelius was profound and correct in his observation in *Jungfrauensohn und Krippenkind* (p. 80) that the infancy narratives were not only a later excrescence to a growing Christology, but were also an addition to Christian preaching. The narratives as they now stand represent the tendency of Christian preaching to describe the wonder of redemption in terms of powerful, superhuman phenomena and to characterize it as a gift of God which penetrates into the confines of temporal existence.

The first understanding afforded by form criticism is that there never was a purely historical witness to Jesus. The description of Jesus' words and deeds was always motivated by a desire to give testimony to faith and formulated for preaching and exhortation in order to convert unbelievers and confirm the faithful. From the standpoint of form criticism the same principle is to be applied to the birth narratives.

2. MacNeill's Criticism of the Lukan Narratives

H. L. MacNeill, of McMaster University, had an article on " The *Sitz im Leben* of Luke 1:5 to 2:20 " in JBL, June, 1949 (Vol. LXV, Part II). His purpose was to find out " just where the contents of these chapters properly belong. What is their social and religious milieu? " (P. 123.)

At the outset, he recognized that these chapters in Luke (chs. 1

and 2) constitute a distinctive section, " one of the many ' unit-sections ' which the Form-Critics are finding in our Gospels," and that they did not originally form a single unit. As they stand, they represent the attempt in the developing Christian community to link or to blend what were originally two separate and distinct movements, viz., those of John the Baptist and of Jesus.

a. *Their relationship to myth and to history*

His discussion is also helpful for a clarification of the literary classification as religious folklore, and the relationship of the characters described therein to history. The narratives are *mythos* in the classical sense of the word, denoting historical material in which, or around which, fancy and imagination have to some degree woven legendary material. Of various kinds of *mythoi* the birth narratives are " high-class and high-powered examples of religious *mythos*." Here MacNeill rightfully challenged Loisy's characterization of them as " lower mysticism and vulgar supernaturalism," [21] and he straightened out many other scholars by insisting that their mythical character does not exclude them entirely from the realm of history. The minimum historical core which must be recognized is the historicity of John and of Jesus. " Even the persons and some of the activities of Zacharias and Elizabeth, of Joseph and Mary, and even possibly of Simeon and Anna may be reckoned, as historical." (P. 125.)

b. *Their* Sitz im Leben *in the primitive Jewish-Christian period*

The form-critical method finally led MacNeill to the conclusion that the material in Luke, chs. 1 and 2, is the precipitate of the life and faith of a religious community rather than the expression of any individual. He disagreed with Dibelius that only v. 34 is an interpolation into this section and preferred to assume that the whole of the story of the virgin birth, either vs. 34 and 35 or vs. 34 through 37, constitutes a somewhat later interpolation into this section. " The dominant thought in this section is not the Virgin Birth but the Messiahship of Jesus." (P. 126.)

Form criticism led him to conclude: (1) in these two chapters there is nothing whatever that is distinctively, necessarily, Chris-

---

[21] Alfred Loisy, *Les Évangiles Synoptiques* I (1907) ; *La Naissance du Christianisme* (1933) ; *Jésus et la tradition évangélique* (1910) .

tian; in these chapters Jesus is not a Christian, but the Messiah of Israel (ch. 2:26); they reflect the thought of Isa. 11:2-4; 42:6-7; Enoch 105; Psalm of Solomon 17:23 ff.; (2) in these two chapters we have pictured an early Jewish community whose members had come to accept Jesus as the " Son-of-David " Messiah (p. 128).

These chapters must be placed, therefore, thought MacNeill, in what is called the primitive Jewish-Christian period, somewhere between A.D. 30 and 70. The emphasis on the " Son-of-David " concept (to the exclusion of the " Son-of-man ") indicates a date in that period as early as possible. The nativity narratives are the product of a community somewhere in Judea, outside Jerusalem, probably not long before A.D. 60 (pp. 129–130).

3. Minear's Criticism of the Matthaean and Lukan Narratives

The results of a half century of critical historical research as they effect the interpretation of the birth narratives were beautifully summarized by Paul S. Minear. His remarkable essay which encompassed less than twenty pages maintains the respectability of the critical historical investigation of the narratives of Jesus' birth. He summarized as no one else ever has the significance of the stories, all according to the principles of modern research.[22] Minear proposed that in coming to an understanding of the nativity legends three important factors must be determined: the *Sitz im Leben*, the *Sitz im Glauben*, and the *Sitz im Loben*. This is how he describes these three categories:

a. *The* Sitz im Leben

The original " life situation " itself includes three factors: (1) the audience knew well the course of the later events in the story of Jesus; narrators and listeners alike thought backward from the period after the cross and the resurrection; the prophetic implications of the two Annunciations, the Magnificat, the Benedictus, and the prophecies of Simeon and Anna were revealed through the later experience, (2) the context for the tradition was provided by all the memories of the history of the church up

22 " The Interpreter and the Birth Narratives," in *Symbolae Biblicae Upsalienses, Supplementhäften Till Svensk Exegetisk Årsbok*, 13 (1950).

to the time of each successive reading, and (3) each individual disciple placed the story within the frame of his own personal experience, orientating it around his recollections of earlier encounters with God's mercy.

b. *Their* Sitz im Glauben

To each believing congregation each situation was also a " faith situation," because its significance stemmed from the contemporaneous relationship of that congregation to God. The plan of God for the salvation of the world which had first been revealed in the death and exaltation of Jesus had been at work (secretly) in all preceding episodes. In each episode of the life of Jesus is contained the whole eternal purpose. " The eyes of faith discern in each episode the major accents of that purpose: God's merciful invitation and stern judgment, the offense created by His word, the creation of a new Adam and a new Israel, the powers of the new age at work in those who seek that new age with all their heart, the manifestation of glory to the humble." (P. 12.) In this way, the whole Gospel furnished the central motifs in the tradition of Jesus' birth. Four motifs are predominant: (1) in the coming of Jesus, God moves decisively toward men in his loving intent to save them (Matt. 1:23; Luke 1:35, 37, 48-53, 55, 70-73) , (2) the expression of the various responses of creation to this divine activity (Zacharias' spontaneous doubt, Elizabeth's and Anna's patient, prayerful expectancy; Herod's wary cruelty and his blind efforts to protect his own autonomy; the overcoming of Joseph's temptation to be offended by prevailing moral standards by trust in the heavenly command; Mary's awareness of probable slanders but pure receptivity to the Holy Spirit, an instant readiness to let the Word of God have its way; the awareness of how even in such a shameful event for Jewish nationalists as the Roman census God uses the humiliation of Israel as the opportunity for its rebirth) , (3) the clear recollection of Jesus' place in the whole history of salvation (in the babe is realized the solidarity of Israel in the one new man; all the generations of faith meet here in a final unity; God in Christ has fulfilled his promises to the fathers; the Son of God was born of woman, born under the Law, born of the flesh, yet at the same time he was born of the flesh and of the spirit, he was a son of Israel-according-to-the-flesh and of Israel-according-to-the-spirit, for in him the two become one) , (4) those who told and heard the stories of Jesus' birth were themselves ministers of reconciliation to other men (the witnesses share the poverty and obscurity of the stable, the infamy and scorn to which Joseph and Mary were subjected; in their lives daily there is on one side the babe; the stories defy the enemies of the cross and bring about victory over their power).

c. *Their* Sitz im Loben

Finally, the birth narratives reflect a " worship situation." " The stories serve to make the Spirit's presence vivid, to bring the life of worshipers within that realm where God's sovereignty is again realized " (p. 17). The materials contained in the narratives which were employed in worship " will convey messages from the Master to his slaves, according to their present duties and temptations. They will convey messages from the slaves to their Master, according to his mysterious ways of ordering their affairs and of guiding their growth in grace " (pp. 17–18).

E. TEXTUAL CRITICISM

During the several generations in which the virgin birth had been examined from the various philosophical, theological, and historical points of view, the textual problems of the virgin birth pericopes came into sharp focus under the bright light of historical analyses.

The chief problem in the infancy narrative of the First Gospel has been the text of ch. 1:16. Much of the criticism of the virgin birth toward the close of the nineteenth century and into the opening years of the twentieth concerned itself primarily with the background of this text which constitutes the final words of the Matthaean genealogy. This aspect of criticism of the birth narratives captivated the imagination of textual critics since Mrs. Agnes Lewis' discovery in 1892 of the Sinaitic Syriac text which reads: " Jacob begat Joseph; Joseph, to whom was betrothed Mary, the Virgin, begat Jesus, who is called Christ."

At about the same time Conybeare had claimed that a passage in the *Dialogue of Timothy and Aquila* may be the true text of Matt. 1:16. " Jacob begat Joseph, the husband of Mary, from whom was born Jesus who is called Christ, and Joseph begat Jesus who is called Christ." This passage, Conybeare said, must be regarded as that which the original author of the dialogue read in his form of Matthew's Gospel. This form, too, he thought best accounts for the variants in the existing sources. " The reading of the great mass of Greek MSS. was derived from it by the simple omission of the words: 'and Joseph begat Jesus who is called Christ.' " [23]

Many scholars have taken the *Syr. Sin.* as the text which reflects the original " Ebionite " tradition of Jesus' natural origin. Before the discovery of this MS. Jesus' natural generation was assumed by most literary critics on the basis of one or both of the following factors: the priority of Mark, the priority of Pauline or other Gospel tradition which implied the natural or Davidic descent of Jesus. This position is stated in Christian Hermann Weisse's *Die evangelische Geschichte* (1838, p. 179), Karl Theodor Keim's *Geschichte Jesu von Nazara* (1867; ET, 1876, pp. 39 ff.), Carl von Weizsäcker's *Das apostolische Zeitalter der Christlichen Kirche* (1886, 1892; ET, 1894, Vol. 1, pp. 19, 127, 218), Heinrich J. Holtzmann's *Hand-Commentar zum Neuen Testament* (1901), and Oskar Holtzmann's *Leben Jesu* (1901; ET, 1904, p. 89). Included among those who used this textual evidence in support of an early tradition of Jesus' natural origin are Rudolf Otto (*Leben und Wirken Jesu nach historisch-kritischer Auffassung,* 1902; ET, 1908, p. 20), W. Bousset (*Jesus,* 1906, p. 6), E. Giran (*Jesus of Nazareth,* 1907, p. 56), C. Torrey (*Studies in the History of Religions,* 1912, p. 303), J. Klausner (*Jesus of Nazareth,* 1925, p. 232), and C. Montefiore (*The Synoptic Gospels,* Vol. II, 1927, p. 3).

In the *Expository Times* of November, 1900, Mrs. Lewis gave her own analysis of Matt. 1:16: " The Genealogy is a purely *official* one, having regard only to the social status of our Lord." All the so-called discrepancies between vs. 16, 18-19-20, and 21 may be satisfactorily explained by a consideration of those social customs which have been ever in vogue among Semitic peoples. From the *social* point of view, Joseph was the foster father of Jesus, and in any register of births in the Temple or elsewhere, he would probably be there described as the *actual* father. The possibility of this was illustrated by her from passages quoted from Robertson W. Smith's *Kinship and Marriage in Early Arabia* and by reference to

---

[23] *Anecdota Oxoniensia,* " The Dialogues of Athanasius and Zacchaeus and of Timothy and Aquila" (1898), p. xxi. In his article in " Academy," Nov. 17, 1894, he noted that the Vatican MS. of Tatian's *Diatessaron* in an Arabic version has the same text of Matt. 1:16 as the Greek " Dialogue."

her own Syriac Palimpsest of the *Protevangelium Jacobi* and *Transitus Mariae*. In this palimpsest, which was composed expressly for the honor of Mary and her perpetual virginity, the angel says to Joseph, " She shall bear *to thee* a son." Mrs. Lewis concluded that the sense in which Joseph was called the father of Jesus (Matt. 1:16) must be understood in the light of the narrative in ch. 1:18-25.

Both Thorburn's *A Critical Examination of the Evidences for the Doctrine of the Virgin Birth* (1908) and Vincent Taylor's *The Historical Evidence for the Virgin Birth* (1920) dealt at length with several theories of interpretation of Matt. 1:16-25. Thorburn and Taylor concluded that the readings of the *Syr. Sin.* in Matt., ch. 1, probably do not represent the original form of the text, the term *egennese* was probably used and understood by the early Christians in an official sense,[24] and the structure of the genealogy is artificial.

Taylor provided us with a complete and comprehensive analysis of the literary and historical textual problems of the virgin birth in the Third Gospel. His study was made principally over against the background of the materials which led P. W. Schmiedel and Usener in their articles in the *Encyclopaedia Biblica* on " Mary " and " Nativity " to conclude that not only was the virgin birth not an original part of the Third Gospel but also that Luke never taught that doctrine.

Taylor agreed that Luke, ch. 2, can be properly understood only when it is recognized that Luke probably did not know of the virgin birth when he wrote this chapter. He conceded that Luke had no knowledge of the virgin birth when he first wrote his Gospel (p. 32). The only conclusion however, which Taylor felt was warranted was that the virgin birth belongs to a later stratum of the Third Gospel. Taylor outlined the textual and stylistic evidence for the Lukan authorship of ch. 1:34 ff. His hypothesis was that ch. 1:34 ff. is an interpolation made by Luke himself on his own material.

Taylor's study is significant for authenticating the New Testament witness to the virgin birth. Belief in the virgin birth existed in influential Christian communities at the time when the First

---

[24] For discussions of " legal " descent, see: Gustaf Dalman, *The Words of Jesus* (1902), pp. 319 ff.; Alan Hugh McNeile, *The Gospel According to St. Matthew* (1915), p. 4; Philip A. Micklem, *St. Matthew* (1917), pp. 7 ff.; Kirsopp and Silva Lake, *An Introduction to the New Testament* (1937).

and Third Gospels were written. Matthew and Luke each in its own way is a different witness to the same tradition. " What is of chief importance is the view that in both Gospels we have, not so much two independent narratives of the Virgin Birth, as rather two independent witnesses to what originally was one and the same tradition " (p. 116). Much is to be said for the view that both expressions point back to a common original, to a primitive belief that Jesus was " born of the Holy Spirit."

The nature of Luke's source has remained a mystery. Taylor himself had noted that the virgin birth tradition cannot be traced to Mark or Q. Later in another writing, *Behind the Third Gospel*,[25] he indicated that Luke, chs. 1 and 2, is a source separate from proto-Luke. In his pamphlet on *The First Draft of Luke's Gospel* (1927), he showed that proto-Luke begins at ch. 3:1. Luke, chs. 1 and 2, then, was not a part of " L " but does rest upon sources which along with " L " Luke incorporated into his writing of the Third Gospel.

Taylor became interested in this subject after the publication of Burnett Hillman Streeter's *The Four Gospels* in 1924. According to Streeter's source theory and theory of composition of the Third Gospel, Luke, chs. 1 and 2, reflects a source distinct from proto-Luke (pp. 150, 165), and Luke himself may have been the person who originally combined Q and L, and then at some subsequent time produced an enlarged edition of his earlier work by incorporating large extracts from Mark and prefixing an account of the infancy (pp. 200, 218). " The first two chapters of Matthew are probably derived from oral sources, but the corresponding section in Luke is more likely to have been found by him in a written document, possibly Hebrew." (P. 225.) Later on, B. S. Easton in his commentary *The Gospel According to St. Luke* (1926) and P. Gardner-Smith in *The Christ of the Gospels* (1938) advocated that Luke, chs. 1 to 2, was part of L. Eventually questions that were associated with this issue were thoroughly discussed by J. M. C. Crum (*The Original Jerusalem Gospel*, 1927), John M. Creed (*The Gospel According to St. Luke*, 1930), William Manson (*The Gospel of Luke*, 1930), Frederick C. Grant (*The Growth of the Gospels*, 1933), and Floyd V. Filson (*Origin of the Gospels*, 1938).

The virgin birth pericopes stand as authentic and integral parts of the narratives in the first two chapters of both the First and

[25] " A Study of the Proto-Luke Hypothesis " (1926), pp. 165–166, 182.

Third Gospels. Even though this may be so, it is, nevertheless, necessary to offer a better explanation than those which have already been set forth for the apparent evidences of " interpolation." By saying that Luke at some time after he had written the bulk of his infancy narrative inserted the virgin birth pericope in his narrative, Taylor hoped to explain why the narrative indicates an interpolative passage. What Taylor actually accomplished was only the maintenance of Lukan authorship of the whole. He did not satisfactorily explain the problem which some scholars have noticed; namely, that ch. 1:34-38 is apparently not in literary harmony with its immediate context.

The best explanation of the literary problem, an explanation which is in keeping with the findings of both form criticism and textual criticism was suggested by Harnack and explained by Firmin Nicolardot in his *Les Procédés de Rédaction des Trois Premiers Evangélistes* (1908). Luke 1:34 ff., the virgin birth pericope, may be explained as the point of juncture between originally individual traditions, i.e., the narratives of John's infancy and the narratives of Jesus' infancy (pp. 169–170). The indications that an interpolator may have been at work on the virgin birth pericope stand out, not because particular parts in the passage are interpolations, but because the virgin birth story was originally a separate narrative and was introduced into the whole narrative as a means of forming a bridge between two originally separate traditions. It is irrelevant whether Luke accomplished this in one or two (or even several) writings. From this it can be seen why it is impossible to remove the virgin birth story from the infancy narratives in the Third Gospel on textual grounds. At the same time, this explains why the whole narrative is not a perfectly smooth literary piece.

Nicolardot's theory on the textual problem in Luke anticipated the solution which a combination of the findings of form criticism and textual criticism achieve. Form criticism has determined the original independence of the narrative of Jesus' miraculous conception from the surrounding infancy narratives. Textual criticism has established the integrity of the virgin birth pericope in the present canonical setting. These facts taken together imply that one hand was responsible for the finished product.

This principle applies to Matthew and to Luke alike. The author of each Gospel had at his disposal the tradition that Jesus was divinely conceived and virgin born. Each had on hand, in addition, other infancy traditions. The materials that each author chose to incorporate into his own Gospel were determined by the particular motives of his own writing. Finally, each author left on the traditions the imprint of his own creative insights. The problem that each faced was that of handling originally separate and sometimes diverse ideas and adapting them to a continuous narrative.

Outside the confines of traditional Judaism and still not in the pagan world at large, but in Hellenistic Judaism, important elements for an understanding of the background for the Biblical idea of the virgin birth are to be found. The traditions of Philo, John the Baptist, and the primitive Christology of the earliest churches all contributed to the historical foundation for the virgin birth.

The Philonic interpretation of supernatural birth implies that divine paternity is responsible for the noble human virtues. In this sense, then, the story of the virgin birth in the New Testament may be understood as an attempt to explain the nature of Jesus. His virtues were divinely begotten. First-century Christians who had come under the influence of Philonic thought would have understood the infancy narratives in this way: Jesus was begotten by God; this concept did not deny male parentage, but rather was intended to complement human paternal participation. Divine begetting supplies the explanation of the mysterious factor which accounted for particular or peculiar virtue, in this case, all the excellencies of Jesus Christ. For Philonic thinkers human parentage on both sides did not suffice to account for the superior personal qualities of an offspring. As in the pagan world, divine begetting explained the mystery of procreation itself, so in Alexandrinian Hellenistic Jewish thought, divine procreation solved the problem of the origin of superior virtues. In this sense too, a famous person was considered to be a child or son of God.

In spite of Harnack's rejection of the possible influence of Philonic thought on the early Christian circles which produced the virgin birth narratives, Philonic thought remains relevant to the question of the interpretation of the virgin birth, if not as a source for the virgin birth, at least as an important influence on

the audience of the birth narratives. What would Philonic thinkers have thought when they read the infancy narratives in Matthew and in Luke?

Guignebert's shrewd observation that even if the virgin birth
tradition had arisen from a mistranslation of Isa. 7:14, this would,
nevertheless, indicate a Hellenistic origin since the mistranslation
that is purported is of the LXX (Hellenistic Judaism), destroys
Harnack's argument against at least the possibility of a link between the infancy narratives and Philonic thought.

Harnack's recognition of the haggadic character of the Matthaean narratives was a noteworthy contribution to the criticism
of the narratives in question. Readers should now be aware, however, also of the haggadic character of the narratives in Luke and
of an even more important fact; namely, that Christian Haggada
drew its materials not only from historical backgrounds that ante-
dated the birth of Jesus but also from events in Jesus' own ministry.

Harnack was on solid ground, too, in his insistence on the distinction between pagan mythology and Christian legend. This distinction in literary type was later brought into even sharper focus
by the form critics. It is unfortunate that the words " myth " and
" legend " must be used with reference to the Biblical narratives,
since in both form and content Christian myth and legend are
so distinctively different from pagan mythology, myth, and legend. Christians may hope that someday a word may be devised
that will do for the word " myth " what *agapē* did for the word
" love."

A principal source and background for the Gospel birth traditions was the double meaning of *pais*, which stems from the LXX
rendering of " servant " as *pais* in Isaiah. In primitive Christianity
(The Acts of the Apostles 4:27, 30), Jesus was God's holy *pais*.
He was the wonderful servant and the wonderful child. The virgin
birth is the mythical expression of the combination of two important early Christian beliefs: that Jesus was the fulfillment of all
human expectations for a redeemer and that Jesus was the embodi-
ment of the world's hope for the appearance of a wonderful child.[26]
In the story of the virgin birth there is a uniting of two streams of
Judaistic tradition and a running together of important Jewish
and Gentile streams of thought.

[26] An excellent and detailed study of " *pais* " is to be found in W. Zimmerli and
J. Jeremias' *The Servant of God* (1957).

Criticism of the development of early Christian theology has produced an important frame of reference for the virgin birth. According to the Christological analysis, the virgin birth is one of several Christological theories in the New Testament which attempts to specify where in Jesus' life his divine nature originated. The consequent scheme is this: the resurrection, the transfiguration, the baptism, the birth, pre-existence. The chronological relationship of these interpretations is not of primary importance. Where the theory of pre-existence belongs chronologically in this scheme is almost impossible to determine. The order in which the others arose in Christian tradition is also elusive. What is important is the reason for the particular form and use of the virgin birth apotheosis. The story of the virgin birth of Jesus makes the idea of the origin of our Lord's sonship comprehensible to the non-philosophical mentality. One of the virtues of the New Testament is the diversity of modes of thought which helps to increase the range of its audience. Diversity of expression in the New Testament with regard to Jesus' origin ought to be taken not as evidence of contradiction in tradition but as a means of appealing to the greatest possible number of people. All the traditions in the New Testament were not directed to the same audience at the same time.

Historians and theologians who say that the doctrine of the virgin birth lowers the notion of Jesus' divinity into the material and physical sphere and does away with his real humanity err in two ways. First of all, it is by no means " lowering " Jesus' divinity to express his origin in pure moral ideology to an audience whose minds had been steeped with grossly sensual traditions about the origins of their gods and heroes. In the second place, the virgin birth does not do away with Jesus' real humanity. It states it. The formula is: conceived by the Holy Spirit and born of the Virgin Mary. Here are divinity and humanity side by side. " Virgin Mary " represents the humanity of Jesus. " Virgin " was relevant to pagan mythologists. " Mary " was relevant to Docetists.

Form criticism made a notable contribution to the understanding of the virgin birth by pointing out that originally the virgin birth was a pericope separate from the rest of the infancy narratives. This justifies the independent study of the virgin birth and helps to prevent the historian from falling into the harmonistic slough which trapped most of the rationalists and supernaturalists. The question of the virgin birth may be considered apart from questions pertaining to the star, the magi, the flight, the shepherds, the census, and all the rest of the incidents in the narratives. This judgment frees the story of the virgin birth from its canonical surroundings which were only secondarily associated with its source and original meaning and at the same time makes possible the stress on its primary significance; namely, its place in the development of Christology and the use of it in the early Christian mission. To form criticism we are indebted for the recognition of the true value of the story of Jesus' virgin birth as an individual literary unit.

The virgin birth cannot be displaced from the Christian faith by removing it from the text either on the basis of an appeal to a possible " natural " original of Matt. 1:16 or by dismissing Luke 1:34 ff. as a later interpolation.[27] On textual grounds these passages remain firmly established in the infancy narratives. The conclusions reached by Thorburn and Taylor on Matthew and Luke represent sound scholarship on the textual problems.

Although the silence of the rest of the New Testament does not necessarily imply either ignorance or denial of the virgin birth on the part of other authors, it is probable that the virgin birth was not a part of the early kerygma, and even upon its adoption into the Evangelical tradition it was not considered to be contradictory to other traditions. It was complementary. The virgin birth tradition is an independent witness to the particular belief of the early Christian community in the nature of Jesus. By being mythic in nature the virgin birth tradition acted as a popularized form of Christology which gave breadth and beauty to faith of early believers. The virgin birth tradition complemented perfectly the more philosophical Christological formulations which are found elsewhere in the Gospels and throughout the New Testament. Each witness has its own rightful place in Christian tradition giving evidence to the varied ways in which statements of belief in Christ's nature and the Christian mission were formulated.

Although it is impossible to determine either in what form the tradition of Jesus' origin from Mary circulated in the primitive

---

[27] For the theory of interpolation, see: Gustav D'Eichthal, *Les Évangiles* (1863) ; Adolf Harnack, *History of Dogma*, Vol. 1 (1897) ; Nathaniel Schmidt, *The Prophet of Nazareth* (1905) ; Alfred Loisy, *Les Évangiles Synoptiques I* (1907) ; Hermann Usener, *Das Weihnachtsfest* (1911) ; Martin Dibelius, *Die Formgeschichte des Evangeliums* (1933) ; Charles G. Montefiore, *The Synoptic Gospels*, Vol. II (1927) ; H. D. A. Major, *The Mission and Message of Jesus* (1938) ; William Scott, *The Gospel Records in the Light of Recent Research* (1941).

Christian community or when it was placed in its present literary canonical settings, its intrinsic value is verifiable, and the Christian community may be assured that its place in the Evangelical narratives was established with integrity.

It is inconceivable that these stories will ever be surrendered; and this can be said, not because they are familiar stories or beautiful stories, but because they are in the profoundest sense true stories.

— John Knox, *Jesus Lord and Christ*

CONCLUSION

KARL BARTH has rendered the church the service of rescuing the virgin birth from theological oblivion and setting it in its proper context. " We may joyously respond ' yes ' to the question — must we believe this? " He went on to add what it is that we are to believe.

The truth of the conception of Jesus Christ by the Holy Spirit and of His birth of the Virgin Mary points to the true Incarnation of the true God achieved in His historical manifestation, and recalls the special form through which this beginning of the divine act of grace and revelation, that occurred in Jesus Christ, was distinguished from other human events.[1]

In his interpretative analysis, Barth referred to the *mystery* of the incarnation and to the virgin birth which is a *sign* of that mystery. " The sign does not prove the thing signified, it communicates it. In other words, this miracle was not necessary for the incarnation. God could have chosen another process, even as Jesus could have done other miracles to signify the same word." [2] For him the virgin birth has noetic character, and on the basis of its noetic character it has a real place in the faith and theology of the church.[3]

Barth's theological judgment is correct, and the realm of the conclusions that he draws encompasses a number of historical truths to which the miracle points. The " noetic " character of the

[1] Barth, *Dogmatics in Outline* (1949) , p. 95.
[2] Barth, *The Faith of the Church* (1958) , p. 86.
[3] W. Norman Pittenger, *The Word Incarnate* (1959) , also rejected the view that the virginal conception is essential to the incarnation. He too distinguished between the metaphorical language of the birth narratives and the metaphysical truth of concepts concerning Jesus' incarnation which appeared elsewhere in the New Testament (pp. 66–67) .

virgin birth suggests a vast panorama of basic elements of the
Christian faith that were relevant to the ancient world and continue to be relevant to modern society.

The Christian concept of the virgin birth of Jesus had as its
background the total experience of the early Christian community,
which consisted of and came into contact with and desired to pro-
claim a message to peoples of diverse historical traditions. The
narratives of Jesus' birth in the New Testament reflect a milieu
of Jewish, Gentile, and Christian elements (Jewish: miraculous
birth motif, the LXX translation of Isa. 7:14, reflection of other
Old Testament passages, the double meaning of *pais* as servant and
child; Gentile: the universal child-savior motif; Christian: the
several primitive Christologies). In order to bring about contact
with non-Christians, the story of Jesus' birth had to be similar to
the stories of the births of the heroes of the other traditions. The
similarity exists at the point of the universal extraordinary birth
motif. The Christian story is different, however, from the others
because of the uniqueness of the personality it describes and the
uniqueness of his teaching that is reflected in it which combined
to leave a profound impression upon his immediate followers.

The canonical narratives of the virgin birth may be generally described as Christian stories in a primarily Hellenistic mode of
thought cast in a Jewish setting and designed to make a universal
appeal.

Because of the later apocryphal connotation of the word " virgin," the original significance of the birth from a *virgin* became
obscured. In early Christian times, both in Gentile and Jewish
circles, " virgin " had a more general and less specific connotation
than it had later on. The later Roman Catholic idea of perpetual
virginity, together with ascetic and Docetic tendencies, has clouded
the original significance of the word. The Christian narrative says
essentially that Jesus' conception took place in a young betrothed
woman. The birth narratives are the mythical forms of Paul's
mythic expressions " born of woman " and the " second Adam." [4]

The next thing to be noticed is not the lack of paternal participation but rather the divine participation in the conception. The
Savior was born within the marriage bond, but because of the
magnificence of his character and personality, his conception had

---

[4] I prefer to distinguish three levels of " mythus ": the language of Paul,
" mythic "; the language of the virgin birth pericopes, " myth "; and the language
of the surrounding birth narratives, " legend."

to be described in terms of divine conception. Only in this way could the divine and human characteristics of Jesus during his ministry be described and accounted for. Essentially the story of Jesus' conception teaches that two factors were at work in his origin: the divine and the human. Originally the emphasis was on God and Mary, the betrothed *woman*. The emphasis on virginity developed in patristic and Roman Catholic tradition and in Greek Orthodoxy in such a way that the birth of Jesus was entirely removed from the marriage relationship. The canonical narratives stand at the bottom of an ascending scale of developing " virgin " tradition.

The primitive Christian kerygma was a message of redemption and incarnation, concerning the one to whom was ascribed divine power. For the primitive Christian community in its Jewish-Gentile mission, Jesus was both Messiah and Savior. In the primitive Christian mind, the effectiveness of the salvation that he wrought could be accounted for only in terms of the direct influence of God upon his life.

The problem for the early Christian community doctrinally was at what point in the life of Jesus the divine power was originally effected. The New Testament bears witness to a number of attempts to place the apotheosis of Jesus. The resurrection, transfiguration, and baptism episodes, and the birth narratives form a series of such doctrinal attempts. These together with the Pauline theory of pre-existence and the Johannine formulation of the Logos doctrine give evidence of the most important early Christian attempts to date the apotheosis of Jesus either at a point in his life or ministry or in eternity.

Historical criticism treads upon treacherous ground when it attempts to supply the chronological order of these several apotheoses based on some evolutionary theory of early Christian doctrinal development. With our present knowledge of the New Testament and early Christian history, it is possible only to delineate the several theories in the New Testament. The data does not allow us to venture more than a guess at the order in which the Epiphany traditions developed. The theory that the Epiphany theories developed in definite " stages " is a superficial explanation of primitive Christian history. It is just as likely that the ideas developed simultaneously but in different areas of the early Christian church.

The New Testament record bears witness to the crystallization of diverse primitive Christian traditions. To unravel this complex

literary deposit and establish precise chronological order of the
ideas portrayed therein can only be conjecture. On the basis of
what the New Testament record reveals, to say that the virgin
birth is the fourth and last stage in a developing Epiphany tradition is to state only that this is so on the basis of the present theories of form and source criticism which are dominated by the
Marcan hypothesis that concerns a Gospel which contains the records of three of the Epiphanies but not the last. The virgin birth
is the fourth and last stage of the Epiphany tradition only in its
present literary form. The idea of the virgin birth itself may have
existed somewhere in the Christian community at the same time
the other Epiphanies were current in Christian tradition, but it
was some time before the idea of virgin birth gained enough importance to become attached to the established tradition and be
placed in the literature of the Christian community.

From what is known of primitive Christian thought, however,
the virgin birth was not a part of the earliest kerygma. The virgin
birth is neither stated nor implied outside the narratives in the
First and Third Gospels. On this basis it does appear that the virgin birth is at least a relatively late accretion to early Christian
Christology. The belief that Jesus was proclaimed Son of God by
his resurrection along with the doctrines of pre-existence and the
Logos certainly antedate the doctrine of the virgin birth as integral to the content of the early Christian evangelizing proclamation.

The doctrine of the virgin birth ought to be understood in relation to the early Christian kerygma as an attempt to popularize
Christology. The Pauline ideas of a resurrection apotheosis or pre-
existence as well as the Johannine theory of the Logos made an
appeal primarily to cultured and educated minds. The virgin
birth tradition was an Epiphany tradition that was akin to the
mentality of the masses. It was popular tradition. It is unrealistic
to state that the virgin birth is in conflict with or contradictory to
the Pauline and Johannine doctrines of Christ. These ideas are
contradictory only in the minds of scholars who assume that the
audience at which the gospel was directed was all of the same mind
and culture. The story of the virgin birth would make an appeal
to the uncultured and the uneducated, to the young and to the
simple, to the oppressed and to the idealistic. An Epiphany dated
at Jesus' birth had great popular and universal appeal because of
the tremendous interest which the miraculous birth and child

motif held in ancient Gentile and Jewish society. The virgin birth
is a secondary doctrine only for those who prefer another to clarify
the doctrine of Christ. To masses of early Christians the virgin
birth was unquestionably of primary significance. It is quite accurate to speak of the virgin birth as a late and primary doctrine.

The stories of the virgin birth became part of the literature of
Christianity at a time when the Christian community was attempting to convert the world to Christ. As they stand in their
respective Gospels they reflect a Jewish-Gentile Christian mission.
The narratives both in Matthew and in Luke are designed to appeal to Jews. Matthew's attaching the birth to prophecy and to the
Davidic line as well as the association of the birth with Bethlehem
is meant to imply and to teach that Jesus Christ is Israel's expected redeemer. The flight into Egypt is intended to associate
Christ with ancient Jewish tradition of deliverance and redemption from bondage. The Herod incident is an attempt to show
that Christ too was subject to the vicissitudes that Israel had had
to tolerate for years at the hands of dictatorial antagonists and
that the new child was immune to these aggressors. This incident
had another implication, however. To the Gentile mind this incident was analogous to the motif in antiquity of the Evil One who
sought the destruction of the newborn babe.

Whereas the Matthaean narrative is primarily Jewish and secondarily Gentile in its character and directive, the Lukan tradition is more of a true mixture of Gentile and Jewish motifs. The
dominant theme in the Lukan tradition is the attempt to merge
the Baptist movement with the Christian. As the Second Gospel
subordinates John to Jesus by the forerunner theory and the
Fourth Gospel effects the reconciliation between the two movements favorable to Christianity by means of the " Lamb of God "
theme, so the Third Gospel is witness to a third means of effect-
ing the subordination of John to Jesus. The birth of Jesus is more
spectacular than the birth of John. Both the mother of the unborn child and the unborn child himself recognize the supremacy
of Jesus, even before Jesus' birth.

The Jewish motifs are obvious in Luke in the language of the
hymns, in Jesus' Davidic significance, in the birth at Bethlehem,
and in the circumcision scene. The more characteristic Gentile
note is struck by the census, the shepherds, the angelic host, the
swaddling clothes, and the pastoral scene. In their canonical form
the virgin birth traditions were meant to effect a complex of pur-

poses, for they had a complex and varied audience.

The virgin birth of Jesus ought to be maintained and believed in the twentieth century as it was in the first and second, an expression of Christology which formulates for the popular, primitive mind worthy and edifying Christian doctrine. This belief and the creedal confession of it are basic to the expression of Christianity as community. The absence of the virgin birth in the contemporary Christian World Mission is unthinkable. The acceptance and understanding of the virgin birth in an ecumenical age is imperative.

The myth of Jesus' origin and the legends that comprise this vignette present in primitive concrete form what New Testament authors record elsewhere in philosophical and abstract modes of thought. By the very nature of the story, the myth in addition encompasses a number of elements, individual ones of which have always been relevant and pertinent to different audiences. The myth of Jesus' origin and the accompanying legends perform a didactic, evangelizing, eclectic, and universalizing function in the church's attempt to communicate to many audiences many significant Christian truths.

The fact that a number of people in modern times interpret the virgin birth literally and insist that the birth narratives are " historical " indicates that even in modern times people think mythically. When a person thinks mythically, he takes myth literally as history. When a person thinks historically, he is able to discern the mythical element in a narrative. The Biblical interpreter who thinks historically sees the story of Jesus' origin as myth. Religiously, the individual who is able to discern the mythical element in the tradition and derive from it its meaning is the individual who has his faith rooted in history. Interpreters who deny the existence of the mythical element in Scripture are the actual mythologists of our time. They who discern, describe, and interpret the mythical element in Scripture maintain for Scripture its historicity and for the Christian religion its historical integrity. The existence of the mythical element in Scripture with the possibility of it being taken as it stands or interpreted provides the basis for its eclectic nature and its inherent universality and makes it possible for its readers to comprise a true " household of believers."

Mankind has always and shall continue to think in mythical categories, to express ideas mythically, and to communicate in

mythical language. Man's understanding of the nature and power
of his own religious ideas will come only as he is able to discern
when he is thinking mythically, when he is reading mythical language, and how to interpret this special and profound literary
category.

Those who insist that the story of the virgin birth be taken literally are simply admitting that they think mythically and are unable to perceive that in the name of history they are actually removing the origin of Jesus from historical connection. Those who
dismiss the virgin birth as a " myth " (in a derogatory sense) are
reflecting their reaction to an interpretation that they know is
wrong and admitting their ignorance of the area in which the
truth is to be found. The " supernaturalist " who is satisfied when
his interpretation of the virgin birth is exclusively the establishment of the story to be what he calls " historical " and the " naturalist " who is satisfied when his interpretation of the virgin
birth is exclusively the establishment of the story as " unhistorical " are misinterpreting in opposite directions the virgin birth of
Jesus.

The virgin birth of Jesus attests the humanity of Christ. The
marvel is that God became man. The central message of the story
of Jesus' origin is that he was born of a woman, a human being.
The fact which the virgin birth represents is that Jesus was a human being. The important word in the story is the proper noun
" Mary." What Paul expressed in the mythic phrase " born of a
woman " and John recorded in the religio-philosophical terminology " the Word became flesh " was put by the authors of the First
and Third Gospels into a mythical formulation, and each surrounded it with several significant legends.

In no way does the virgin birth obscure or obstruct the doctrine
of Jesus' humanity. The virgin birth obscures the humanity of
Jesus and his true incarnation only when it is seen through the
eyes of the Romanist who Marianizes it, the naturalist who ra-
tionalizes it, the supernaturalist who de-historicizes it, the historian
who demythologizes it, and the theologian who subcategorizes it.
The virgin birth enhances the incarnation. The word pictures
which the Gospel authors drew are subtle but forceful statements
in behalf of Jesus' humanity for a society and for primitive mentality which thought that the Savior was not or could not be human. The Savior was real! Amidst all the Christological speculation that followed the resurrection it was necessary to hold before

the world and the church the fact that Jesus was human in every sense of the word.

As the resurrection stands for the " Godness of Jesus," so the virgin birth attests the " humanness of Christ." [5] These two Christian facts stand at the end and at the beginning of the written Christian tradition in witnessing to history's most stupendous event — the incarnation.

Because of the mythical form into which this truth was cast, Christianity was able to evangelize the ancient world. The story of Jesus' origin in its Biblical form established a natural bridge between the Christian community and non-Christian society. The closest association between Christian and pagan tradition was at the point of the narratives of the birth of gods and heroes. Not only were these traditions the most comparable, they were also the most popular. The Christian story made it possible for God's Word concerning incarnation to be communicated to the hearts of the masses of men. Although Douglas Edwards was of the " Machen School " and insisted that the virgin birth was neither a legend nor a dogma but a fact in history, by his reverse and incorrect literary analysis of the narrative he did reach the correct conclusion when he said, " Had it not been for the Virgin Birth it is highly improbable that the Doctrine of the Incarnation would have ever gained a prominent lodging in the human mind " (*The Virgin Birth in History and Faith*, 1943, p. 142).

The Christian myth stood out in sharp contrast to pagan mythologies. From the Evangelical narrative it was apparent that Jesus was a real human being. In the early centuries of Christianity when the church was in most intimate association with pagan mythologies the church fathers consistently used the story of the virgin birth as an argument for Jesus' humanity. Also, this story was the vehicle by which the church conveyed to a morally corrupt world its insistence on sexual purity and its belief in the sanctity of marriage.

The story of the virgin birth represents in mythical form two of Christendom's principal logical propositions: that God acted in history and that monogamous marriage is civilization's most important social institution. Among the great tragedies within Christian history have been the Protestant Fundamentalists' perversion

[5] I prefer these expressions to Tillich's substitution of " eternal God-man-unity " or " Eternal God-Manhood " for " divine nature " and " human nature " (Tillich, *op. cit.*, p. 149).

of the first proposition and the Roman Catholics' corruption of the second. The former's insistence on the so-called "historicity" of the virgin birth and on the association of it exclusively with the deity of Jesus has actually deprecated its historical value. The latter's speculation which had its outgrowth in monasticism and in Marianism inadvertently prevented the church from making a real moral impact on society. The result has been the Protestant heresy of associating the virgin birth exclusively with the deity of Jesus and the Roman Catholic heresy of deriving from the virgin birth a Docetic theology of Mary. Each in its own separate, distinctively different, decisive way has destroyed the Biblical, orthodox significance of the virgin birth. The total result has been that Christ has been made to be irrelevant both in his person and in his redemptive power to multitudes in modern society.

The virgin birth is a positive affirmation of the sanctity of marriage. In the narrative of Jesus' birth a preview glimpse is given of the Savior's own teaching on sex and marriage. Over against such religious and moral orders as the Essenes and those of the Qumran community, who did not believe in marriage, the Lord advocated it. Over against the promiscuous and polygamous practices of the Gentile world, Christ proposed the necessity of one marriage for life.

What is set forth in the record of Jesus' ministry as a bold and provocative moral injunction (Mark 10:6 ff.) is portrayed in the narrative of his origin with poetic beauty and esthetic sensitivity. The couple is betrothed. The marriage bond has been established. Within this relationship God acted. The atmosphere is charged with ethical purity and moral vigor. Those who receive this story with faith accept premarital chastity, heterosexuality, and monogamous marriage as a divinely ordained way of life. The fact that Jesus himself never married casts no disparagement on the institution. The demands of his mission superseded all of his family relationships. Actually the fact that the unmarried teacher advocated marriage makes an even stronger case for the institution. Jesus' life and teaching present history's strongest statement of the imperative of moral integrity and the sanctity of marriage. The story of his origin presents the most sensitive suggestion of the necessity and beauty of the sanctity of sex and morality in marriage.

The stories of Jesus' nativity are excellent examples of "Christian Midrashic haggada" on a number of Christian convictions.

The convictions concern more than the relationship of the Christian community by faith to the heritage that it shared with Judaism.[6] The stories of the birth of Jesus in the New Testament more than being midrashic haggada on Old Testament passages and concepts are midrashic haggada on Christian ethical teachings. The birth narratives, then, are " Christian Midrashic haggada " which reflect the following Christian convictions based on the teaching of Jesus and the faith of the earliest church: the unity of God and man in Christ, the sanctity of sex, the necessity of monogamy and fidelity in marriage, the superiority of Christianity over astrology, the superiority of Christianity over the Baptist movement, the fulfillment of Judaism in Christianity, the universality of the gospel, and the inevitability of the success of the Christian mission. The birth narratives performed a dual evangelizing and catechizing function in presenting these beliefs both outside and within Christian circles.

These ideas were expressed in mythical form, since it was only in this form that primitive peoples could grasp these truths, believe them, and have religious, ethical, moral, and social behavior motivated in their lives. Millions of believers throughout the ages have had a confrontation with God in Christ and have been inspired to moral and ethical behavior when reverently attending to the story of Jesus' origin long before they were able to comprehend intellectually the rationale of Christian ethics and be challenged by it. Often even after they have met the intellectual challenge of Christianity they find their convictions strengthened and their lives enriched from fresh glimpses at the truth and beauty which stream from the infancy narratives.

As the history of the human race is the history of the individual, so will the virgin birth of Jesus always have its place both in the history of Christianity and in the life of every believer. The story of God's wonderful *pais* (child-servant) speaks in every age to

---

[6] See M. D. Goulder and M. L. Sanderson, *St. Luke's Genesis* in *Journal of Theological Studies*, April, 1957. " The Lukan Genesis is a devout and learned man's meditation on the beginning of our redemption in the light of ancient prophecy, written either in an enlightened reverence for the reality behind the symbol, or a conviction that God must have, and had, fulfilled the scriptures." To them, as Matthew had presented Jesus as the second Moses, so Luke presented Jesus as the new Jacob (cf. Gen., ch. 37). " Fulfilments of Old Testament prophecy stand side by side with new outpourings of Holy Spirit to complete the pattern of the new Genesis " (pp. 12–30).

God's children of any age the Christian message of incarnation and redemption.

The time may not be far away when the whole church will confess, " I believe in God the Father Almighty, Maker of heaven and earth: and in Jesus Christ his only Son our Lord: who was conceived by the Holy Ghost, born of the Virgin Mary . . ."

BIBLIOGRAPHY

A Committee of the Oxford Society of Historical Theology, *The New Testament in the Apostolic Fathers*. Clarendon Press, 1905.

Albright, William F., " The Names Nazareth and Nazorean." JBL, Vol. LXV (December, 1946).

Altaner, Berthold, *Patrology*, trans. by Hilda C. Graef. Herder and Herder and Thomas Nelson & Sons, 1960.

Anselm, *Cur Deus Homo?* The Religious Tract Society, London, 1886.

Aquinas, Thomas, *The Summa Theologica*, Part III. Burns, Oates & Washbourne, Ltd., 1926.

Aristides, Marcianus, " The Apology of Aristides." 2d ed., by Joseph Armitage Robinson, *Texts and Studies*, Vol. 1, No. 1. Cambridge University Press, 1893.

Augustine, Saint, in Nicene and Post-Nicene Fathers, Vol. III. William B. Eerdmans Publishing Co., 1956.

Bacon, Benjamin, *The Story of Jesus and the Beginnings of the Church*. The Century Company, 1927.

Bacon, Benjamin, *Studies in Matthew*. Henry Holt and Company and Constable & Co., Ltd., 1930.

Bahrdt, Karl Friedrich, *Ausführung des Plans und Zwecks Jesu. In Briefen an Wahrheit suchende Leser*. Vol. 2 of eleven volumes. August Mylius, 1784–1792.

Bahrdt, Karl Friedrich, *Briefe über die Bibel im Volkston. Eine Wochenschrift von einem Prediger auf dem Lande*. J. Fr. Dost, 1782.

Bardsley, Herbert James, *Reconstructions of Early Christian Documents*. Society for Promoting Christian Knowledge, 1935.

Barth, Karl, *Church Dogmatics*. Vol. IV, " The Doctrine of Reconciliation." Part I. T. & T. Clark, 1956.

Barth, Karl, *Credo*. Charles Scribner's Sons and Hodder and Stoughton, Ltd., 1936.

Barth, Karl, *Dogmatics in Outline*. S.C.M. Press, Ltd., 1949.

Barth, Karl, *The Faith of the Church*. Meridian Books, Inc., 1958.

Barton, George A., *Semitic and Hamitic Origins.* Oxford University Press, 1934.

Barton, George A., *A Sketch of Semitic Origins.* The Macmillan Company, 1902.

Barton, George A., " Some Influences of Apollos in the New Testament." JBL, Vol. XLIII (1924).

Barton, George A., *Studies in New Testament Christianity.* University of Pennsylvania Press, 1928.

Bate, Herbert Newell, *The Sibylline Oracles.* The Society for Promoting Christian Knowledge, 1918.

Bauer, Bruno, *Christus und die Cäsaren. Der Ursprung des Christentums aus dem römischen Griechentum.* Eugen Grosser, 1877.

Bauer, Bruno, *Kritik der Evangelien und Geschichte ihres Ursprungs,* I, II. Gustav Hempel, 1850–1851.

Bauer, Bruno, *Philo, Strauss, und das Urchristenthum.* Gustav Hempel, 1874.

Bauer, Bruno, *Das Urevangelium und die Gegner die Schrift:' Christus und die Caesaren' von Bruno Bauer.* Eugen Grosser, 1880.

Bauer, Walter, *Das Leben Jesu im Zeitalter der neutestamentlichen Apokryphen.* J. C. B. Mohr, 1909.

Baur, Ferdinand Christian, *Das Christenthum und die christliche Kirche der drei ersten Jahrhunderte.* L. Fr. Fues, 1853.

Baur, Ferdinand Christian, *The Church History of the First Three Centuries,* 3d ed. Williams and Norgate, 1878.

Beard, J. R., *Voices of the Church.* Simpkin, Marshall and Co., 1845.

Bergeur, Georges, *Some Aspects of the Life of Jesus from the Psychological and Psycho-Analytic Point of View.* ET, Harcourt, Brace and Co., 1923.

Bernard, J. H., *Studia Sacra.* Hodder and Stoughton, 1917.

Bethune-Baker, James, *Early Traditions About Jesus.* Cambridge University Press and The Macmillan Company, 1930.

Bethune-Baker, James, *An Introduction to the Early History of Christian Doctrine.* Methuen & Co., 1903; 9th ed., 1951.

Beyschlag, Willibald, *Neutestamentliche Theologie,* I, II. E. Strien, 1891. ET, Vol. 2, T. & T. Clark, 1896.

Bierer, Dora, " Renan and His Interpreters." *The Journal of Modern History,* Vol. XXV, No. 4 (December, 1953).

Bigandet, P., *The Life or Legend of Gaudama, the Buddha of the Burmese,* Vol. 1, 3d ed. Trübner & Co., 1880.

Blakeney, Edward K., *The Epistle to Diognetus.* S.P.C.K., 1943.

Blunt, Alfred W. F., " The Apologies of Justin Martyr." *Cambridge Patristic Texts.* Cambridge University Press, 1911.

Bornhäuser, Karl, *Die Geburts- und Kindheitsgeschichte Jesu.* Druck und Verlag von C. Bertelsmann, 1930.

Bousett, Wilhelm, *Jesus,* 3 Auflage. J.C.B. Mohr, 1907. ET, G.P. Putnam's Sons, 1906.

Bowen, C. R., *Studies in the New Testament.* The University of Chicago Press, 1936.

Box, G. H., *The Virgin Birth of Christ.* Sir Isaac Pitman and Sons, Ltd., 1916.

Breasted, James H., *Ancient Records of Egypt,* Vol. 2. The University of Chicago Press, 1906.

Breasted, James H., *Development of Religion and Thought in Ancient Egypt.* Charles Scribner's Sons, 1912.

Briggs, Charles A., *New Light on the Life of Jesus.* Charles Scribner's Sons, 1904.

Briggs, Charles A., " The Virgin Birth of Our Lord." *American Journal of Theology,* Vol. XII, No. 2 (April, 1908) .

Bruce, A. B., " The Synoptic Gospels." *The Expositor's Greek Testament,* Vol. I. W. Robertson Nicoll. Dodd, Mead and Co., 1902.

Brunner, Emil, *The Mediator.* The Westminster Press and Lutterworth Press, 1947.

Budge, E. A. Wallis, *The Gods of the Egyptians,* 2 vols. Methuen & Co., 1904.

Budge, E. A. Wallis, *The History of the Blessed Virgin Mary and the History of the Likeness of Christ; Luzac's Semitic Text and Translation Series.* Vol. IV, *The Syriac Texts.* Luzac and Co., 1899. Vol. V, ET.

Budge, E. A. Wallis, *Legends of Our Lady Mary the Perpetual Virgin and Her Mother Hannâ.* Oxford University Press, 1933.

Bultmann, Rudolf, *Die Erforschung der synoptischen Evangelien.* Alfred Töpelmann, 1930.

Bundy, Walter E., *Jesus and the First Three Gospels.* Harvard University Press, 1955.

Burkitt, F. Crawford, *Christian Beginnings.* University of London Press, Ltd., 1924.

Burkitt, F. Crawford, *Evangelion Da-Mepharreshe,* Vol. II. Cambridge University Press, 1904.

Burkitt, F. Crawford, *Jesus Christ.* Blackie & Son, Ltd., 1932.

Burlingame, Eugene W., *Buddhist Legends,* Part I. Harvard Oriental Studies, Vol. 28. Harvard University Press, 1921.

Burrows, Millar, *The Dead Sea Scrolls.* The Viking Press and Martin Secker & Warburg, Ltd., 1955.

Burton, Ernest D., and Matthews, Shailer, *The Life of Christ.* The University of Chicago Press, 1901.

Cadbury, Henry J., *The Making of Luke-Acts.* The Macmillan Company, 1927.

Cadbury, Henry J., *The Style and Literary Method of Luke.* Harvard

Theological Studies, VI. Harvard University Press and Oxford University Press, 1920.

Campbell, Joseph, *The Masks of God: Primitive Mythology.* Viking Press, 1959.

Carpenter, Joseph Estlin, " Buddhist and Christian Parallels: the Mythological Background." *Studies in the History of Religions,* ed. by D. G. Lyon and G. F. Moore. The Macmillan Company, 1912.

Carpenter, Joseph Estlin, *The First Three Gospels,* 2d ed. American Unitarian Association, 1890. (Lindsey Press, London.)

Carus, Paul, *Virgil's Prophecy on the Saviour's Birth.* The Open Court Publishing Co., 1918.

Case, Shirley Jackson, *The Historicity of Jesus.* The University of Chicago Press, 1912.

Chalmers, Lord, *Further Dialogues of the Buddha,* Vol. II. *Dialogues of the Buddha,* Part V. *Sacred Books of the Buddhists,* Vol. VI, ed. by Mrs. T. W. Rhys Davids. Oxford University Press, 1927.

Charles, R. H., *The Ascension of Isaiah.* Adam and Charles Black, 1900.

Cheyne, Thomas K., *Bible Problems.* Crown Theological Library, Vol. VIII. G. P. Putnam's Sons, 1904.

Church Fathers, in Nicene and Post-Nicene Fathers, New York Christian Literature Company. *Eusebius,* Vol. 1, 1890; *Athanasius,* Vol. 4, 1892; *Gregory of Nyssa,* Vol. 5, 1893; *Jerome,* Vol. 6, 1893; *Ambrose,* Vol. 10, 1896.

Clemen, Carl, *Primitive Christianity and Its Non-Jewish Sources.* T. & T. Clark, 1912.

Clemen, Carl, *Religionsgeschichtliche Erklärung des neuen Testaments.* Alfred Töpelmann, 1924.

Clement of Alexandria, *Clemens Alexandrinus; Die Griechischen Christlichen Schriftsteller,* Band 12, 15, 17 von Otto Stählin. J. C. Hinrichs'sche Buchhandlung, 1905, 1906, 1909.

Clough, A. H., *Plutarch's Lives,* Vol. 1. The Athenaeum Society, 1905.

Cone, Orello, *Gospel-Criticism and Historical Christianity.* G. P. Putnam's Sons, 1891.

Conrady, Ludwig, *Die Quelle der kanonischen Kindheitsgeschichte Jesus'.* Vandenhoeck und Ruprecht, 1900.

Conybeare, Fred C., " The Dialogues of Athanasius and Zacchaeus and of Timothy and Aquila." *Anecdota Oxoniensia.* Clarendon Press, 1898.

Conybeare, Fred C., *The Historical Christ.* The Open Court Publishing Co., 1914.

Conybeare, Fred C., *Myth, Magic, and Morals.* Watts and Co., 1909.

Cornford, F. M., *Greek Religious Thought.* E. P. Dutton & Co., 1923.

Couchoud, Paul-Louis, *The Book of Revelation,* trans. from the French by C. B. Bonner. Watts & Co., 1932.

Couchoud, Paul-Louis, *Le Mystère de Jésus*. F. Rieder et C^le Éditeurs, 1924.

Couchoud, Paul-Louis; Alfaric, P.; and Bayet, Albert, *Le Problème de Jésus et les origines du Christianisme*. Les oeuvres représentatives, 1932.

Cowell, E. B., *Buddhist Mahāyāna Texts*. Part I, *The Buddhakarita of Asvaghosha; Sacred Books of the East*, ed. by F. Max Müller. Vol. XLIX. Clarendon Press, 1894.

Creed, John M., *The Gospel According to St. Luke*. Cambridge Greek Testament. Cambridge University Press and Macmillan & Co., Ltd., 1930.

Crum, J. M. C., *The Original Jerusalem Gospel*. Constable & Company, Ltd., 1927.

Cullmann, Oscar, *The Christology of the New Testament*. The Westminster Press and S.C.M. Press, Ltd., 1959.

Cumont, Franz, *The Mysteries of Mithra*. The Open Court Publishing Co., 1903.

Dalman, Gustaf, *Die Worte Jesu*, Band I, Zweite Auflage. J. C. Hinrichs'sche Buchhandlung, 1930. ET from first German edition of 1898 by T. & T. Clark, 1902.

Darmesteter, James, *Zend-Avesta*, Part II; *Sacred Books of the East*, ed. by F. Max Müller. Vol. XXIII. Clarendon Press, 1883.

Davids, T. W. Rhys, *Buddhist Birth Stories or Jātaka Tales*, Vol. I. Houghton Mifflin & Co., 1880.

Davids, T. W. Rhys, *Dialogues of the Buddha, Dīgha Nikāya*, Part I. *Sacred Books of the Buddhists*, ed. by F. Max Müller, Vol. II. Henry Frowde, 1899.

Davids, T. W. Rhys, *Dialogues of the Buddha, Dīgha Nikāya*, Part II. *Sacred Books of the Buddhists*, ed. by T. W. Rhys Davids, Vol. III. Henry Frowde, 1910.

De Bunsen, Ernest, *The Angel-Messiah of Buddhists, Essenes, and Christians*. Longmans, Green & Co., 1880.

D'Eichthal, Gustav, *Les Évangiles*. Tome Deuxième. Librairie De L. Hachette, 1863.

Descartes, René, *Discourse on the Method of Rightly Conducting the Reason and Seeking the Truth in the Sciences* (1637). The Open Court Publishing Co., 1910. Many other editions.

Dibelius, Martin, *Die Formgeschichte des Evangeliums*. J. C. B. Mohr, 1919, 1933.

Dibelius, Martin, *From Tradition to Gospel*. Charles Scribner's Sons and I. Nicholson & Watson, Ltd., 1935.

Dibelius, Martin, *Gospel Criticism and Christology*, I. Nicholson & Watson, Ltd., 1935.

Dibelius, Martin, *Jesus*. Walter de Gruyter & Co., 1939 and 1949. ET, The Westminster Press, 1949.

Dibelius, Martin, *Jungfrauensohn und Krippenkind; Sitzungsberichte der Heidelberger Akademie der Wissenschaften. Philosophisch-historische Klasse,* 4. Heidelberg: Carl Winters Universitätsbuchhandlung, 1932.

Dillmann, August, " Der Prophet Jesajas," 5 Auflage; *Kurzgefasstes Exegetisches Handbuch zum Alten Testament,* Fünfter Band. S. Hirzel, 1898.

Diogenes Laërtius, *Lives of the Philosophers.* H. G. Bohn, 1853.

Doane, Thomas William, *Bible Myths.* J. W. Bouton, 1883.

Dodd, C. H., *The Gospels as History: A Reconsideration.* The Manchester University Press, 1938.

Dodd, C. H., *History and the Gospel.* Charles Scribner's Sons and James Nisbet & Co., Ltd., 1938.

Donaldson, James, *A Critical History of Christian Literature.* Vol. II, *The Apologists.* The Macmillan Company, 1866.

Drews, Arthur, *Die Christus-mythe.* Eugen Diederichs, 1909, 1911. ET, T. F. Unwin, 1910, and The Open Court Publishing Co., 1911.

Drews, Arthur, *The Witnesses to the Historicity of Jesus.* The Open Court Publishing Co., 1912.

Dupuis, Charles F., *Origine de tous les cultes, ou, Religion universelle,* I, II, III. H. Agasse, 1796.

Dutt, Manmatha Nath., *Mahābhārata,* 3 vols. H. C. Dass, 1895–1905.

Eagleson, Walter F., *The Virgin Birth* (pamphlet). The Judicial Commission of the Presbyterian Church, Philadelphia, 1928.

Easton, Burton Scott, *The Gospel According to St. Luke.* Charles Scribner's Sons and T. & T. Clark, 1926.

Easton, Burton Scott, *The Gospel Before the Gospels.* Charles Scribner's Sons, 1928.

Ebrard, Johannes Heinrich A., *Wissenschaftliche Kritik der evangelischen Geschichte.* Heyder und Zimmer, 1841–1842, 1850, 1868. ET by T. & T. Clark, 1863.

Ecumenical Councils, The Seven, in Nicene and Post-Nicene Fathers, Vol. 14. Charles Scribner's Sons, 1900.

Edelstein, E. J., and Ludwig, *Asclepius.* Johns Hopkins Press, 1945.

Edersheim, Alfred, *The Life and Times of Jesus the Messiah,* 2 vols. ET from the German edition of 1883, by William B. Eerdmans Publishing Co. and Longmans, Green & Co., Ltd., 1943.

Edmunds, Albert J., *Buddhist and Christian Gospels,* Vol. 1. Innes and Sons, 1914.

Edwards, Douglas, *The Virgin Birth in History and Faith.* Faber & Faber, Ltd., 1943.

Eisler, Robert, *The Messiah Jesus and John the Baptist.* The Dial Press, 1931.

Eisler, Robert, *Orpheus — the Fisher.* J. M. Watkins, 1921.

Enslin, Morton, *Christian Beginnings.* Harper & Brothers, 1938.

Enslin, Morton, "The Christian Stories of the Nativity." JBL, Vol. LIX, Part III (September, 1940).

Erdman, E., *The Homilies of St. John Chrysostom.* Vol. X on *The Gospel According to St. Matthew* in Nicene and Post-Nicene Fathers. William B. Eerdmans Publishing Co., 1956.

Erdmann, Gottfried, *Die Vorgeschichten des Lukas- und Matthäus-Evangeliums und Vergils vierte Ekloge.* Vandenhoeck & Ruprecht, 1932.

Erman, Adolf, *A Handbook of Egyptian Religion.* A. Constable & Co., 1907.

Erman, Adolf, *The Literature of the Ancient Egyptians.* Methuen & Co., 1927.

Erman, Adolf, *Die Märchen des Papyrus Westcar.* W. Spemann, 1890.

Ewald, Heinrich, *Geschichte Christus' und seiner Zeit,* Fünfter Band. *Die Geschichte des Volkes Israel,* Dritte Ausgabe. Göttingen: in der Dieterich'schen Buchhandlung, 1867.

Fairbairn, A. M., *Studies in the Life of Christ,* 4th ed. Hodder and Stoughton, 1885.

Farrar, Frederic W., *The Gospel According to St. Luke.* Cambridge Greek Text for Schools and Colleges. Cambridge University Press, 1891.

Fausböll, V., *The Sutta-Nipāta. Sacred Books of the East,* ed. by F. Max Müller. Vol. X, Part II, 1st ed. Clarendon Press, 1881.

Ferré, Nels F. S., *The Sun and the Umbrella.* Harper & Brothers, 1953.

Fiebig, Paul, *Jüdische Wundergeschichten des neutestamentlichen Zeitalters.* J. C. B. Mohr, 1911.

Filson, Floyd V., *Origin of the Gospels.* Abingdon Press, 1938.

Finegan, Jack, *The Archeology of World Religions.* Princeton University Press, 1952.

Foakes-Jackson, F. J., and Lake, Kirsopp, *The Beginnings of Christianity,* Vol. II. Macmillan & Co., Ltd., 1922.

Foakes-Jackson, F. J., *St. Luke and a Modern Writer.* W. Heffer and Sons, Ltd., 1916.

Foucaux, Ph. Ed., *Rgya Tch'er Rol Pa.* Paris: Imprimé par autorisation du gouvernement a L' Imprimerie Nationale, 1848.

Frankfort, H. and H. A., and others, *The Intellectual Adventure of Ancient Man.* The University of Chicago Press, 1946.

Friess, Horace L., and Schneider, Herbert W., *Religion in Various Cultures.* Henry Holt and Company, 1932.

Garbe, Richard, *India and Christendom.* The Open Court Publishing Co., 1959.

Gardner, Percy, *A Historic View of the New Testament.* Adam and Charles Black, 1901.

Gardner-Smith, P., *The Christ of the Gospels.* W. Heffer and Sons, Ltd., 1938.

Gefecken, John, *Die Oracula Sibyllina; Die Griechischen Christlichen Schriftsteller.* J. C. Hinrichs'sche Buchhandlung, 1902.

Gilbert, George H., *Greek Thought in the New Testament.* The Macmillan Company, 1928.

Gilbert, George H., *Jesus.* The Macmillan Company, 1912.

Giran, Étienne, *Jesus of Nazareth.* The Sunday School Association, London, 1907.

Godet, Frederic, *Commentaire sur l'évangile de Saint Luc.* First published in 1869. ET from second French edition, *A Commentary on the Gospel of St. Luke,* Vol. 1, 4th ed. T. & T. Clark, 1887.

Goguel, Maurice, *Au Seuil de L'évangile Jean-Baptiste.* Payot, 1928.

Goguel, Maurice, *Jésus.* Payot, 1950.

Goguel, Maurice, *Jésus de Nazareth — Mythe ou Histoire?* Payot, 1925. ET by T. F. Unwin, Ltd., 1926.

Goguel, Maurice, *La Vie de Jésus; Jésus et les origines du Christianisme,* I. Payot, 1932. ET by George Allen & Unwin, Ltd., 1933.

Goodspeed, Edgar J., *Die ältesten Apologeten.* Vandenhoeck & Ruprecht, 1914.

Goodspeed, Edgar J., *A History of Early Christian Literature.* The University of Chicago Press, 1942.

Goodspeed, Edgar J., *Strange New Gospels.* The University of Chicago Press, 1931.

Gordon, Cyrus. *The Living Past.* The John Day Company, 1941.

Gordon, Cyrus, *The Loves and Wars of Baal and Anat.* Princeton University Press, 1943.

Gore, Charles, *Dissertations on Subjects Connected with the Incarnation.* John Murray and Charles Scribner's Sons, 1895.

Gore, Charles, *Jesus of Nazareth.* Oxford University Press and Henry Holt and Company, 1929.

Grant, Frederick C., *The Gospels — Their Origin and Their Growth.* Harper & Brothers and Faber & Faber, Ltd., 1957.

Grant, Frederick C., *The Growth of the Gospels.* Abingdon Press, 1933.

Grant, Frederick C., *An Introduction to New Testament Thought.* Abingdon-Cokesbury Press, 1950.

Gressmann, Hugo, *Das Weihnachts-Evangelium auf Ursprung und Geschichte untersucht.* Vandenhoeck & Ruprecht, 1914.

Grützmacher, Richard H., *Die Jungfrauengeburt: Biblische Zeit- und Streitfragen,* II Serie, Heft 5. Edwin Runge, 1906. ET by Eaton & Mains, 1907.

Guignebert, Charles A., *Jésus.* Paris: La Renaissance du Livre, 1933. ET by Alfred A. Knopf and Kegan Paul, 1935.

Guignebert, Charles A., *Des Prophètes à Jésus. Le Monde juif vers le temps de Jésus.* Paris: La Renaissance du Livre, 1935. ET by Kegan Paul, 1939.

Gunkel, Hermann, *Zum religionsgeschichtlichen Verständnis des Neuen Testaments.* Vandenhoeck & Ruprecht, 1903.

Hall, G. Stanley, *Jesus the Christ, in the Light of Psychology.* Doubleday, Page & Co., 1917.

Hardy, Edward R., ed., *Christology of the Later Fathers.* The Library of Christian Classics, Vol. III. The Westminster Press and S.C.M. Press, Ltd., 1954.

Harnack, Adolf, *The Date of the Acts and of the Synoptic Gospels.* Crown Theological Library, Vol. XXXIII; New Testament Studies IV. G. P. Putnam's Sons, 1911.

Harnack, Adolf, *Dogmengeschichte, Grundriss der theologischen Wissenschaften.* J. C. B. Mohr, 1893, 1914, 1922. ET in Theological Translation Library. Roberts Brothers and T. & T. Clark, 1897.

Harnack, Adolf, *Luke the Physician.* G. P. Putnam's Sons and Williams and Norgate, 1907.

Harnack, Adolf, *What Is Christianity?* G. P. Putnam's Sons and Williams and Norgate, 1901.

Harris, J. Rendel, *The Odes and Psalms of Solomon.* Cambridge University Press, 1909.

Hartland, Edwin Sidney, *The Legend of Perseus,* Vols. 1 and 2. David Nutt, 1894.

Hartland, Edwin Sidney, *Primitive Paternity, The Myth of Supernatural Birth in Relation to the History of the Family,* Vols. 1 and 2. David Nutt, 1909.

Hase, Karl August Von, *Das Leben Jesu.* Johann Friedrich Leich, 1829; Breitkopf und Härtel, 1840 and 1865.

Headlam, Arthur C., *Jesus Christ in History and Faith.* John Murray and Harvard University Press, 1925.

Hegel, George Wilhelm Friedrich, *Lectures on the Philosophy of Religion.* ET from second German edition by Kegan Paul, Trench, Trubner & Co., Ltd., 1895.

Hennell, Charles C., *An Inquiry Concerning the Origin of Christianity.* T. Allman, 1838.

Hess, Johann Jakob, *Geschichte der drey letzten Lebensjahre Jesu,* I, II, III. Johannes Bayrhoffer, 1773–1774.

Hess, Johann Jakob, *Lebensgeschichte Jesu.* Achte, vom Verfasser neu bearbeitete Auflage. Zürich, 1822.

Hilgenfeld, Adolf, *Die Evangelien nach ihrer Entstehung und geschichtlichen Bedeutung.* S. Hirzel, 1854.

Hippolytus, *Hippolytus,* Erster Band: *Exegetische und Homil. Schriften; Die Griechischen Christlichen Schriftsteller.* J. C. Hinrichs'sche Buchhandlung, 1897.

Hippolytus, *Hippolytus Werke,* Dritter Band: *Refutatio Omnium Haeresium; Die Griechischen Christlichen Schriftsteller,* 26. J. C. Hinrichs'sche Buchhandlung, 1916.

Hitchcock, Francis R. M., *Irenaeus of Lugdunum*. Cambridge University Press, 1914.

Hobart, William Kirk, *The Medical Language of St. Luke*. Hodges, Figgis, and Co., 1882.

Hobbes, Thomas, *Leviathan*, 1651. Cambridge University Press, 1904.

Hoben, Allan, *The Virgin Birth*. The University of Chicago Press, 1903.

Hoffman, Jean G. H., *Les Vies de Jésus et le Jésus de l'histoire. Acta Seminarii Neotestamentici Upsaliensis Edenda Curavit*, ed. A. Fridrichsen, Vol. XVII. Paris: Prostant apud, Messageries Évangeliques Distributeur, 1947.

Holtzmann, Heinrich J., und anderen, *Hand-Commentar zum Neuen Testament*, Erster Band. J. C. B. Mohr, 1901.

Holtzmann, Heinrich J., *Die synoptischen Evangelien*. Wilhelm Engelmann, 1863.

Holtzmann, Oskar, *Leben Jesu*. J. C. B. Mohr, 1901. ET by Adam and Charles Black, 1904.

Hopkins, Edward W., *India Old and New*. Charles Scribner's Sons, 1901.

Horner, George, *Pistis Sophia*. S.P.C.K., 1924.

Horner, I. B., *The Collection of Middle Length Sayings* (Majjhima-Nikāya), Vols. I, II, III. Luzac and Co., 1954, 1957, 1959.

Houtsma, M. Th., ed., *The Encyclopaedia of Islam*. Luzac and Co., 1913.

Hughson, Shirley C., *Modernism and the Birth of Christ* (pamphlet). Holy Cross Press, 1924.

Hume, David, *Enquiry Concerning the Principles of Morals* (1751). Clarendon Press, 1894.

Hume, David, *A Treatise on Human Nature* (1739–1740). Longmans, Green & Co., 1874.

Irenaeus, *Irenaeus*. Massueti, Domni Renati, Paris, 1710. Reprinted in *Patrologie Greco-Latine*, Tomus VII. Paris: Excudebatur et Venit apud J.–P. Migne Editorem, 1857.

Jackson, A. V. Williams, *Zoroaster*. The Macmillan Company, 1899.

Jacobi, Hermann, *Gaina Sūtras*, Part I. *Sacred Books of the East*, ed. by F. Max Müller. Vol. XXII. Clarendon Press, 1884.

James, Montague Rhodes, *The Apocryphal New Testament*. Clarendon Press, 1924, 1926.

James, Montague Rhodes, *Latin Infancy Gospels*. Cambridge University Press, 1927.

Jensen, Peter, *Das Gilgamesh-Epos in der Weltliteratur*, Erster Band. Karl J. Trübner, 1906.

Jensen, Peter, *Hat der Jesus der Evangelien wirklich gelebt?* Neuer Frankfurter Verlag, 1910.

Jensen, Peter, *Moses, Jesus, Paulus, drei Varianten des babylonischen Gottmenschen Gilgamesh*. Neuer Frankfurter Verlag, 1909.

Jeremias, Alfred, *Das Alte Testament im Lichte des alten Orients*. Dritte Aufl. J. C. Hinrichs, 1916.

Jeremias, Alfred, *Babylonisches im Neuen Testament*. J. C. Hinrichs'sche Buchhandlung, 1905.

Jones, J. J., *The Mahāvastu*, Vol. 1. *Sacred Books of the Buddhists*, Vol. xvi. Luzac and Co., 1949.

Jones, J. J., *The Mahāvastu*, Vol. 2. *Sacred Books of the Buddhists*, Vol. xviii. Luzac and Co., 1952.

Josephus, Flavius, *The Works of Flavius Josephus*. T. Nelson and Sons, 1860.

Jülicher, Adolf, *Einleitung in das Neue Testament*. J. C. B. Mohr, 1894, 1931. ET by Smith, Elder & Co., 1904.

Jülicher, Adolf, *Hat Jesus gelebt?* N. G. Elwert, 1910.

Jurji, Edward J., *The Great Religions of the Modern World*. Princeton University Press, 1947.

Kalthoff, Albert, *Das Christus-Problem Grundlinien zu einer Sozialtheologie*, Zweite Auflage. Eugen Diederichs, 1903.

Kalthoff, Albert, *Die Enstehung des Christenthums*. Eugen Diederichs, 1904.

Kant, Immanuel, *Die Religion Innerhalb der Grenzen der Blossen Vernunft*, 1794; *Sämmtliche Werke*. Leopold Voss, 1838.

Keim, Karl Theodor, *Geschichte Jesu von Nazara*, Zweiter Band. Drell, Füssli, 1867. ET by Williams and Norgate, 1876.

Kepler, Thomas S., *The Jesus of Formgeschichte*. New Testament Studies, ed. by Edwin Booth. Abingdon-Cokesbury Press, 1942.

Klausner, Joseph, *Jesus of Nazareth*. The Macmillan Company and George Allen & Unwin, Ltd., 1925.

Kleist, James A., *The Epistles of St. Clement of Rome and Ignatius of Antioch*. The Newman Bookshop, 1946.

Klostermann, E., *Das Lukasevangelium*, Zweite Auflage, *Handbuch zum Neuen Testament*, 5. J. C. B. Mohr, 1929.

Knowling, R. J., *Our Lord's Virgin Birth and the Criticism of Today*. S.P.C.K., 1904.

Knox, John, *Jesus Lord and Christ*. Harper & Brothers, 1958.

Knox, John, *Marcion and the New Testament*. The University of Chicago Press, 1942.

Knox, Wilfred L., *Some Hellenistic Elements in Primitive Christianity*. Oxford University Press, 1944.

Knox, Wilfred L., *The Sources of the Synoptic Gospels*, Vol. 2, *St. Luke and St. Matthew*. Cambridge University Press, 1957.

Kraeling, Carl, *John the Baptist*. Charles Scribner's Sons, 1951.

Krenkel, Max, *Josephus und Lucas*. H. Haessel, 1894.

Lactantius, works of, *Divine Institutes,* Book IV, Vols. 1 and 2. T. & T. Clark, 1871.

La Grange, P. M.-J., *Évangile Selon Saint Luc.* Quatrième Édition. Paris: Librairie Victor Lecoffre, J. Gabalda, Éditeur, 1927.

Lake, Kirsopp, *The Apostolic Fathers;* The Loeb Classical Library, I. William Heinemann, 1912.

Lake, Kirsopp and Silva, *An Introduction to the New Testament.* Harper & Brothers, 1937.

Lang, Andrew, *The Homeric Hymns.* Longmans, Green & Co., 1899.

Lange, Johann Peter, *Das Leben Jesu,* 3 Bücher. Heidelberg, 1844–1847. ET, *The Life of the Lord Jesus Christ,* Vol. 1. Smith, English, and Co., 1872.

Lange, Johann Peter, *Theologisch-homiletisches Bibelwerk, Erster Theil: Das Evangelium nach Matthäus.* Velhagen und Klasing, 1857.

Law, Bimala Churn, *The Minor Anthologies of the Pali Canon,* Part III. *Sacred Books of the Buddhists,* Vol. IX. Oxford University Press, 1938.

Lawson, J., *The Biblical Theology of Saint Irenaeus.* Epworth, 1948.

Leipoldt, Johannes, *Sterbende und auferstehende Götter.* A. Deichert, 1923.

Lessing, Gotthold Ephraim, *Gesammelte Werke,* Zeiter Band. G. T. Göschen'sche Verlagshandlung, 1855.

Lewis, Agnes Smith, *Light on the Four Gospels from the Sinai Palimpsest.* Williams and Norgate, 1913.

Lietzmann, Hans, *The Beginnings of the Christian Church.* Charles Scribner's Sons, 1937.

Lietzmann, Hans, "The Gospel Portrait of Jesus." *Contemporary Thinking About Jesus,* ed. by Thomas S. Kepler. Abingdon-Cokesbury Press, 1944.

Lightfoot, Joseph Barker, *The Apostolic Fathers,* revised texts. Macmillan & Co., Ltd., 1907.

Lightfoot, Robert H., *History and Interpretation in the Gospels.* Harper & Brothers and Hodder and Stoughton, Ltd., 1934.

Lightfoot, Robert H., *Locality and Doctrine in the Gospels.* Hodder and Stoughton, Ltd., 1938.

Lobstein, Paul, *The Virgin Birth of Christ,* trans. from the French edition of 1890. G. P. Putnam's Sons, 1903.

Locke, John, *A Commonplace-Book to the Holy Bible.* From the 5th London edition. The American Tract Society, n.d.

Locke, John, *An Essay Concerning Human Understanding.* Clarendon Press, 1894.

Locke, John, *An Essay on Human Understanding,* 2 vols. Ward, Lock and Co., n.d.

Loisy, Alfred, *Les Évangiles synoptiques I.* Ceffonds-près Montier-en-Der (Haute-Marne), 1907.

Loisy, Alfred, *Jésus et la tradition évangélique*. Émile Nourry, 1910.

Loisy, Alfred, *La Naissance du Christianisme*. É. Nourry, 1933. ET by George Allen & Unwin, Ltd., 1948.

Loofs, Friedrich, *Leitfaden für seine Vorlesungen über Dogmengeschichte*. M. Niemeyer, 1889.

Loofs, Friedrich, *Leitfaden zum Studium der Dogmengeschichte*, 5. M. Niemeyer, 1950.

Loofs, Friedrich, *What Is the Truth About Jesus Christ?* Charles Scribner's Sons, 1913.

Luckenbill, Daniel David, *Ancient Records of Assyria and Babylonia*, Vols. 1 and 2. University of Chicago Press, 1926, 1927.

Machen, John Gresham, *The Virgin Birth of Christ*. Harper & Brothers, 1930.

MacNeill, H. L., " The *Sitz im Leben* of Luke 1:5 to 2:20." JBL, Vol. LXV (June, 1946).

Major, H. D. A.; Manson, T. W.; and Wright, C. J., *The Mission and Message of Jesus*. E. P. Dutton and Co., Inc. and I. Nicholson & Watson, Ltd., 1938.

Manson, William, *The Gospel of Luke*. Hodder and Stoughton, 1930.

Maspero, G., *The Dawn of Civilization*. D. Appleton and Co., 1894.

Mayer, Arnold, *Le Christ Mythique*. Imprimerie Paul Richter, 1912.

McCown, Chester C., *The Search for the Real Jesus*. Charles Scribner's Sons, 1940.

McNeile, Alan Hugh, *The Gospel According to St. Matthew*. Macmillan & Co., Ltd., 1915; 3d reprint, 1949.

Mead, G. R. S., *Did Jesus Live 100 B.C.?* London and Benares: Theosophical Publishing Society, 1903.

Mead, G. R. S., *The Gnostic John the Baptizer*. John M. Watkins, 1924.

Melito, Bishop of Sardis, *The Homily on the Passion*. Studies and Documents, XII, ed. by K. and S. Lake. London: Christophers, 1940.

Meyer, Heinrich August Wilh., " Markus und Lukas." *Kritisch exegetischer Kommentar über das Neue Testament*, Zweite Auflage. Vandenhoeck & Ruprecht, 1846. ET from fifth German edition, T. & T. Clark, 1880.

Micklem, Philip A., *St. Matthew*. Methuen & Co., 1917.

Minear, Paul S., " The Interpreter and the Birth Narratives." *Symbolae Biblicae Upsalienses, Supplementhäften Till Svensk Exegetisk Årsbok*, 13. Uppsala: Wretmans Boktryckeri A.–B., 1950.

Mitra, Rajendralala, *The Lalita-Vistara*, 3 vols. *Bibliotheca Indica*. Calcutta: the Asiatic Society, 1882.

Moffatt, James, *An Introduction to the Literature of the New Testament*. Charles Scribner's Sons and T. & T. Clark, 1915.

Montefiore, Charles G., *The Synoptic Gospels*, Vol. II, 2d ed. Macmillan & Co., Ltd., 1927.

Morgan, James, *The Importance of Tertullian in the Development of Christian Dogma.* Kegan Paul, Trench, Trubner & Co., Ltd., 1928.

Moss, C. B., *The Virgin Birth,* The Congress Books, No. 5. London: The Society of SS. Peter & Paul, 1923.

Moulton, James Hope, *Early Zoroastrianism.* Williams and Norgate, 1913.

Müller, F. Max, *Nidānkathā, Jātaka. Sacred Books of the Buddhists,* Vol. I. Henry Frowde, 1895.

Müller, F. Max, *Vedic Hymns,* Part I. *Sacred Books of the East,* Vol. XXXII. Clarendon Press, 1891.

Murray, Gilbert, " The Future of Religion." *The Modern Churchman,* Vol. XLIII, No. 3 (September, 1953) .

Neander, Johann August Wilhelm, *Das Leben Jesu Christi.* Friedrich Perthes, 1837, 1852. ET from the 4th German edition by Harper & Brothers, 1849.

Nebe, A., *Die Kindheitsgeschichte unseres Herrn Jesu Christi nach Matthäus und Lukas.* Greiner und Pfeiffer, 1893.

Nicolardot, Firmin, *Les Procédés de rédaction des trois premiers evangélistes.* Librairie Fischbacher, 1908.

Nilsson, Martin P., *The Historical Hellenistic Background of the New Testament.* Harvard University Press and Oxford University Press, 1941.

Noack, Ludwig, *Der Ursprung des Christenthums,* I, II. Friedrich Fleischer, 1857.

Norden, Eduard, *Die Geburt des Kindes; Studien der Bibliothek Warburg.* B. G. Teubner, 1924.

Notovitch, Nicholas, *La Vie inconnue de Jésus Christ.* Paris: Ollenforf, 1894. ET by Rand, McNally & Co., 1894.

Oates, Whitney J., and O'Neill, Eugene, Jr., *The Complete Greek Drama,* 2 vols. Random House, 1938.

Olshausen, Hermann, *Biblischer Commentar über sämmtliche Schriften des Neuen Testaments zunächst für Prediger und Studirende,* Band I. *Die drei ersten Evangelien.* August Wilhelm Unzer, 1837. ET by T. & T. Clark, 1847.

Orr, James, *The Virgin Birth of Christ.* Charles Scribner's Sons, 1907.

Osiander, Johann Ernst, *Apologie des Lebens Jesu, gegen den neuesten Versuch, es in Mythen aufzulösen.* L. F. Fues, 1837.

Otto, Johann K., *Corpus Apologetarum Christianorum saeculi secundi,* Vol. 9. Jenae, 1872.

Otto, Rudolf, *Life and Ministry of Jesus,* trans. from the third German edition. The Open Court Publishing Co., 1908.

Palmer, Frederic, *The Virgin Birth.* The Macmillan Company, 1924.

Paulus, Heinrich Eberhard Gottlob, *Das Leben Jesu, als Grundlage einer Geschichte des Urchristentums,* I, II. Carl Winter, 1828.

Petersen, E., *Die Geburt des Heilandes. Religionsgeschichtliche Volks-bücher,* herausgegeben von Fr. Michael Schiele, I. Reihe, 17. Heft. J. C. B. Mohr, 1909.

Pfeiffer, Robert H., *History of New Testament Times.* Harper & Brothers and Adam and Charles Black, 1949.

Pfleiderer, Otto, *Die Entstehung des Christentums.* J. F. Lehmanns, 1905. ET by B. W. Huebsch, 1906.

Pfleiderer, Otto, *Die Entwicklung der protestantische Theologie in Deutschland seit Kant.* Freiburg, 1891. ET by Swan Sonnenschein & Co., 1893.

Pfleiderer, Otto, *Das Urchristenthum seine Schriften und Lehren, in geschichtlichen Zusammenhang beschrieben.* George Reimer, 1887, 1902. ET in 4 vols. by G. P. Putnam's Sons, 1906–1911.

Philo, The Loeb Classical Library. William Heinemann, Ltd. *De Cherubim,* Vol. 2, 1929; *Quod Deus Immutabilis Sit,* Vol. 3, 1930; *De Congressu Quaerendae Eruditionis Gratia,* Vol. 4, 1932; *De Migratione Abrahami,* Vol. 4, 1932; *De Mutatione Nominum,* Vol. 5, 1934; *De Abrahamo,* Vol. 6, 1935.

Pittenger, W. Norman, *The Word Incarnate: A Study of the Doctrine of the Person of Christ.* Harper & Brothers and James Nisbet & Co., Ltd., 1959.

Plinius Secundus, C., *Natural History,* Vol. 1, Libri I, II. William Heinemann, Ltd., 1938.

Plummer, Alfred, *An Exegetical Commentary to the Gospel of S. Matthew.* Elliot Stock, 1909.

Plummer, Alfred, *The International Critical Commentary; On the Gospel According to S. Luke,* 4th ed. T. & T. Clark, 1908.

Plumptre, E. H., *The Gospel According to St. Luke.* Cassell, Petter, Galpin and Co., 1879.

Pollock, Bertram, *The Virgin's Son,* 2d ed. John Murray, 1920.

de Pressensé, Edmond D., *Jésus-Christ, son temps, sa vie, son oeuvre.* Charles Meyrueis, 1865.

Pritchard, James B., *Ancient Near Eastern Texts.* Princeton University Press, 1950.

Quastin, Johannes, *Patrology,* Vol. II. *The Ante-Nicene Literature After Irenaeus.* Spectrum Publishers, 1953.

Rahlfs, Alfred, ed., *Septuaginta id est Vetus Testamentum Graece Luxta LXX Interpretes.* Stuttgart: Privilegierte Württembergische Bibelanstalt, 1935.

Ramsay, W. M., *The Bearing of Recent Discovery on the Trustworthiness of the New Testament,* 4th ed. Hodder and Stoughton, Ltd., 1920.

Ramsay, W. M., *Was Christ Born at Bethlehem?* G. P. Putnam's Sons and Hodder and Stoughton, Ltd., 1898.

Randolph, B. W., *The Virgin Birth of Our Lord*. Longmans, Green & Co., 1903.

Rank, Otto, *The Myth of the Birth of the Hero*. Vintage Books, 1959.

Rawlinson, George, *The History of Herodotus*, Vol. 1. The Appleton Co., 1875.

Redlich, E. Basil, *Form Criticism*. Duckworth, 1939.

Reimarus, Hermann Samuel, *Fragmente des Wolfenbüttelschen Ungennannten*. George Reimer, 1895, Fünfte Auflage. ET by Williams and Norgate, 1879.

Reinach, Salomon, *Orpheus, Histoire générale des religions*, Troisième Édition. Alcide Picard, 1909. ET by G. P. Putman's Sons, 1909.

Renan, Ernest, *Vie de Jésus*, Septième Édition. Chez B. Paetz, 1863. *Histoire des origines du Christianisme*, I, Calmann Levy, 1876. ET from 23d French edition by Little, Brown and Co., 1929.

Resch, Alfred, *Texte und Untersuchungen zur Geschichte altchristlichen Literatur*, X. Band, Heft 5. *Aussercanonische Paralleltexte zu den Evangelien*, Fünftes Heft, *Das Kindheitsevangelium nach Lucas und Matthäus*. J. C. Hinrichs'sche Buchhandlung, 1897.

Richardson, Alan, *An Introduction to the Theology of the New Testament*. S.C.M. Press, Ltd., and Harper & Brothers, 1958.

Richardson, Alan, ed., *A Theological Word Book of the Bible*. S.C.M. Press, Ltd., and The Macmillan Company, 1950.

Richardson, Cyril, *The Christianity of Ignatius of Antioch*. Columbia University Press, 1935.

Richardson, Cyril, ed., *Early Christian Fathers*. The Library of Christian Classics, Vol. I. The Westminster Press and S.C.M. Press, Ltd., 1953.

Riddle, Donald W., *The Occasion of Luke–Acts*. Reprint from *The Journal of Religion*, Vol. X, No. 4 (October, 1930).

Riddle, Donald W., and Hutson, Harold H., *New Testament Life and Literature*. University of Chicago Press, 1946.

Ritschl, Albrecht, *The Christian Doctrine of Justification and Reconciliation*. First German edition 1870–1874. ET by T. & T. Clark; 2d ed., 1902.

Robertson, Archibald T., *Luke the Historian in the Light of Research*. Charles Scribner's Sons and T. & T. Clark, 1920.

Robertson, Archibald T., *Word Pictures in the New Testament*. Richard R. Smith, Inc., 1930.

Robertson, John M., *Christianity and Mythology*, 1900. Second edition, enlarged, Watts and Co., 1910.

Robinson, Father Paschal, *The Writings of Saint Francis of Assisi*. The Dolphin Press, 1906.

Robinson, Joseph A., *St. Irenaeus, The Demonstration of Apostolic Preaching*. S.P.C.K., 1920.

Royds, T. F., *The Virgin Birth of Christ* (pamphlet). No. VIII of *Papers in Modern Churchmanship.* Longmans, Green & Co., 1925.

Sadler, M. F., *The Gospel According to St. Luke,* 4th ed. George Bell and Sons, 1892.

Sanday, William, *The Life of Christ in Recent Research.* Oxford University Press, 1907.

Sanday, William, *Outlines of the Life of Christ.* Longmans, Green & Co., Ltd., and Charles Scribner's Sons, 1905.

Sanday, William, and others, *Criticism of the New Testament.* Charles Scribner's Sons, 1902.

Schaff, Philip, *The Person of Christ.* American Tract Society, 1865.

Schanz, Paul, *Commentar über das Evangelium des heiligen Lucas.* Franz Fues, 1883.

Schenkel, Daniel, *Das Charakterbild Jesu.* C. W. Kreidel, 1873.

Schlatter, D. A., *Das Evangelium des Lukas.* Calwer Vereinsbuchhandlung, 1931.

Schleiermacher, Friedrich Ernst Daniel, *Der Christliche Glaube nach den Grundsätzen der evangelischen Kirche in Zusammenhange dargestellt.* Otto Hendel, 1821. ET from second German edition by T. & T. Clark, 1928.

Schleiermacher, F. E. D., *Das Leben Jesu.* Georg Reimer, 1864.

Schleiermacher, F. E. D., *Über die Schriften des Lukas.* Erster Theil. G. Reimer, 1817.

Schmidt, Nathaniel, *The Prophet of Nazareth.* The Macmillan Company, 1905.

Schmidt, Paul W., and Von Holzendorff, Franz, *A Short Protestant Commentary on the Books of the New Testament,* Vol. I, 3d ed. Williams and Norgate, 1882.

Schmiedel, P. W., *Jesus in Modern Criticism.* Adam and Charles Black, 1907.

Schonfield, Hugh J., *The Lost " Book of the Nativity of John."* T. & T. Clark, 1929.

Schweitzer, Albert, *Die psychiatrische Beurteilung Jesu.* J. C. B. Mohr, 1913. ET by The Beacon Press, Inc., 1948.

Schweitzer, Albert, *Von Reimarus zu Wrede.* J. C. B. Mohr, 1906. 2 neu bearb. *Geschichte der Leben-Jesu-Forschung,* 1913. ET Adam and Charles Black, Ltd., and The Macmillan Company as *The Quest of the Historical Jesus,* 2d ed., 1926.

Scott, Ernest F., *The Fourth Gospel.* T. & T. Clark, 1926.

Scott, Ernest F., *The Literature of the New Testament.* Oxford University Press and Columbia University Press, 1936.

Scott, William, *The Gospel Records in the Light of Recent Research.* Edwards Brothers, Inc., 1941.

Seeberg, Reinhold, *Text-Book of the History of Doctrines,* I. Philadelphia: Lutheran Publishing Society, revised, 1905.

Seydel, Rudolf, *Die Buddha-Legende und das Leben Jesu nach den Evangelien.* Otto Schulze, 1884.

Seydel, Rudolf, *Das Evangelium von Jesu in seinen Verhältnissen zu Buddha-Sage und Buddha-Lehre.* Breitkopf und Härtel, 1882.

Sheen, Fulton J., *Life of Christ.* McGraw-Hill Book Co., Inc., 1958.

Sīlācāra, Bhikkhu, *The Majjhima Nikāya.* Vols. 1 and 2. Walter Markgraf, 1912.

Sīlācāra, Bhikkhu, *The Majjhima Nikāya,* 2d ed. Oskar Schloss, 1924.

Smith, J. Frederick, *Studies in Religion Under German Masters.* Williams and Norgate, 1880.

Smith, Harold, *Ante-Nicene Exegesis of the Gospels,* Vol. 1. S.P.C.K., 1925.

Smith, Robertson W., *Kinship and Marriage in Early Arabia,* new ed. Adam and Charles Black, 1903.

Smith, William Benjamin, *Ecce Deus.* Eugen Diederichs, 1911.

Smith, William Benjamin, *Der vorchristliche Jesus nebst weiteren Vorstudien zur Entstehungsgeschichte des Urchristentums.* Alfred Töpelmann, 1906.

Smyth, Charles, " Christianity and Secular Myths." *Theology,* Vol. LII, No. 362 (October, 1949).

Soltau, Wilhelm, *Die Geburtsgeschichte Jesu Christi.* Dieterich'sche Verlagsbuchhandlung, 1902. ET by Adam and Charles Black, 1903.

Stählin, Leonhard, *Kant, Lotze, and Ritschl.* T. & T. Clark, 1889.

Stanton, Vincent H., *The Gospels as Historical Documents,* 3 vols. Cambridge University Press, 1903, 1909, 1920.

Stapfer, Edmond, *Jésus-Christ, sa personne, son autorité,* I, II, III. ET of Vol. 1, by Charles Scribner's Sons, 1900.

Steinmetzer, Franz X., *Die Geschichte der Geburt und Kindheit Christi und ihr Verhältnis zur babylonischen Mythe. Eine religionsgeschichtliche Untersuchung.* Aschendorff, 1910.

Stendahl, Krister, ed., *The Scrolls and the New Testament.* III, " John the Baptist in the New Light of Ancient Scrolls," W. H. Brownlee. Harper & Brothers, 1957.

Straton, John Roach, *The Virgin Birth — Fact or Fiction?* George H. Doran Co., 1924.

Strauss, David Friedrich, *Das Leben Jesu.* C. F. Osiander, 1835. Dritte Auflage, 1838.

Strauss, David Friedrich, *Das Leben Jesu für das deutsche Volk bearbeitet.* F. A. Brockhaus, 1864.

Strauss, David Friedrich, *The Life of Jesus.* ET from the fourth German edition. 2d edition in one vol. Swan Sonnenschein & Co., 1892.

Streeter, Burnett Hillman, *The Four Gospels.* Fourth impression, revised. Macmillan & Co., Ltd., 1930.

Suetonius, *Suetonius,* Vol. 1. The Macmillan Company, 1924.

Sweet, Louis Matthew, *The Birth and Infancy of Jesus Christ*. The Westminster Press, 1906; reprinted, 1907.

Sweetman, J. Windrow, *Islam and Christian Theology*, Vol. I. Lutterworth Press, 1945.

Taylor, Vincent, *Behind the Third Gospel*. Clarendon Press, 1926.

Taylor, Vincent, *The First Draft of Luke's Gospel*. S.P.C.K., 1927.

Taylor, Vincent, *Formation of Gospel Tradition*. Macmillan & Co., Ltd., 1933.

Taylor, Vincent, *The Historical Evidence for the Virgin Birth*. Clarendon Press, 1920.

Terry, Milton S., *The Sibylline Oracles*. Hunt & Eaton, 1890.

Tertullianus, Quintus Septimus Florens, *Tertulliani, Opera Omni; Patrologiae Latinae*, Tomus I. Parisiis, apud Garnier Fratres, Editores et J.–P. Migne Successors, 1879; Tomus II. Parisiis, Excudebat Migne, 1844.

Tertullian, *De Spectaculis*. Migne, J.–P., *Patrologiae Latinae*, Tomus I. Paris, 1844.

Tholuck, Friederic Augustus, *Die Glaubwürdigkeit der evangelischen Geschichte, zugleich eine Kritik des Lebens Jesu von Strauss*. Friedrich Perthes, 1837.

Thomas, Edward, *The Life of Buddha*. Kegan Paul, Trench, Trubner & Co., Ltd., 1927.

Thorburn, Thomas James, *A Critical Examination of the Evidences for the Doctrine of the Virgin Birth*. S.P.C.K., 1908.

Thorburn, Thomas James, *Jesus the Christ: Historical or Mythical?* T. & T. Clark, 1912.

Thorburn, Thomas James, *The Mythical Interpretation of the Gospels*. Charles Scribner's Sons, 1916.

Tillich, Paul, *Systematic Theology*, Vol. 2, *Existence and the Christ*. University of Chicago Press and James Nisbet & Co., Ltd., 1957.

Tollinton, Richard Bartram, *Clement of Alexandria*, Vols. I and II. Williams and Norgate, 1914.

Torrey, Charles Cutler, *Documents of the Primitive Church*. Harper & Brothers, 1941.

Torrey, Charles Cutler, *Translations Made from the Original Aramaic Gospels. Studies in the History of Religions*. The Macmillan Company, 1912.

Toy, Crawford Howell, *Quotations in the New Testament*. Charles Scribner's Sons, 1884.

Turmel, Joseph, *Histoire des dogmes*, II. Paris: Les Éditions Rieder, 1932.

Turmel, Joseph, *La Vierge Marie. Christianisme*. Paris: F. Rieder et Cte Éditeurs, 1925.

Usener, Hermann, *Religionsgeschichtliche Untersuchungen*, I. Theil.

Das Weihnachtsfest. Zweite Auflage, Friedrich Cohen, 1911. (Erste Aufl., 1899.)

Van Oosterzee, J. J., *Das Evangelium nach Lukas. Theologisch-homiletisches Bibelwerk; Des Neuen Testaments,* Dritter Theil. Velhagen und Klasing, 1859. ET by Charles Scribner's Sons, 1867, 3d ed.

Venturini, Karl Heinrick, *Natürliche Geschichte des grossen Propheten von Nazareth,* Erste Aufl., Copenhagen, 1800–1802.

Völter, Daniel, *Die Evangelischen Erzählungen von der Geburt und Kindheit Jesu, kritisch Untersucht.* Heitz und Mündel, 1911.

Volkmar, Gustav, *Jesus Nazarenus und die erste christliche Zeit mit den beiden ersten Erzählern.* Caesar Schmidt, 1882.

Walker, Alexander, *Apocryphal Gospels, Acts, and Revelations.* Ante-Nicene Christian Library, Vol. xvi. T. & T. Clark, 1870.

Warschauer, Joseph, *The Historical Life of Christ.* The Macmillan Company, 1927.

Webb, Clement C. J., *Kant's Philosophy of Religion.* Clarendon Press, 1926.

Weinel, Heinrich, *Jesus im neunzehnten Jahrhundert.* J. C. B. Mohr, 1903, neue Bearbeitung, 1907.

Weiss, Bernhard, *Das Leben Jesu,* I, II. First published in 1882. Cotter, 1902. ET by T. & T. Clark, 1883.

Weiss, Bernhard, *Die Vier Evangelien.* J. C. Hinrichs'sche Buchhandlung, 1900.

Weiss, Johannes, *Jesus von Nazareth Mythus oder Geschichte?* J. C. B. Mohr, 1910.

Weiss, Johannes, *Das Urchristentum,* 1914 (completed after his death by Rudolf Knopf). Vandenhoeck & Ruprecht, 1917. ET by Wilson-Erickson Inc., 1937.

Weisse, Christian Hermann, *Die evangelische Geschichte kritisch und philosophisch Bearbeiter.* Erster Band. Breitkopf und Härtel, 1838.

Weizsäcker, Carl von, *Das apostolische Zeitalter der Christlichen Kirche.* J. C. B. Mohr, 1886. Zweite, neu bearbeitete Auflage, 1892. ET by G. P. Putnam's Sons, 1894–1895, 2 vols.

Wernle, Paul, *Die Anfänge unserer Religion.* J. C. B. Mohr, 1901. ET by G. P. Putnam's Sons, 1904.

Wernle, Paul, *The Sources of Our Knowledge of the Life of Jesus.* Philip Green, 1907.

Wescott, Brooke F., *Introduction to the Study of the Gospels.* The Macmillan Company, 1887.

West, E. W., *Bundahish; Pahlavi Texts,* Part 1: *Sacred Books of the East,* ed. by F. Max Müller, Vol. V. Clarendon Press, 1880.

West, E. W., *Pahlavi Texts,* Part V. *Sacred Books of the East,* ed. by F. Max Müller, Vol. XLVII. Clarendon Press, 1897.

White, Lynn, Jr., "Christian Myth and Christian History." *Journal of the History of Ideas,* Vol. III, No. 2 (April, 1942).

Wilke, Christian Gottlob, *Der Urevangelist*. G. Fleischer, 1838.

Wilkinson, J. H., *Four Lectures on the Early History of the Gospels*. The Macmillan Company, 1898.

Williams, A. Lukyn, *Adversus Judaeos*. Cambridge University Press, 1935.

Willoughby, Harold R., *Pagan Regeneration*. The University of Chicago Press, 1929.

Windisch, Ernest, *Buddha's Geburt*. B. G. Teubner, 1908.

Worcester, Elwood, *Studies in the Birth of the Lord*. Charles Scribner's Sons, 1932.

Wright, F. A., *Fathers of the Church*. E. P. Dutton & Co., 1929.

Wright, William Kelley, *A History of Modern Philosophy*. The Macmillan Company, 1941.

Zahn, Theodor, *Das Evangelium des Lukas*, I. *Kommentar zum Neuen Testament*, III. A. Deichert'sche, 1913.

Zimmerli, W., and Jeremias, J., *The Servant of God. Studies in Biblical Theology*, No. 20. S.C.M. Press, Ltd., and Alec R. Allenson, Inc., 1957.

INDEX

(Asterisk indicates reference in footnote.)

AUTHORS

SUBJECTS AND SOURCES

TEXTS

APOCRYPHAL SOURCES